ACTIVIST MEDIA

ACTIVIST MEDIA

Documenting Movements and Networked Solidarity

GINO CANELLA

RUTGERS UNIVERSITY PRESS

New Brunswick, Camden, and Newark, New Jersey, and London

Library of Congress Cataloging-in-Publication Data

Names: Canella, Gino, author.
Title: Activist media: documenting movements and networked solidarity / Gino
Canella.
Description: New Brunswick: Rutgers University Press, 2022. | Includes
bibliographical references and index.
Identifiers: LCCN 2021028279 | ISBN 9781978824348 (paperback) | ISBN
9781978824355 (cloth) | ISBN 9781978824362 (epub) | ISBN 9781978824379 (mobi) |
ISBN 9781978824386 (pdf)
Subjects: LCSH: Documentary films—Social aspects—United States. | Documentary
films—Political aspects—United States. | Radicalism in mass media.
Classification: LCC PN1995.9.D6 C36 2021 | DDC 302.23/4—dc23
LC record available at https://lccn.loc.gov/2021028279

A British Cataloging-in-Publication record for this book is available from the British
Library.

www.rutgersuniversitypress.org

Manufactured in the United States of America

For my parents, Sarvey and Maria Canella

CONTENTS

CONTENTS

ACTIVIST MEDIA

INTRODUCTION

A strike wave is rippling across the United States. Led by rank-and-file workers and backed by broad community support, workers in health care, education, technology, manufacturing, and hospitality are fighting back against austerity—demanding union representation, living wages, fairer working conditions, dignity, and respect. These workers are flexing the strike muscle at a time when support for unions is high: according to a 2020 Gallup poll, public approval of unions in the United States is at 65 percent, a dramatic rebound from unions' record-low approval of 48 percent in 2009, during the Great Recession.[1]

Despite these favorability ratings, however, news media portrayals of working people are inconsistent, inaccurate, or nonexistent. In *No Longer Newsworthy: How Mainstream Media Abandoned the Working Class*, Christopher R. Martin showed how commercial mainstream media have historically produced business-friendly coverage of labor issues; these stories have also depicted unionized workers as hard-hat-wearing white men in the manufacturing and trade industries.[2] In recent years, labor organizers and grassroots media makers have begun rejecting these outdated caricatures by producing and sharing multiracial, multiethnic, and feminist stories that highlight the diversity of the working class.[3] To contend with declining membership in the United States (as a result of various legal decisions and increasingly casualized labor relations), unions are using media to organize members, promote workplace campaigns, respond to demands for racial and gender justice, and explain to broader publics why a strong labor movement is essential to a democratic society.[4] Many of these campaigns do not focus on, or even mention, "bread-and-butter" union issues, such as contracts, wages, and benefits; rather, these campaigns use media to communicate fairness, communal responsibility, and justice.[5]

As the U.S. labor movement is reviving its militant history, uprisings for racial justice are proclaiming that Black lives matter. By creating podcasts, magazines, and videos, and sharing them on social media, activists are demanding an end to systemic racism and creating a burgeoning left media infrastructure in which organizers can communicate directly with members and supporters on a range of issues; reframe issues of race, class, citizenship, and gender; and highlight the connections among work, identity, and public resources.

Various terms have been used to describe activists' media practices (for example, "community media," "citizens' media," "movement media," and "radical alternative media"). I use the term "activist media" to examine a series of documentary films I produced in partnership with the Service Employees International Union (SEIU) Local 105 and with Black Lives Matter 5280 (BLM5280) in Denver, Colorado, between August 2015 and May 2018. Activist media are the use of media and technology by grassroots organizers to (1) interrupt social, political, and journalistic discourses about race, class, gender, ability, citizenship status, and labor; (2) complement and enhance on-the-ground organizing efforts, such as canvassing, direct actions, and community meetings; and (3) identify and network a broad-based coalition of people committed to social and political change.[6]

I rely on Donatella della Porta's work on social movement media to examine activist media as material social practices rooted in communication and democracy. This framework, della Porta argued, acknowledges "the agency power of social movements in the construction of democracy and communications, rather than considering political and media institutions only as structural constraints."[7] The institutional and structural constraints that activists must navigate—within media, society, and politics—are many. From social media's algorithmic biases and surveillance mechanisms that disproportionately target Black activists, to politicians and mainstream media outlets that delegitimize activists' campaigns as "too radical" or unrealistic, activists who champion revolutionary politics face considerable obstacles.

Although these structural constraints may compel activists to compromise their demands or limit the scope of their campaigns, I examine how SEIU Local 105 and BLM5280 navigated institutional constraints and used media to promote people's agency, amplify their demands for justice, and network broad-based community support. I understand activist media not *as* media, but rather as a series of social practices that occur with and through media. This understanding is in conversation with researchers who have examined how the material conditions in which activists operate influence the formation and organization of social movements. In *Digital Rebellion: The Birth of the Cyber Left*, Todd Wolfson analyzed Independent Media Center (IMC; also known as Indymedia) and its coverage of the 1999 World Trade Organization (WTO) protests in Seattle, Washington. Indymedia is a global network of independent media makers that has been both celebrated for challenging dominant narratives about neoliberal globalization and also critiqued for a rejection of hierarchy, which, some argue, contributed to Indymedia's decline.

Wolfson examined media's affordances and structural limitations by focusing on the connections between media, technology, and activists' on-the-ground organizing. He provided historical context for contemporary media activism by reviewing the Zapatista Army of National Liberation (EZLN) in Chiapas, Mexico. Wolfson argued that journalists and researchers who focused solely on the Zapatistas' use of media—specifically, newsletters and community radio—failed to offer a deeper critique of the sociopolitical and material conditions in which these groups organized.[8] By fostering relationships based on "dialogue, patience, and community," and proclaiming, "One NO to neoliberal capitalism, many YESES," Wolfson argued that the Marxist revolutionaries and the Indigenous Mayans of Chiapas promoted a plurality of voices and identified a common threat (i.e. neoliberal globalization).[9] The material conditions in which these relationships were forged informed organizers' communication strategies and helped them craft a coherent and compelling message—one that drew international attention and support from journalists, politicians, and human rights organizations.[10]

Similarly, filmmaker and media scholar Angela J. Aguayo argued in her book *Documentary Resistance: Social Change and Participatory Media* that media are not simply cultural texts but are also a "force of social influence." Focusing on documentary film, she wrote that although the "documentary object" is important, "we should also study the participatory publics that emerge around documentary media, asking how production and circulation of documentary discourse reveal the key players (individual, institutional, governmental) and historical networks shaping the influence of films."[11] Through a first-person account of my activist media projects with BLM5280 and SEIU Local 105, I explore the social relationships embedded within media to understand how the production and distribution of documentary discourse illuminates the micro-practices of democracy.

As democracies around the world are in crisis—among other reasons, because pseudo-populist and authoritarian leaders have exposed liberal democracies' failures—it is necessary to address how power functions within activist media. Chris Robé traced the history of anarchist video and noted how social inequalities and capitalism's contradictions are often reflected in activists' media practices.[12] A notable example Robé reviewed from the late 1960s was the tensions between New York Newsreel, a documentary filmmaking collective, and the League of Revolutionary Black Workers, an umbrella organization of union organizers in Detroit, Michigan. During production of *Finally Got the News* (1970), a documentary about labor unions, workers' rights, and the connections between racial and economic justice, filmmakers debated revolutionary versus reformist approaches to justice and struggled to agree on the film's narrative. Despite numerous attempts from some in the video collective to eschew racial, gendered, and class privileges in their video activism, Robé concluded that "the countercultural politics of the video guerrillas embody the contradictions of a movement that both wants to challenge capitalism's hegemony while still being deeply indebted to its inequities and emerging neoliberal practices."[13] To expose the racial and class contradictions that characterized my activist filmmaking, I interrogate my positionality to SEIU Local 105 and BLM5280 as a white, male documentarian; I reflect on how collaborative media making operates on a continuum of collaboration in which participants must navigate difference, embrace conflict, and contribute when and how they are able.

This book addresses activist media's potential and limitations and contributes to ongoing debates about media, politics, and democracy. By reviewing the planning, production, and distribution of activist media, I investigate *the social* within social media, social movements, and social networks. I define the social as a complex matrix of people, emotions, and material conditions that promote and constrain meaning and action. The social can be strengthened or eroded throughout all stages of activist media—production, exhibition, or reception. Because the social is the foundation upon which networks are built, organizers must address the social conditions in which their movements operate in order to organize publics and build durable infrastructures capable of claiming power. I bring a humanistic approach to activist media to recognize that the people who produce and are represented in media are intimately connected to one another and to nature.

I discuss my documentary filmmaking within the social, political, and historical contexts in which it occurred and review how the communicative practices within activist media have the potential to foster meaningful relationships among community organizers. These relationships, in turn, politicize the narratives and aesthetics that activists use in their media. Because activist media and grassroots organizing are inherently communicative social practices, these practices create spaces for media makers and organizers to navigate and embrace their political, ideological, and identity differences; define and broadcast their values; and practice empathic listening and "care-full" organizing.

By focusing on the relationships among SEIU Local 105, BLM5280, and other community groups in Colorado, I theorize activist media practices—filming, interviewing, writing, editing, community exhibitions, and social media distribution—as social practices that are informed by the political subjectivities and emotions of the people involved. Although activist media alone will not bring about the revolutionary change that is needed to achieve a democratic and just society, these practices provide organizers with opportunities to strategize about their campaigns, communicate with one another and with diverse publics, and receive real-time feedback from supporters and detractors.

Activist media are a method through which organizers and researchers can script new visions for social and political life. This book examines activist media in relation to the contemporary political moment in 2022, in which the rhetoric of austerity and neoliberalism (e.g., competitive individualism, "free markets," and entrepreneurialism) has worn thin among working people. Activists from Chile to Iraq to Hong Kong are taking to the streets to demand an end to extreme inequality, climate change and ecological collapse, and the gutting of the commons and shared public resources.[14] Following the 2016 election of Donald Trump, millions of people around the world participated in the Women's March on January 21,

2017. A week later, thousands demonstrated in airport terminals across the United States to protest the Trump administration's "Muslim ban," which restricted travelers from seven Muslim-majority countries from entering the United States. In April 2017, thousands more marched to champion science and environmental justice. And in the summer of 2020, the largest global protest movement for racial justice took to the streets and demanded an end to state violence against Black people. My filmmaking emerged out of this anger and energy; I used media to enter this moment, join these movements, and uplift a political project that centers the labor of women, people of color, and immigrants in the struggle for justice. This book provides evidence for how co-creative research creates opportunities for scholars to contribute to social movements' communication and organizing strategies. Producing activist media in partnership with grassroots organizers and studying these practices, however, demands more than simply consulting with movements. This work requires highlighting the grassroots epistemologies emanating from the streets and leveraging them to decolonize knowledge production and imagine new forms of social and political life.

As publics vigorously debate the language of race, class, gender, and citizenship, it is essential to review the media and communication strategies that activists use to broadcast their values to publics and create networks of support. Despite organized labor's decline in membership and political influence in the United States since the 1970s, unions have been promoting narratives that reject the logic of neoliberalism and celebrate the multiracial and multigenerational composition of the labor movement. Although only 10.7 percent of wage and salary workers in the United States are members of a union (down from 20.1% in 1983), there are positive signs that unions are reclaiming their radical roots.[15] The documentary films I made with SEIU Local 105 and BLM5280, for example, critiqued how racial capitalism has, for decades, divided working people along superficial identity lines and cultural issues. I examine how activist media created physical and online spaces for these groups to practice radical pluralistic politics.

Activist media have the potential to promote solidarity among working people because these practices ask participants to embrace their differences and recognize their shared struggles. Building relationships through media does not mean compromising revolutionary visions of justice for reformist approaches to politics but does require acknowledging the needs and material conditions of working people. Historian Thomas Frank has argued that the Democratic Party abandoned working people's needs in the 1970s, when it turned away from unions in favor of credentialed professionals from Silicon Valley and Wall Street.[16] Many political scientists and journalists have examined this trend, and the decline of working people's material conditions, to make sense of Donald Trump's appeal to working class voters: Was it animated by racial resentment, loss of status, or economic anxiety? Within this sociopolitical and historical context, I offer nuanced analyses of racial and class politics and argue that activist media rewrite the script on tired and simplistic narratives that racialize and dehumanize people. Through my work with organizers in Colorado, I demonstrate how activist media have the potential to promote meaningful and difficult dialogues among publics. Dialogue is not about sacrificing one's principles; rather, it is about patience, active listening, and developing relationships based on earned trust, mutual respect, and accountability. In order to endure, movements must build resilient infrastructures and promote political education through radical and unapologetic messaging. Activist media create the social conditions in which movements can begin to build the capacities and material resources needed to claim power.

The book begins by reviewing theories of democracy, media power, and networks. I then provide a brief history of radical alternative media and trace how the logics of new technologies have often mirrored social movement dynamics. I offer the case study of SEIU and BLM5280.

Chapter 1 provides the theoretical framework needed to interrogate *the social* and *the political* within activist media. Critical cultural studies informs my approach to activism, social movements' communication strategies, and how grassroots organizers network and sustain campaigns for justice.

Chapter 2 introduces the organizations I worked with and situates my activist media within the tradition of militant ethnographic filmmaking. This chapter highlights how co-creative research operates along a continuum of collaboration in which participants do not contribute equally during all stages of production and distribution; rather, participants make meaningful contributions grounded in accountability and transparency. I provide historical context for my media making by reviewing how technological evolutions—from analog to digital, and film to video—have influenced activists' media practices.

Chapters 3, 4, and 5 present the case study, organized into thematic chapters that reflect the typical documentary production cycle: pre-production, production and post-production, and distribution. Chapter 3 (*pre-production*) discusses how attending community meetings hosted by BLM5280 and SEIU Local 105 built trust between myself and key organizers and provided me with the political education I needed to infuse our films with compelling narratives and radical aesthetics. Chapter 4 (*production and post-production*) offers textual analyses of our documentary media. I discuss how I visualized BLM5280 and Local 105's politics through media by centering the voices of women and people of color and by crafting anti-capitalist and antiracist stories about the labor movement. Chapter 5 (*distribution and exhibition*) reviews the multifaceted distribution strategies we used to promote our activist media. I detail these distribution methods to interrogate the impact and engagement industry that has emerged around documentary. With the proliferation of streaming services and the relatively low production costs associated with documentaries, studios and distributors are eager to capitalize on documentary's commercial potential. Documentaries about social justice—

which appeal to broad audiences and offer the potential for award prestige—are increasingly desirable and marketable. Because there is so much competition within media, impact and engagement consultants help filmmakers brand their films, identify an audience, and market social justice. Having an "impact" or "engaging" with a community, however, is not about creating slogans or measuring online metrics; rather, engagement is using media to promote deliberative, intentional organizing.

The conclusion reflects on how co-creative research forces scholars to engage with grassroots epistemologies, defy academic conventions, and reject intellectual elitism. I conclude by assessing the risks and labor associated with co-creative research and address the need to break artificial boundaries within the academy that restrict and prevent new knowledges from emerging.

As social networks and activist media evolve, researchers must update the theoretical and methodological frameworks they use to study these phenomena. Visual and multimedia storytelling in partnership with communities provides researchers with opportunities to intervene in and contribute to community organizing campaigns that promote justice. Through films, podcasts, and magazines, activists are broadcasting and visualizing new ways to reimagine society and challenging the limits of acceptable discourse. Researchers and journalists should learn from these efforts and recognize how information—regardless of the form in which it is expressed or the venue in which it is distributed—either reinforces the status quo or scripts an alternative vision for an equitable and just society. By grabbing my camera, listening humbly to my community partners, and documenting their fight for justice, I produced activist media in solidarity with the collective struggle for liberation.

1 · ACTIVIST MEDIA, POWER, AND NETWORKED PUBLICS

Media and politics are increasingly colliding in explosive ways, complicating how researchers, media makers, and activists conceive of democracy, politics, and the social. These complex dynamics between media and politics raise provocative questions: What is the political? What does it mean to participate meaningfully in civic life through media? Who has the ability to access the public sphere and contribute to conversations that seek to change it? Attempts to address how activists use media to engage with politics often focus on Twitter, Facebook, and smartphones, emphasizing the online platforms and digital technologies that activists use to promote social justice. This focus on media and technology, however, fails to account for how the communicative practices that occur with and through media are enhanced or hindered by technology, or for how the mediation of activism has broader implications for organizing and democracy. I examine my media making with Service Employees International Union (SEIU) Local 105 and Black Lives Matter 5280 (BLM5280) through political and social theories of democracy to understand activist media practices as material social practices that foster participants' political subjectivity and encourage them to exert their agency. Although media allow activists to visualize and amplify their messages for social justice, the current networked media ecosystem demands that we ask serious questions about how media interact with, and reshape our conceptions of, social life. This chapter reviews theories of democracy, media power, and networks to argue that activists' media practices reflect the uneven, contentious, and hopeful dynamics at the heart of democracy.

Activists' media practices have been discussed using various terms—participatory, alternative, community, and social movement media—but John Downing's term "radical alternative media" is instructive for thinking about activist media's relationship with democratic practice.[1] Downing included the word "radical," he explained, because "alternative media is almost oxymoronic. Everything is, at some point, alternative to something else."[2] "Radical," on the other hand, comes from the Latin *radix* or *radic-* and means "root." Activist media practices, including street art, video, and community radio, therefore, are not simply cultural productions, but social activities that get to *the root* of politics. Downing outlined various dynamics that characterize radical media, and one of these dynamics is that radical media are democratic. He described how radical media are structured *vertically* and *laterally* to challenge hegemonic power structures (a point addressed later in this chapter), and he encouraged researchers to theorize radical media as the "complex *socio*technical institutions they actually are."[3]

In line with this argument, I review my media making by recognizing how media's affordances are connected to the personal relationships embedded in the production and distribution of media. I focus on how these relationships network the messaging of grassroots groups across space and time and connect the organizing of activists working to build a mass movement committed to justice. Rather than reinforce a binary between mainstream corporate media and activist media, I celebrate the diversity of activist media practices and acknowledge that when media interacts with the social—online, in the streets, or at community meetings—activists can create the capacity and scale needed to claim symbolic and political power.

Also analyzing social movement media's relationship with politics and the social, Clemencia Rodriguez, Benjamin Ferron, and Kristin Shamas suggested theoretical and methodological approaches best suited for studying these phenomena.[4] To understand both activists' media practices and the technologies and platforms that activists use to make and share media, the authors argued that the practices, devices, and online platforms must be situated within their historical, political, and socioeconomic contexts. Chapter 2 provides historical context on the evolution of activist media and situates my project within its local socioeconomic environment. This chapter, though, begins by detailing exactly what I mean by "the social."

THE SOCIAL FORCE OF DOCUMENTARY MEDIA

John Grierson powerfully discussed documentary's relationship with the social in a 1939 essay in the *Fortnightly Review*. Grierson argued that the early documentary movement's "basic force . . . was social not aesthetic. . . . We were interested in *all* instruments which would crystalize sentiments in a muddled world and create a will toward civic participation."[5] Although visual aesthetics and the technologies used to produce media are indeed important—and I consider them throughout the book—Grierson understood that documentary, at its core, is about civic participation, political education, and community engagement. Recognizing how the relationships among community organizers and activists are developed, fractured, or maintained through media suggests that media making has the potential to create movements' infrastructures and network movements' politics.

Investigating the social within activist media requires examining how the political ideologies of movements shape activists' media practices and influence their visual aesthetics. Focusing on the social and material relations embedded in activist media understands media, politics, and language as contested sites of struggle. Therefore, activist media create spaces to study how framing and networking occur within the contemporary media ecosystem.

Radical Alternative Media

Chris Atton built on John Downing's theorization of radical media by arguing that the social is fundamental to the production and distribution of alternative media: "Any model must consider not simply the differences in content and medium/ carrier (and its dissemination and delivery) but how communication as a social (rather than simply an informational) process is construed. . . . What is radical about the communication processes (as instances of social relations) employed by that media?"[6]

Atton argued that the "transformatory potential of the media" is found in "process and relation."[7] He recognized the contradictions inherent in alternative media, including the surveillance mechanisms embedded within social media. Moving beyond creating counter-information and developing real political power means creating spaces in which to produce media, identify with allies, and promote solidarity through political education. The social in activist media recognizes how the relational dynamics among participants structure the narratives movements use and hold participants accountable throughout the making and sharing of media.

Similar to Atton and Downing, Peter Funke, Chris Robé, and Todd Wolfson offered the concept of "media-suturing" to argue that filming, editing, and distribution are not "endpoint[s] unto themselves," but ways to build grassroots collectives and "re-forg[e] a contemporary working class identity."[8] Although the authors focused on a community media center that teaches video production skills to community organizers and encourages them to use these skills to tell their own stories, I use "media-suturing" to describe how media texts, the communication strategies employed by activists, and the distribution strategies participants use to promote these texts to audiences have the potential to unite—or "suture"— grassroots groups.

In the past decade, analyses of radical media have evolved in parallel to digital media. As Google, Apple, Facebook, and Amazon have claimed monopoly power over the communication infrastructures on which activists rely to communicate and organize, a more critical and skeptical tone about the potential of activist media has emerged. Utopian rhetoric about social media's ability to democratize information is no longer helpful. Because the scale and reach of these platforms is so large, however, many activists argue that ceding these digital spaces to far-right reactionary movements is also unwise.

As mentioned in the introduction, Todd Wolfson balanced techno-deterministic and techno-utopian visions of activist media in his analysis of contemporary movements that rely heavily on digital media. Wolfson argued that twenty-first century movements—for example, Occupy Wall Street, Black Lives Matter, and the Arab Spring uprisings—emerged from the logics of the New Left of the 1960s and, therefore, reflect some of those movements' characteristics.[9] For example, Occupy and BLM favor a horizontal, nonhierarchical structure based on leaderless (or leaderfull) organizing. These movements, Wolfson contended, favor "radical democratic revolution[ary]" approaches to social change. He situated the "Cyber Left" in relation to the New Left, because, he argued, "to understand a specific period of resistance, it is vital to look at historical antecedents as well as the current socioeconomic environment."[10] I situate my documentary filmmaking with SEIU Local 105 and BLM5280 in its historical and socioeconomic contexts in chapter 2 and examine how the local dynamics in Colorado influenced the activist media practices that we used.

Democratizing Documentary and the Problems with Participation

Before we delve further into activist media, it is important that we explore the promise and pitfalls of democracy. Using media to foster vibrant social relationships and to promote democratic civic participation presents several profound challenges: fragmented publics must overcome their differences and collaborate on how best to achieve their goals. Understanding how movements bridge differences—in organizing spaces and through messaging strategies—requires reconceptualizing the classic bourgeois public sphere described by Jürgen Habermas.[11] Nancy Fraser critiqued Habermas's conception of the public sphere in which citizens unite to express their opinions and debate public affairs, and offered the term "subaltern counterpublics." Counterpublics, she argued, further democracy by allowing a plurality of citizens to speak "in one's own voice" and serve as "training grounds for agitational activities directed toward wider publics."[12] Similarly, Judith Butler understood voice and style as crucial aspects of political participation and identity formation.[13] Critiques of so-called "identity politics," commonly associated with the New Left movements that fought for civil rights, gay rights, and women's rights, were made, Butler argued, by a "hegemonic Left" that sought to "'include' through domestication and subordination precisely those movements that formed in part in opposition to such domestication and subordination."[14] Relying on Louis Althusser's notion of the "apparatus," Butler argued that challenges to capitalist ideology are inherently material practices. [15] "Even if homophobia were conceived only as a cultural attitude," she wrote, "that attitude should still be located in the apparatus and practice of its institutionalization."[16]

Although Habermas updated his theory of the public sphere, he remained skeptical that a cacophony of competing voices can engage effectively in politics and public deliberation.[17] Most relevant for my analysis of activist media is Habermas's comment on the role of *presentation*. He wrote, "Only through their controversial presentation in the media do such topics reach the larger public and subsequently gain a place on the 'public agenda.'"[18] As activist media makers leverage social media to share their media and place their issues on the public agenda, they do so while navigating the contradictions within the contemporary media eco-system. Because social media privilege content that elicits emotions, telling complex and nuanced stories about structural and institutional inequalities is a challenge. Linking the struggle for Black liberation with stories about the labor movement requires highlighting the personal stories of organizers and connect-ing them with the not-so-glamorous aspects of community organizing. Commu-nity meetings and canvassing do not make for exciting visual storytelling, and these images are unlikely to go viral on Twitter. But these practices are essential to build-ing long-term campaigns for change. Although emotional stories elevate activists' messages in crowded online environments, organizers often reminded me that anger and rage can burn movements out.

John Downey and Natalie Fenton considered the dilemma of presentation in the public sphere by discussing publicity and "counter-publicity."[19] They argued that, rather than viewing activist media as being constrained by social media, these practices must be understood within a broader power analysis. "A cultural poli-tics of counter-publicity can be founded neither on abstract ideals of universality nor on essentialist notions of community," Downey and Fenton wrote. "Rather, it has to begin by understanding the complex dynamics of existing public spheres and counter-public spheres, their embeddedness in global and local contexts, [and] their unstable make-up. . . . And then, importantly, any counter-publicity must be evaluated against the constant power of cultural and economic capital and accumulation."[20]

A power structure analysis helps activists interrogate the public sphere by forc-ing them to ask: Who is included within the public sphere, whose voices matter, and how is participation regulated? Henry Jenkins is notable within media and cultural studies for promoting a hopeful view of online activities and digital media with his term "participatory culture."[21] Jenkins argued that the cultural politics of youth fan cultures, such as remixing popular culture, provide people with oppor-tunities to challenge representations presented in commercial media, engage in civic life, and recognize their agency.

Carole Pateman argued, however, that participation must be understood in rela-tion to classical liberal conceptions of democracy, which were founded on notions of the enlightened individual capable of engaging in thoughtful debate and ratio-nal deliberation about matters of civic importance.[22] Offering a model of democ-racy that complicates representative, minimalist conceptions of democracy, Pate-man argued that "'participation' refers to (equal) participation in the making of decisions, and 'political equality' refers to equality of power in determining the outcome of decisions, a very different definition from that in the contemporary theory."[23] Pateman later revised her argument and wrote that deliberation is not synonymous with democracy and that true participation is about "democratizing democracy."[24] Pateman doubted democracy's potential in advanced global capitalist societies and remained skeptical about the value of engaged citizenship, which she said is increasingly aligned with consumerism.

In *Digital Keywords*, an update of Raymond Williams's classic book *Keywords*, Rasmus Kleis Nielsen examined democratic participation by arguing that analyses of digital technologies and media have focused too heavily on the connection between media and maximalist notions of democracy.[25] Technology's relationship to democracy, Nielsen argued, has matured from a "utopian/dystopian dichotomy" to a "complex realism," in which an empty "it's complicated" conclusion has emerged.[26] To move past this and understand "how democracy is complicated, where, under what conditions, what it means, and for whom," I examine how social movements utilize media to promote online and off-line participation in the public sphere and use media to network across movements.[27]

Recognizing how publics and counterpublics navigate their ideological and identity differences is central to understanding democratic participation. Chantal Mouffe theorized participation among competing publics and offered the term "radical democracy." She argued that political organizing "requires the existence of multiplicity, of plurality, and of conflict, and sees in them the *raison d'être of politics*."[28] Mouffe, however, drew a crucial distinction between politics and the political.[29] In calling for a politics based on "agonistic pluralism," Mouffe argued that activists' antagonisms "take many different forms and can emerge in diverse social relations." Often, however, these antagonisms avoid institutional politics, which leads to their domestication.[30]

Understanding how a plurality of voices, styles, and identities compete for attention and recognition within the contemporary media ecosystem is a challenge. While leveraging social media and online networks to craft intersectional narratives about justice and build power to challenge global capitalism, activists must confront the contradictions within digital media. Jodi Dean offered perhaps the most searing critique of political participation that occurs largely online, arguing that the Left's emphasis on identity and online metrics has created a form of "post-politics," which is based on "democratic drive" and an obsession with circulation.[31] Focusing on democracy as the "underlying supposition," Dean wrote, "provides the basic vocabulary of law and politics . . . [and] invoke[s] our 'ambient milieu.'"[32] Filming rallies and demonstrations with BLM5280, a Black-led social movement that centers the work of Black women and girls, and with SEIU Local 105, a predominantly Hispanic labor union, demanded that I work through this milieu and engage in regular discussions with organizers about how to represent, through media, radical and antagonistic conceptions of democracy and anti-capitalist politics.

The recent outpouring of activist energy around the world—from France, Chile, Iran, and Hong Kong—has given optimism to the idea that as more people appear politically active, this energy will translate into more democracy. Dean, however, cautioned against this logic by suggesting that as politics and activism become increasingly visible, they become increasingly performative. Protest loses its efficacy online, she wrote, because it is diluted in the spectacle of "media-stream."[33] Networked communications create what Dean called "communicative capitalism," which she defined as "participation in information, entertainment, and communication technologies in ways that capture resistance and intensify global capitalism."[34] Inspired by Lacanian psychoanalysis and by Slavoj Žižek's critique of symbolic efficiency, Dean is concerned with how social media and participatory culture further the personalization of politics and contribute to the decline of shared meaning. [35] According to Dean, social media privilege narratives about the liberated individual and commodify activism, creating a "pseudo-democracy," which is guided by a market logic and appears separate from collective or communitarian approaches to justice.[36] By embracing a politics based on drive, Dean argued, "we perpetually miss our goal and get satisfaction through this very missing. Or we don't even have an actual goal and we take the absence of a goal to be a strength. We talk, complain, and protest."[37] Dean asserted that communicative capitalism distracts organizers from realizing long-term political goals and instead is obsessed with celebrating "small victories and momentary pleasures." Creating a socialist alternative, she wrote, "requires amplifying the collective desire that can cut through these affective networks."[38]

Publishing media within this context, therefore, requires considering how affect and emotions influence activists' media and organizing practices. Emotions can distract organizers—by forcing them to respond to the latest social media controversy—and have the potential to fracture movements. Researchers have examined how social media tailor users' news feeds to match their personal preferences, creating filter bubbles and information silos. A common misconception, however, is that social media show us only messages that we agree with. To provoke a reaction, these sites also show us messages we fiercely disagree with, hoping we will click, argue, repeat; this cycle keeps us on the sites and creates more opportunities for the companies to sell us ads. This intense emotional environment creates a double bind for activists. On one hand, a viral message can spread across a global network and expand the movement's geographic reach. On the other hand, being in a constant state of heightened emotions can fatigue organizers and cause burnout. Social media are an effective space for organizers to keep up with announcements about meetings, rallies, and canvassing efforts and to view all of the multimedia produced to document and promote these activities. Activist media makers should leverage these affordances of social media but remain focused on how media can foster the social relationships among movement members that are required to realize radical democracy.

REVOLUTIONARY VISIONS OF RACE, LABOR, AND GENDER

Producing media about social justice, with narratives that connect antagonistic and pluralistic publics, requires grappling with the tensions between racial and class politics. Race and racial categories have been produced historically, socially, and juridically through culture, policy, and discourse. Activist media that promote racial justice, therefore, must be grounded in critical race and feminist analyses. This framework provides a prism through which to understand the structural inequalities confronting Black Americans and other marginalized groups and offers activists a language through which to communicate their demands for justice.

In *Black Is a Country: Race and the Unfinished Struggle for Democracy*, Nikhil Pal Singh provided a thorough intellectual history of Black thinkers—including Martin Luther King Jr., W. E. B. Du Bois, E. Franklin Frazier, C. L. R. James, and others. Singh traced the evolution of Black radical thought and explored the tensions among reform and revolutionary approaches to racial justice. He argued that these tensions reveal the struggle at the core of democracy: namely, how to conceive of the public.[39] A consistent debate throughout this scholarship, Singh showed, is the distinction Black scholars have made between "integration" and "assimilation." Frazier, for instance, was concerned with the assimilation of radical Black thought within academia. He perceived a lack of interest among Black intellectuals in addressing the question of cultural and social integration within the United States and its liberal democratic institutions.[40] These questions, Frazier argued, are fundamental to understanding how Black people have shaped the democratic societies in which they have lived. According to Frazier, as the Black U.S. intellectual "goes his merry way discussing such matters as the superficial aspects of the material standard of living among Negroes and the extent to which they enjoy civil rights," there is no consideration for the role slavery played in the "pulverization of their social life . . . and annihilation of their personality through the destruction of their cultural heritage."[41] The focus on improving the material standards of Black people in the United States, he argued, has often come at the expense of deeper examinations of Black culture and its connection to the social.

Through films, photography, and written essays, BLM5280 creates physical and digital spaces in which to both critique the political economic conditions of Black people and also to visualize and celebrate Black culture. BLM5280 challenges stereotypical and dominant narratives about Black people presented in mainstream media by highlighting the complexity of Blackness.

As contemporary social movements such as BLM increasingly use social and digital media to revise and update history, shape our views about the present, and offer alternative futures, they define the political terrain. For example, challenging the collective memory of Martin Luther King Jr. revives debates about violence versus nonviolence, democracy and freedom, and assimilation and integration. King is often cited by liberals as an advocate for peace and nonviolent civil disobedience during the civil rights movement of the 1950s and 1960s. Situating King within the long civil rights movement—which encompasses slavery, the New Deal, Jim Crow, and today—means acknowledging how he radically challenged U.S. exceptionalism, white supremacy, and global capital. King addressed the uprisings across the United States and connected them to U.S. state violence in Vietnam, effectively calling out the hypocrisy of legitimate versus illegitimate forms of violence.

Citizenship and freedom, King argued, are linked to exploitation and militarism. This international perspective is essential for understanding King within a tradition of radical Black scholarship that continues to influence movement thought and culture today. King's critiques of structural racism and systemic oppressions, for example, shed light on how contemporary movements for racial justice critique state violence waged against racialized subjects and spaces—domestically and internationally. King's radical edge is often lost amid MLK Day celebrations that champion multicultural diversity; but that edge is essential for movements that seek to develop language that critiques how nation-states limit participation in and access to the public sphere.

Malcolm X's intellectual evolution also reveals a shift in Black activism in the United States, from a politics focused primarily on racial injustices to a politics focused on a systemic critique of state violence, economic inequality, and U.S. imperialism. Although Malcolm X offered conflicting statements on the role that white allies play in the struggle for Black liberation, he acknowledged in January 1965 that his understanding of Black nationalism, which advocated for a separate nation for Black people in the United States, was "alienating people who were true revolutionaries."[42] This comment is instructive for understanding how Malcolm X and other Black Power activists of the 1960s emphasized the centrality of race while also highlighting broader systems of injustice. "We are living in an era of revolution, and the revolt of the American Negro is part of the rebellion against the oppression and colonialism which has characterized this era," he said. "It is incorrect to classify the revolt of the Negro as simply a racial conflict of black against white, or as purely an American problem. Rather, we are today seeing a global rebellion of the oppressed against the oppressor, the exploited against the exploiters."[43]

Singh also reflected on how "New Deal liberalism" influenced Black intellectuals struggling with reform versus revolutionary approaches to racial justice. New Deal liberalism, he argued, constructed racial boundaries between liberal individuals and civic-republicanism and created binaries that must be interrogated by movements seeking equality: "the market versus the state, the private and the public, the defense of liberty and the goal of equality."[44] Dog whistle politics that promote "law and order," he wrote, heighten moral panics about Black Americans. Caricatures of welfare queens and drug criminals, which were popularized by southern Republican politicians in the 1960s and continue to be used by politicians and public figures today, "drive a wedge between people at, or near, the bottom of society."[45] And these wedges are often driven with media and popular culture (e.g., George H. W. Bush's Willie Horton campaign advertisement).[46]

Cornel West, one of the most prominent Black intellectuals and public scholars today, has offered vehement critiques of liberalism and the elitism of the Democratic Party. Some of his most potent ire has been directed at neoliberalism, which, he has said, is based on an individualistic ethos that prevents a multiracial, multi-generational, and multiethnic movement from forming. In *Race Matters*, West broke the binary between "liberal structuralists," who believe that systemic fail-ures of federal and local governments are responsible for poverty and crime within Black communities, and "conservative behaviorists," who believe that moral fail-ings of the individual are at the root of social problems; instead, West offered a "politics of conversion" grounded in compassion and communal love.[47] The Black community, West wrote, is afflicted by nihilism, "a disease of the soul" which is best "tamed by love and care."[48] West argued that "racial reasoning" is an insuffi-cient way to break nihilism, because that reasoning is built on the false narrative that Black authenticity is associated with closing ranks within the Black commu-nity and ignoring the struggles of Black women and gay Black men. Instead, West advocated for developing accountable Black leadership and "Black cultural democ-racy" that moves both Black and white communities closer to collective libera-tion.[49] As discussed further in the next chapter, BLM5280 promotes the Black-centered activism that West advocated by not simply recognizing the diversity of ways that one can be Black in America but by rejecting "the pervasive patriarchy and homophobia in black American life."[50]

The tensions between "racialist" and redistributive approaches to justice are also prominent in W.E.B. Du Bois's work. Although some have argued that Du Bois reduced his analyses of race to the economic and material needs of Black people, he stressed the importance of language and culture and recognized how racist policies rely on a cultural apparatus that creates and legitimizes racist ide-ologies. These ideologies provide "an otherwise abstract capitalist market with one of its most reliable mechanisms of value-differentiation."[51] Analyses of racial justice, therefore, do not need to "go beyond" race; rather, the long civil rights move-ment's "worldly, heterogeneous, insurgent, participatory, and disorderly" character-istics reveal how race and racial categories are central to defining democracy and granting citizenship.[52] Activist media, as heterogeneous, participatory, and dis-orderly practices, must embrace the tensions within collaboration and realize the potential it offers. The social is animated during moments of friction. Apply-ing care, practicing empathy, and showing love during these moments of friction provide movements with the tools they need to navigate these tensions and real-ize change.

Black feminism has also deeply informed the political trajectory of radical social movements and has promoted nuanced representations of Blackness within the public sphere. BLM was founded on, and its organizing is informed by, the principles of Black feminism. Angela Davis is one of the foremost scholars of Black feminism. She argued that although Black liberation is led by women of color, it appeals to multiracial unity that works across the color line.[53] "The only line we draw is one based on our political principles," she wrote.[54] Davis used the analogy of a pyramid to describe how class situates women and oppressions in society, placing white, bourgeois women at the top of this hierarchy. The gains they achieve remain at the top of the pyramid and do not yield material change for those below these women (the gains do not "trickle down"). Situated at the bottom of the pyramid, working-class women of color animate social justice, because, as Davis wrote, when "those at the nadir of the pyramid win victories for themselves, it is virtually inevitable that their progress will push the entire structure upward. The forward movement of women of color almost always initiates progressive change for all women."[55]

Davis's analysis is in conversation with the approach to Black liberation of the Combahee River Collective (CRC). Founded in 1974 in Boston, Massachusetts, CRC provided the intellectual and political space for Black women who felt that white feminism and male-dominated civil rights movements did not go far enough to ensure the collective liberation of all oppressed people. Standing in solidarity with anti-colonial struggles in Algeria and Vietnam, CRC's statement reveals the radical roots of "identity politics": "We need to articulate the real class situation of persons who are not merely raceless, sexless workers, but for whom racial and sexual oppression are significant determinants in their working/economic lives. Although we are in essential agreement with Marx's theory as it applied to the very specific economic relationships he analyzed, we know that his analysis must be extended further in order for us to understand our specific economic situation as Black women."[56]

The legacy of CRC provides the framework necessary for articulating the interlocking oppressions of racism, capitalism, and patriarchy. Intersectional Black feminism has been vocalized throughout the Black Lives Matter movement. Davis, for example, expressed intersectional politics during her speech at the 2017 Women's March in Washington, D.C. Speaking to a crowd of nearly half a million people gathered on the Washington Mall, she championed collective resistance through art, music, political education, and protest—movement tactics that, she argued, are needed to fight heteronormative patriarchy, white supremacy, and institutional racism. "This is a women's march and this Women's March represents the promise of feminism against the pernicious powers of state violence," Davis said. "An inclusive and intersectional feminism that calls upon all of us to join the resistance to racism, to Islamophobia, to anti-Semitism, to misogyny, to capitalist exploitation. Yes, we salute the Fight for $15. We dedicate ourselves to collective resistance."[57]

The Women's March and the subsequent Women's Strike on March 8, 2017, have been critiqued for being led by and centering the voices of privileged, white women.[58] Davis's comments, however, represent a key strategy through which women of color and marginalized people, including queer and trans people and immigrants, are leading resistance efforts and fights for social justice—they are demanding not only to be included in the public sphere but also to have a stake in shaping an equitable and just public sphere that meets the needs of all people.

Davis's global anti-capitalist critique fits within a historical tradition of Black feminism that has consistently urged movements to frame their struggles through solidarity and love. Audre Lorde, a writer, poet, and organizer with the CRC, influences BLM's politics in this way. Lorde critiqued how global capitalism exacerbates inequalities through an "institutionalized rejection of difference" that divides people based on race, ethnicity, religion, and gender.[59] This rejection of difference causes confusion and fear among people and creates groups of "outsiders" who are needed as "surplus people."[60]

Combating this system with radical love and care, Lorde wrote, is essential. "As members of such an economy we have *all* been programmed to respond to the human differences between us with fear and loathing and to handle that difference in one of three ways: ignore it, and if that is not possible, copy it if we think it is dominant, or destroy it if we think it is subordinate. But we have no patterns for relating across our human differences as equals. As a result, those differences have been misnamed and misused in the service of separation and confusion."[61]

Lorde understood how shared struggles are strategically papered over or erased by political and financial elites that benefit from fractured and divided publics. Activist media creates physical and digital spaces in which organizers can name their shared struggles, share stories that animate and embrace their differences, and begin to network the collective power of people at the bottom of the pyramid.

STORYTELLING AND MEDIA POWER

Because information and meaning are constructed and spread within networked communications, activist media must be examined through the lens of framing and media power. Publicizing social movements' demands to build solidarity among grassroots groups requires injecting a subversive discourse into the public sphere and challenging dominant framings of political, economic, and social issues. Shifting public opinion and conducting consciousness-raising on issues that are misunderstood, underreported, or absent from public debate have been key features of social movements throughout history. While networked media has indeed expanded the geographic reach of contemporary social movements— enabling activists to broadcast injustices in real time and encouraging supporters across the globe to rise up in solidarity against these injustices—the form that activists use to package their messages, and the platforms activists use to connect with publics, present challenges. Social media are largely driven by visual storytelling, so grassroots media makers often utilize the language of film and video to communicate their issues and values. Film is effective for developing characters and creating a mood for the movement. Through editorial and technical decisions, such as adding music or using different lenses, activists use the language of film to create compelling stories that resonate with audiences. These techniques, however, also have the potential to reinforce neoliberalism by amplifying individual narratives at the expense of collective and systemic solutions.

In networked society, meaning is constructed online and off-line through complex relations of power. The struggle for meaning, therefore, must consider how power constrains the (visual) language activists use to frame social justice and how political, social, and media institutions respond to activists' frames. Antonio Gramsci's concept of "hegemony" and Manuel Castells's concept of "counterpower" are useful for theorizing how the production and distribution of media have implications for how activists claim symbolic power and build the social and institutional capacity needed to achieve real change.[62]

Analyzing activist media through *framing* highlights the social nature of knowledge production and acknowledges the challenges movements encounter when attempting to mobilize publics in networked society. Erving Goffman introduced the concept of framing in 1974 to describe how people make sense of information.[63] Frames, he argued, clarify issues by making certain pieces of information more salient for readers or viewers. Researchers have generally approached framing by identifying what frames journalists and news organizations apply to issues, reviewing their story choices, sources, and the language used to "frame" issues. Kevin Carragee and Wim Roefs, however, offered the "media hegemony thesis" to encourage scholars to consider frames not as storytelling devices but as social processes that occur in relation to the political economy of media.[64] This approach, Carragee and Roefs argued, recognizes the power structures embedded in the production and distribution of news and information and understands framing as a social and relational practice.

Gramsci's concept of hegemony helps us understand framing as a set of social practices, because he argued that power is contested not within texts but across a variety of social and political terrains. Social movements, he argued, engage in framing during the *war of maneuver*, which includes the actions taken during revolutionary struggle; and during the *war of position*, which includes how activists disseminate their ideas, influence public discourse, and seek to gain social and political leverage. Counter-hegemony and framing are commonly associated with the war of position; activist media makers inject seemingly radical ideas into public discourse, illuminate new ways for organizing social and political life, and seek to gain influence. The war of maneuver—the *actions* taken during revolutionary struggle—also represents framing practices: devising strategy, communicating plans, and organizing direct actions require that activists identify their comrades, develop relationships, and think through values and goals.

Similarly, Castells argued that meaning and power must be understood within the complexity of the networked social relations in which people live. Counterpower, he wrote, is an essential component in the framing processes that activists engage in within networked communications.[65] "Social power throughout history, but even more so in the network society, operates primarily by the construction of meaning in the human mind through processes of communication," he wrote.[66] Like Gramsci and Castells, Stuart Hall recognized that hegemony, like democracy, "is not a 'given' and permanent state of affairs, but has to be actively won and *secured*: it can also be lost."[67] Understanding that hegemony is an ongoing process, Hall argued that there are "dominant codes" embedded in language, which support status quo economic, political, and social orders, but that social movements utilize counter-strategies to contest these codes.[68]

Raymond Williams also theorized hegemony as a constant, writing that hegemony "does not just passively exist as a form of dominance. It must continually be renewed, recreated, defended, and modified. It is also continually resisted, limited, altered, challenged by pressures not at all of its own."[69] Examining the struggle over meaning and symbolic power has implications for activist media makers as well as for media studies scholars, because the struggle for meaning reveals how the tensions within society emerge and are represented through language and culture; further, the struggle for meaning shows who has the material and cultural resources needed to produce media, contest dominant codes, and offer new visions of society. Because activist media are often under-funded or produced on a volunteer basis by grassroots media makers committed to justice, these projects rely on the strength of their social networks—networks that are formed and maintained through dynamic power relations.

Producing media and art to radically critique injustice and inequality raises questions about how frames are constructed and how media privilege or constrain the distribution of certain frames over others. Nick Couldry encouraged media and cultural studies scholars to develop media ethics that recognize people's agency and their ability to *listen*. The listening that Couldry suggested requires an informed, engaged citizenry, which may be more of an ideal than a reality at a time of political polarization and extreme inequality. But if social movements and activist media makers wish to frame, distribute, and organize, through media, campaigns that promote social justice, a useful place to begin thinking about power relations is ethics.

Frames not only emerge within ethical social relationships, Couldry argued, but also operate as political strategy. "Regardless of the expansion of political actors, political change . . . must be grounded in transformations of how people evaluate political action, which in turn *depends on how society's concerns and needs get framed*," he wrote (emphasis added). "Such framing of 'the political' requires alliances across the divides of gender, age, ethnicity and class. Changing how 'the political' is framed is difficult, and this reduces the chances for even the most resourceful new networked actors to wield wider political influence."[70]

It is challenging to frame politics and create stories that resonate with various publics, especially for organizers in online spaces. Increasing the visibility of grievances through protest and public actions is one strategy movements utilize to claim power; equally important are the communicative strategies that social movements employ to tell their stories and amplify their values to wider publics. Framing social justice and politics, therefore, is related to Couldry's concept of *digital storytelling*, which, he wrote, is "the whole range of personal stories now being told in potentially public form using digital media resources."[71] Viewing stories in this way recognizes activist media as a conduit of information through which organizers network publics and put pressure on institutions.

Because stories elicit emotional responses and connect structural issues to viewers' everyday lives, filmmakers often rely on narrative strategies that emphasize individual personalities and characters. Joe Lambert stressed the empathic role of digital storytelling in networked society. "Story sharing and listening create compassion, and offer a huge dose of humility," he wrote. "While opinions may not change, certainly a deeper civility can be engendered, a kind of civility that is rapidly disappearing from our culture."[72] Relying on personal narratives' empathic power is certainly a legitimate strategy for filmmakers and grassroots media makers trying to connect art with activism; but, as Couldry cautioned, storytelling must be viewed alongside the "unjust distribution of society's resources . . . [and] the unequal distribution of 'symbolic power.'"[73] Because news media have historically applied conflict frames to social movements that emphasize violence and are episodic in nature, movements often develop communication strategies that challenge these dominant, negative portrayals of their movements and members.[74]

Exploring meaning through hegemony and media power complicates the emancipatory potential that some scholars have given to social movement media and networked communications. Media power understands meaning-making as a historical and material process that is constantly in motion.[75] By reviewing the communication strategies used in the activist media I produced with SEIU Local 105 and BLM5280, I consider how meaning and language are complicated relational processes that require significant labor and emotional intelligence from activists and organizers. The online and off-line methods that activists use to disseminate media, reveal the multifaceted distribution efforts that organizers use to influence publics and network their movements.

AFFECTIVE PUBLICS AND NETWORKING MOVEMENTS

As discussed earlier, media elicits an emotional reaction. Researchers have found that emotional intensity is the best predictor for whether people will share content online—whether the emotions are positive or negative is largely irrelevant. Therefore, emotions are important considerations for activists who create and share media and organize campaigns online. Zizi Papacharissi used the term "affective publics" to describe publics who are awakened emotionally through sharing online content. These already animated crowds present movements with opportunities to spread their messages and bring more people in.[76] In contrast to Dean,

Papacharissi embraces affective media and argued that online activities conducted by movements—such as the use of hashtags and distribution of memes and short videos—are "storytelling structures that sustain a modality of engagement that is primarily affective."[77]

As media studies scholars, social scientists, and journalists focus on big data, machine learning, and artificial intelligence, they often fail to consider *emotional intelligence*. I reflect throughout this project on the "emotional turn" in media studies and argue that the emotions within activist media alter how researchers and filmmakers document, perceive, and analyze movements.[78] Embracing emotion also avoids a central problem within most framing research, namely that "it 'cools' the analysis of movement thinking by separating [framing processes] from the deeply felt passions and value commitments that motivate action."[79] Because social media are often toxic spaces filled with misinformation, hate speech, and false news, it is important to understand how emotions affect the activities that occur on these sites. Emphasizing facts or data as the best way to win an argument or successfully persuade your opposition fails to recognize how emotions are data and are often the expression of people's lived experiences and personal truths. Emotions expressed in public and shared through media have the potential to change reality. Emotional stories reflect our values and construct the social.

Audre Lorde argued that emotion is data. "Anger is loaded with information and energy," she wrote.[80] By examining the communication and distribution strategies of the activist media I produced in collaboration with BLM5280 and SEIU Local 105, I argue that activist media create affective bridges between organizers and among local grassroots organizations. Utilizing the personal stories of activists and labor organizers to make working people's lives visible and their stories legible within the public sphere, our media connected individuals with systemic critiques and situated their labor and emotions in a broader context of communal resources and shared responsibility.

Affect informed all stages of our media production and distribution. Navigating the sometimes turbulent emotions of movements demands patience and sensitivity from all participants. Although emotions can be a useful political tactic, affect is not an effective *strategy*. As Lorde cautioned, "anger expressed and translated into action in the service of our vision and our future is a liberating and strengthening act of clarification, for it is in the painful process of this translation that we identify who are our allies with whom we have grave differences, and who are our genuine enemies."

Activist media makers construct and raise the movement's vision by translating the emotional intelligence of crowds into stories that narrate and visualize the struggle for meaning, truth, and power. Emotional intelligence is a method through which to witness truth emerging at the nexus of affect and people's material conditions. This is where scholar-activists must operate: collecting evidence, embracing emotion, and communicating why it matters. Researchers and activist media practitioners should use affect to produce stories that untangle the complexities and contradictions of an increasingly interconnected and, at times, disorienting world.

Building affective bridges requires understanding how power functions within what Manuel Castells called *networked society*. Castells argued that media "constitute by and large the space where power is decided. . . . Media are the space of power making, not the source of power holding."[81] Castells argued that internet-based forms of communication promote "mass self-communication."[82] This is problematic for movement building, because the logic of mass self-communication is based on a cult of personality that eschews collective subjectivity in favor of personal branding and self-promotion.

Social movements have capitalized, though, on mass self-communication by highlighting specific causes, such as women's rights, gay and transgender rights, and racial justice, Castells argued. These group identities occasionally cohere within networked society and form nodes of *counterpower* that disrupt and resist institutional power. Castells's theory of counterpower, however, did not consider the material conditions of those operating within networked society, what resources activists need in order to challenge hegemony, and how symbolic power operates within the public sphere. Additionally, Castells failed to acknowledge how the range of channels on which symbolic messages are displayed and broadcast makes it difficult for voices to unify around a shared political project.

Castells' theory of networked society asserted that because contemporary society is more connected than ever before thanks to digital media, the production and dissemination of messages via networks provides actors with a wider range of opportunities to claim symbolic power. Nick Couldry questioned this conclusion and asked, "What *is* a 'social practice' in Castells' view?"[83] Couldry reworked Castells's framework and explicated the social as a set of material and relational practices that operate through what Couldry calls the "myth of the mediated centre."[84] This myth naturalizes the concentration of power within certain institutions (the culture industries, broadly, and specifically, the journalism and film industries and social media companies).[85] Because so much of social life is mediated, Couldry attempts to deconstruct the myth that all institutions—political, educational, and economic—are media institutions. Castells and Couldry both agree that societies are more interconnected today, thanks in part to media and technology. But recognizing the distinction between "the media" and "the social" means acknowledging how media power disrupts and connects the two.

W. Lance Bennett and Alexandra Segerberg described the relationships among media, networks, and the social by examining how the personal stories of movement actors are framed.[86] They argued that contemporary movements (such as BLM, Occupy Wall Street, and the Arab Spring), which rely heavily on digital media, often craft *personal action frames* based on individual members' stories. These frames create "digitally enabled action networks."[87] Although these networks,

Bennett and Segerberg wrote, "cast a broader public engagement net using inter-active digital media and easy-to-personalize action themes," they struggle to realize "the familiar logic of *collective* action" (my emphasis added).[88] Distributing per-sonalized messages on social media has the potential to reach a large number of people in a variety of geographic locations and mobilize allies quickly to partici-pate in direct actions; however, the authors acknowledged, media will not alter "the fundamental principles of organizing collectives."[89] The fundamental princi-ples of organizing are listening, empathizing with others, and conducting politi-cal education. But social media and online networks are not always conducive to this work. Therefore, Bennett and Segerberg's critique is crucial for analyzing activ-ist media practices—interviewing organizers, documenting protests, and hosting film screenings—as cyclical and interdependent processes that complement move-ments' on-the-ground organizing (e.g., signing petitions, public community meet-ings, and direct actions). This framework recognizes the complex social and political dynamics movements must navigate to frame their issues and exert counterpower within networked society. As movements mature and learn how to navigate the pitfalls and potentials of media, I show how organizers are being deliberate and acting strategically with activist media.

Activist media that reframe the contemporary labor movement and network the struggle for social justice are also understood through Asef Bayat's concept of "nonmovements." Nonmovements are the everyday actions of social life that have the potential to spark larger mobilizations.[90] Bayat argued that dispersed and networked movements typically lack a formal or hierarchical structure, and this fluidity places them at a considerable disadvantage when attempting to fight a com-mon threat. The material relations among individuals, collectives, and publics are essential for developing collective power. "While making gains in nonmovements takes place individually through direct practices," Bayat wrote, "the defense of gains often takes place collectively, when a common threat turns the subjects' passive network into active communication and organized resistance."[91] Although it is important to utilize personal narratives in activist media, a concerted effort must be made to place these narratives in their social and political context and identify a common threat. My activist media with SEIU Local 105 and BLM5280 framed movement actors and union organizers not as exceptional characters or anecdotal cases but as members of a collective fighting against neoliberal economics, aus-terity, and racist patriarchal capitalism.

Network analysis recognizes that the bridges between grassroots organizations are built and sustained through communication and media. These bridges con-nect various and disparate nodes of thought and action across space and time. Rather than thinking of a power structure with a dominant core at the center, and movements and activists operating as subversive counterpublics exerting pressure from the outside, Frances Fox Piven understood the relational nature between movements and institutions as *interdependent power*.[92] Interdependent power is a strategy by which activists and subaltern classes impact politics by attaching themselves to political institutions. Although some activists wish to avoid institutionalization and decry the commercialization of politics, interdependent power explains social movement's rhetorical practices as networking effects. Interdependence examines the strengths and weaknesses of the network at various points and explores media production and distribution in relation to other actors and institutions. For Piven, power is "not concentrated at the top but is potentially widespread" and relies on a theory of the social rooted in "cooperative life."[93] Cooperation is essential for reclaiming the social within media. The production and distribution of activist media are collaborative processes that require input and feedback, at all stages, from actors across the network. Collaborative and networked media reveal how activist media practices, informed by the principles of democracy, foster shared communal values and promote participants' agency. Organizing with and through media means that grassroots filmmakers must literally and figuratively zoom in and out of protests and organizing: zooming out to reveal the broader historical and social perspectives, which helps organizers understand the boundaries and limitations of their network; zooming in to focus on individuals, their agency at specific moments, and the emotions that animate the social. Both perspectives show how a hybrid activist media strategy is needed to alter the political and economic institutions that allocate the material resources of everyday life.

FILMMAKING AS MILITANT CO-RESEARCH

As a documentary filmmaker who wanted to contribute to social justice campaigns and lend my technical expertise to labor organizers and community activists, I view my filmmaking and community-based research as communication activism for social justice research (CAR), a form of engaged communication scholarship in which researchers work with community groups, intervene to promote justice, and document these interventions.[94] My research and filmmaking with SEIU Local 105 and BLM5280 focuses on three key interventions: (1) interrupting social and political discourses that devalue and dehumanize working people; (2) critiquing objectivity and arguing that attempts at neutrality by researchers and journalists reinforce status quo racial capitalism and constrain progress; and (3) creating spaces in which organizers can unapologetically discuss the intersecting oppressions of race, class, gender, and citizenship status and strategize about how to eliminate them.

The activist media practices discussed throughout this book arose from and were informed by my "social justice sensibility" that recognizes and values the humanity of all people.[95] Thus, I sought not only to write about my experiences working with activists but also to "intervene into discourses and study the processes and outcomes of their interventions. In so doing, [scholars] strive to make a difference *through* research rather than *from* research by hoping that someone else will use the research to make a difference."[96]

Filming protests, attending public meetings, conducting interviews with activists and community organizers, and writing articles about my work were the ways I documented and publicized the organizing and communication strategies that these groups used. I also used my media as conversation starters with friends, peers, and family; when people viewed my films online or at a public screening, I used these opportunities to discuss my research and filmmaking, build on the themes raised in the films, and discuss how movement culture shapes history and reimagines social life. Writing about and reflecting on my work as an activist filmmaker presented numerous opportunities for me to theorize media for social change and review the social practices embedded in community organizing. Writing about this work also offered me opportunities to reflect on the challenges of narrating, through media, the competing visions and diverse identities within movements.[97]

Because CAR is a form of applied communication research, which, at a minimum, requires researchers to offer recommendations to the groups that the researchers work with so that those groups can improve their communication practices, my reflections are offered in the hopes that my lessons learned will be available for researchers, filmmakers, and activists seeking to leverage media to build power. With its emphasis on practical application and offering recommendations, applied communication research is often misperceived as a form of consulting. This critique comes from the false binary that some scholars have made between *basic research*, which focuses on theory testing, and *applied research*, which focuses on community-based interventions.[98]

Grounded in theories of democracy, media power, and networks, however, this project attempts to dismantle the false binary between theory and praxis. I illuminate how my filmmaking with progressive activists in Colorado may be applicable to other groups seeking to employ media in their organizing efforts. I offered SEIU Local 105 and BLM5280 my technical expertise and professional skills as a visual storyteller and documentary filmmaker and crafted stories in the hope of supporting their campaigns of social justice, in keeping with the notion that applied communication researchers are "motivated not only to understand the world, but also to change it in some respect, with luck, in a positive direction."[99] Our films animated and mobilized already committed allies, injected radical and subversive discourses into the public consciousness, and expanded these groups' local and global organizing networks.

Using art and popular culture to intervene in discourses about political and social inequalities has a long tradition in CAR. John McHale, for example, produced a documentary film, *Unreasonable Doubt*, about the wrongful conviction of a man on death row in Missouri and studied its outcomes.[100] In collaborating with local anti-death-penalty organizations to distribute the film, McHale noted the variety of functions that media serve for local organizing: "educating people, mobilizing advocates, aiding lobbying efforts, and facilitating media coverage."[101] As McHale explained, documentaries that seek "social reform and change will have more influence if they are linked to the larger mobilization of social activists with respect to the issue on the table."[102] In other words, it is not enough to produce footage of a demonstration and post it to social media; there must be considerable efforts from organizers to use the footage in various social and political arenas to effect change. My efforts to build trust with local organizations, and to ensure that our media could serve these groups' organizing, are discussed in chapter 3 as the "pre-production" of activist media.

To use media as activism is a lofty goal; but artists have, for generations, viewed photography, painting, and music as forms of resistance. Marwan Kraidy theorized art as activism in his analysis of the Arab Spring by describing graffiti, music, and poetry as *creative insurgency*—art that is intricately connected with violent and physical forms of resistance, such as protests and self-immolation.[103] Creative insurgency, he wrote, plays a "documentary role that broadens the impact of revolutionary action. . . . As a theory of power, creative insurgency rejects the distinction between mind and body, persuasion and compulsion, symbolic and physical violence. Creative insurgency is a social process."[104] Activist media, as a social process that documents resistance, occurs in relation to direct actions, union negotiations, and community meetings and emphasizes how art is not political in and of itself but does have the potential to broaden the physical and rhetorical spaces in which power is contested and won.

CONCLUSION

Pursuing co-creative research that has "impact" and "engages" with communities has become a popular trend within higher education, particularly as these institutions struggle to maintain their legitimacy. Des Freedman offered a thoughtful critique of this trend. He argued that media and communication scholars who pursue public scholarship with an activist orientation must critically examine "fundamental questions of power and injustice."[105] Placing power and justice at the heart of my activist media practices was crucial to informing my collaborative filmmaking with an ethic of care. As Freedman wrote, "methods are neither innocent nor self-sufficient and . . . what animates our methodological choices are our chosen theoretical frameworks and preferred political commitments, in particular our willingness to press for change or to justify the status quo."[106] Drawing on the work of Edward Said, Freedman noted that engaged political scholarship does not necessarily require researchers to shout and march in the streets. [107] He did argue, however, that "the work of intellectuals should be intimately and explicitly linked to their normative positions and should be in solidarity with movements that seek to realise them."[108]

Social theory, framing, and media power provide a conjunctive theoretical and methodological framework through which to investigate my normative positions as a researcher and filmmaker. This framework allows me to ask philosophical questions about activist media's relationship to justice, social life, and the furtherance of democracy. Informing my aesthetic and editorial decisions through my political commitments responds to Freedman's suggestion that research is never neutral—it is always part of a political, social, and cultural project that either reinforces the status quo or challenges it in order to bring about a more just world. By situating the social relations embedded in activist media next to the struggle over meaning and power within networked society, I embraced the dialectic between process and product and utilized methods that allowed me to pursue activist interventions through media.

2 · MOVEMENTS AND MEDIA
Structures and Evolution

The structure and organization of social movements have generated a great deal of debate among scholars and activists. To understand how movements network—internally and with affiliated, like-minded progressive organizations, both online and in their local and global contexts—I review Service Employees International Union Local 105 and Black Lives Matter 5280 in their broader social and historical contexts. Connecting the legacy of labor struggles with the legacy of racial justice demands recognizes how movements have historically produced and exhibited media to develop meaningful relationships among organizers and community members. Discussing the personal and professional relationships that I developed with SEIU and BLM5280 understands communication and media's role in networking grassroots alliances among organizers, and the discussion illuminates the challenges and limitations of using activist media for movement building. This chapter provides historical background on the uneven alliances between the labor movement and racial justice activists in the United States. I argue that the organizational logics and communicative practices of these movements have evolved in relation to the evolutions in digital media and technology. This chapter traces these evolutions in relation to video ethnography and argues that although digital media and new communication technologies offer contemporary movements some affordances, the contradictions within digital media mirror the contradictions that have long existed within social movements. Overcoming these contradictions through an ethic of care rooted in democracy and solidarity asks media practitioners, researchers, and organizers to examine their practices within networked media power.

I collaborated with SEIU Local 105 and BLM5280 for about three years, between August 2015 and May 2018, attending and documenting, through video and photography, direct actions and community meetings and engaging with these organizations on social media, including sharing and commenting on Facebook and Twitter posts and uploading videos directly to these groups' accounts. I relocated from Colorado in 2018, but I continue to stay in contact with both organizations, primarily through social media and email. Although these organizations share some similarities, this project focuses on my efforts as a filmmaker-researcher navigating racial, gendered, and socioeconomic differences between the members of these organizations and myself. Through building meaningful connections and trust with these groups, I explore errors, frustrations, joys, and excitements that I experienced during this project, and I offer a narrative account of my experiences as an activist media maker. Insights and reflections offered here are meant for those engaged in, studying, and organizing campaigns to promote radical change.

Although scholars have suggested that video production and art have the potential to foster civic participation and promote change, I complicate these often celebratory analyses by examining activist media as creative citizenship rooted in democracy.[1] Christian Fuchs defined *participatory democracy* as a "society in which all decisions are made by those who are concerned by them and all organizations (workplaces, schools, cities, politics, etc.) are controlled by those who are affected by them."[2] By following these principles and focusing on the social force of documentary, I engaged community organizers' participation in activist media, not by using a DIY (do-it-yourself) approach but, rather, through co-creative do-it-with-others (DIWO) methods. In contrast to documentary projects in which filmmakers remain detached, neutral observers and view their participants as "subjects," DIWO operates on a continuum of collaboration that demands additional ethical considerations from all participants. These considerations, which include sharing editorial control and rethinking authorship, level the filmmaking hierarchy and view participants as peers in civic life and as allies in the furtherance of democracy (as opposed to directors or individual artists). Thus, DIWO "provides a progressive re-working of documentary's historic role in the public sphere, as an open space for dialogue and a stage for the performance of citizenship."[3] Like "participation" (discussed in chapter 1), "citizenship" is also a somewhat ambiguous term. I rely on Graham Murdock's definition that citizenship is "the right to participate fully in social life with dignity and without fear, and to help formulate the forms it might take in the future."[4] Regular and thoughtful attention to my role as a filmmaker-researcher in relation to my community partners' allowed me to be a creative citizen who produced media that documented, visualized, and exhibited powerful and thoughtful representations of movements that are seeking to change the world.

MOVEMENTS FOR LABOR AND RACIAL JUSTICE

Service Employees International Union Local 105

Service Employees International Union is an international labor union with more than 150 local branches that represents nearly two million workers—primarily, in the fast-food, health care, and janitorial sectors. SEIU is "united by the belief in the dignity and worth of workers and the services they provide and dedicated to improving the lives of workers and their families and creating a more just and humane society."[5] SEIU is one of many union organizations within the broader U.S. labor movement, and these organizations often differ in how they advocate for workers' rights. In 2005, SEIU, along with the International Brotherhood of Teamsters, split from the American Federation of Labor and Congress of Industrial Organizations (AFL-CIO) over fundamental disagreements about how to organize workers. Andrew L. Stern, then president of SEIU, acknowledged the shifting nature of U.S. and global labor markets, saying: "Our world has changed, our economy has changed, employers have changed. But the AFL-CIO is not willing to make fundamental change."[6] SEIU was interested in fighting for workers' rights through direct actions and social movement-style unionism (e.g., public rallies and marches). The AFL-CIO, which represents, primarily, workers in building trades, skills, and manufacturing industries, was focused on institutional politics and contract negotiations—often described as "bread-and-butter" labor issues.[7] Along with several other unions, such as the United Farm Workers of America and the Communication Workers of America, SEIU now is an affiliate of the Change to Win coalition. SEIU Local 105 is affiliated with the AFL-CIO, and it often collaborates with organizers from various unions in Colorado and across the United States.

Although the structure of organized labor unions can be quite complex, and internal disagreements about how best to advocate for workers continue, structure is what provides SEIU locals the capacity to respond to and coordinate with community organizations. Institutional capacity means SEIU locals often have the resources needed, for example, to conduct research about the region and its workforce, arming the locals with crucial information during contract negotiations or local ballot initiatives. This study focuses on my partnership with SEIU Local 105 in Denver, Colorado, and I do not intend to generalize my conclusions or to suggest that they apply to all labor unions. Rather, the goal is to examine how structure within this local promotes or hinders democracy and to understand how activists' media practices mirror the structure of the movements with which they are aligned.

Although the Denver metro region's population growth in recent years is similar to that of other U.S. cities, specifically urban areas in Texas and North Carolina, Denver is not representative of national trends. According to the U.S. Census Bureau, the Denver metro population grew 2.1 percent in 2015, a rate more than double the national average.[8] This rapid pace of urban development has placed affordable housing and gentrification at the center of many organizing campaigns conducted by SEIU Local 105 and BLM5280. These campaigns often highlight problems related to the quality of life of low-wage workers in the service industry—workers who, primarily, are immigrants, women, and people of color. Figures from the Bureau of Labor Statistics, for example, showed that in 2016, Black and Hispanic workers made up about 40 percent of those in service occupations.[9] The neoliberal assault on workers' ability to organize has altered dramatically union membership over the past forty years. In 1979, U.S. labor peaked at 21 million workers, but in 2003, that number fell to 15.8 million.[10] The stereotype of mostly white and male union members is false. According to a 2016 U.S. Department of Labor population survey, 46 percent of union members were women, 12 percent were African American or Black, and 17 percent were Hispanic.[11] Reflecting these national numbers, many of Local 105's members are Mexican immigrants.

Structural inequalities exacerbated by population growth and associated increases in the cost of living disproportionately affect low-wage and part-time workers in the service industry. Highlighting these inequalities has been central to the Fight for $15 campaign, which SEIU has been instrumental in promoting. The campaign began in 2012 when several hundred fast-food workers in New York City demanded an increase to the minimum wage; organizers with the Fight for $15 have focused largely on the gross disparity between workers' pay and the compensation of chief executive officers (CEOs). An "Executive Paywatch" analysis released by the AFL-CIO found that CEOs of the companies making up the Standard and Poor's 500 (S&P 500) stock index made 347 *times* more than the average worker.[12] The Fight for $15 has since grown into an international coalition of more than three hundred chapters representing home care workers, retail employees, and adjunct faculty.[13] Several cities across the United States, including Seattle, San Francisco, Los Angeles, and New York City, have implemented a $15-per-hour minimum wage, and, after collective bargaining negotiations with SEIU Local 1199, the Massachusetts state legislature raised the hourly pay of home health care workers to $15 in 2018.[14] Organized labor in the United States has seen steep declines in its membership and weakened political influence since the 1970s, as a result of capital flight to the Global South and China, "right-to-work" laws in southern U.S. states, and automation and technological innovation.[15] But millions of U.S. workers have rallied behind the Fight for $15 and other organized labor campaigns that are demanding fairer working conditions and higher wages—often based in union membership—for service-sector employees.

SEIU Local 105 has seized on this energy and approaches organizing through a social justice framework that pursues workers' rights and dignity for all. The local represents 7,100 home health care workers, property service workers, and janitors in the Denver metro area and, by its nature, Local 105 is networked, both at local and international levels. Its network is connected internally with affiliated SEIU chapters and externally with grassroots community groups and labor coalitions. A hybrid approach to union and community organizing allows Local 105 to work on both contract negotiations and broader issues championed by social movements, local activists, and the local's members—for example, health care, immigration reform, education, environmental issues, and housing. Local 105's networking efforts must also be understood within the complex history of strained relationships among immigration justice organizers, racial justice activists, and labor union leaders. Francesca Polletta discussed these tensions between civil rights activists and labor organizers and argued that disagreements among these groups often stemmed from the unequal distribution of power in leadership roles between Black worker members and their white counterparts.[16] Mae Ngai similarly described how Mexican immigrants were often vilified by labor organizers during the 1940s and 1950s for driving down wages in the agricultural industry and for "taking" well-paying middle-class jobs from U.S. workers.[17]

Kim Moody provided a comprehensive history of U.S. labor unions in his socialist pamphlet and working paper, "The Rank and File Strategy."[18] Moody examined how internal tensions between rank-and-file members and union bureaucracies, which have often been racialized and gendered, have hindered the U.S. labor movement's ability to promote class consciousness rooted in working-class solidarity. Notable for examining how activist media network movements across space and time, Moody showed how Latino and African American union members used newsletters and pamphlets to inject a militant and antagonistic framing into their union campaigns; these discourses sought to upend the post–World War II consensus in which industrial and trade unions benefited from capitalist expansion. These radical messages promoted strikes, mobilized community support, and challenged the mostly white and male union leaders, who preferred to maintain the status quo through orderly professional bargaining with management.

Local 105 has attempted to navigate this history by highlighting how labor struggles, although rooted in class, are interconnected with race, gender, sexual orientation, and immigrant rights. Local 105's leadership made a concerted effort to feature Spanish-speaking members at rallies and in interviews I conducted for the documentary films. Organizers also avoid the "model minority" stereotype and focus instead on shared communal values and the agency and humanity of all people. Interviews and audio clips from rallies were included in my activist media with English subtitles to make clear the intersectional and international struggles of working people and to push back against media and political discourses that divide working people along identity issues and seek to criminalize immigrants. Highlighting members' voices and community allies in our activist media framed Local 105 as a union that uses a rank-and-file strategy based on democratic participation and grounds its issues in solidarity and justice.

Black Lives Matter 5280

Black Lives Matter is "not a moment, but a movement . . . [and] is a call to action and a response to the virulent anti-Black racism that permeates our society." The movement was formed in 2013 by Alicia Garza, Opal Tometi, and Patrisse Cullors, after George Zimmerman was acquitted in the shooting death of seventeen-year-old Trayvon Martin in Florida. In 2014, after the murder of eighteen-year-old Michael Brown in Ferguson, Missouri, Black Lives Matter grew beyond being a social media hashtag and became an international network of social justice activists, with various official and unofficial chapters in the United States and Canada.[19]

Securing official numbers of BLM membership and chapters is somewhat difficult; a search of Facebook and Twitter reveals roughly forty BLM chapters, but this number may be somewhat inflated because anyone can create a social media account and a website and declare that they are "part of the movement." The movement's reliance on digital media—smartphones, email, and social media, specifically—creates a networked and hybrid movement consisting of semiautonomous local chapters that operate with a somewhat horizontal structure. Although each chapter conducts its organizing and creates its leadership structure somewhat differently, Black Lives Matter 5280 promotes core leaders who conduct political education with members and allies, organize actions in partnership with affiliated grassroots groups, and manage the organization's social media and public communication. By avoiding the pitfalls of horizontalism—a strategy relied on by other recent movements, such as Occupy Wall Street, in which consensus and deliberation were paramount—BLM5280 instead uses a structure in which members and core organizers are accountable to one another and the larger movement.

BLM avoids privileged membership based on social capital, education, gender, ability, citizenship status, and sexual orientation. As a white male, however, my membership in and affiliation with BLM5280 required sensitivity, and my efforts to produce documentaries for one local chapter reveals the challenges and contradictions that activist media makers face when collaborating with movements. Although my project details specific elements of activist media—creating and sharing video, photography, and text, primarily, on social media—my attendance at community meetings and direct actions also provides guidance for grassroots media makers about where, when, and how to plug in to civic and political life.

I wrestled throughout my media making with the racial and class privileges that have long been associated with radical alternative media and activist video collectives. Explaining in detail my efforts to navigate these organizing spaces not only offers insights on how to produce radical media as a thoughtful and compassionate comrade in the fight for liberation but also illuminates how BLM5280 uses short films, social media, public demonstrations, and community meetings to bridge antagonistic politics with messages of love and community. By embracing what Chantal Mouffe called "radical democracy," BLM simultaneously antagonizes elected officials and broader publics through protest (e.g., during the presidential primary campaigns in 2016, BLM activists protested both Bernie Sanders and Hillary Clinton) and strategically pursues campaigns that advocate for policy reform. As Mouffe explained, "a project of radical, plural democracy . . . requires the existence of multiplicity, of plurality, and of conflict, and sees in them the *raison d'être of politics*."[20]

When the New Left movements of the 1960s and 1970s began pursuing justice by focusing on members' identities, critics argued that the movements furthered the personalization of politics and moved away from collective struggle.[21] I contest these arguments by showing how BLM5280 grows out of, and is informed by, the U.S. civil rights movement and links the struggles of Black people to all global struggles for liberation. In fact, a recent incident revealed just how committed BLM5280 is to the principles of democracy. Following the global protests for racial justice and against police violence in 2020, ten local chapters, including BLM5280, expressed concern with Patrisse Cullors's appointment as executive director of the Black Lives Matter Global Network (BLMGN). Under the hashtag #BLM10, the organizers wrote: "Despite years of effort, no acceptable internal process of accountability has ever been produced by BLMGN and these recent events have undermined the efforts of chapters seeking to democratize its processes and resources."[22] The demand for democracy and accountability from movement organizers speaks to the internal struggles that all movements navigate in relation to leadership, funding and resources, and deciding whose voices matter.

Co-founder Alicia Garza argued that BLM is committed to social justice through "solidarity with all oppressed people who are fighting for their liberation [because] we know that our destinies are intertwined."[23] By supporting multiple identities and modes through which members produce and disseminate representations of Blackness, queerness, gender, and sexuality, BLM shows the potential of, and contradictions inherent in, radical democratic politics and antagonistic pluralism. In its first six years, BLM5280 has cultivated a network of formal and informal connections using a variety of movement tactics, including producing and disseminating activist media; attending Denver city council hearings to advocate for affordable housing and police reform; founding a "Freedom School," which offers youth political education about inequities and racial literacy; and hosting community meetings. Because mainstream media often mischaracterize BLM and its supporters as dangerous or violent, BLM5280 uses activist media to challenge these representations, strengthen its relationship with supporters, and sustain itself through moments of high and low visibility.

Three Black women, Amy Brown, Bianca Williams, and Reverend Dawn Riley Duval, founded BLM5280 in May 2015. Brown, Williams, and Duval organize with the movement in various capacities, but they have mostly shifted the core organizing duties to others in the movement. These women were instrumental in crafting BLM5280's vision and facilitating my participation as an activist media maker with the group. The chapter's mission statement reads, in part:

Our chapter is part of a national movement, aligned in Black love, power, and liberation, embodying the declaration that Black Lives Matter—regardless of gender identity, gender expression, sexual identity, immigration location or status, gang affiliation, profession, ability, economic status, and religious beliefs or disbelief. . . . Also in keeping with the national movement, BLM5280 centers and celebrates the lives and leadership of Black women and girls, aligning all Black people in love, power, and liberation. Our work is to cultivate communities of abundant joy where all Black people are emboldened and empowered to lead, love, heal, and thrive.[24]

BLM is often framed in the news media as controversial, which delegitimizes the movement and its demands.[25] I wanted to understand how these framings are perceived and challenged by movement members and how they affect BLM's internal organizing and communication strategies. I discovered through a Facebook search in August 2015 that a recently founded BLM chapter in Colorado was hosting monthly community meetings. I did not want to observe BLM5280 from a distance—watching social media and news coverage about the movement—so I began attending these meetings in Denver. While there, I observed BLM5280's meeting practices, participated in group activities at meetings, interviewed co-lead and co-founder Amy Brown and other members and allies, filmed and produced three short videos for the movement, and conducted a qualitative ethnographic analysis of BLM5280's Facebook page. Moving between BLM5280's online and off-line spaces allowed me to observe and appreciate the diversity of tactics that the movement uses. My analyses do not seek to generalize to the BLM movement or to suggest that BLM5280 is representative of all chapters. Each of BLM's chapters has unique methods for recruiting new members, communicating with other chapters and the national "headquarters," and pursuing policy campaigns. BLM5280 functions both independently and cooperatively with the Black Lives Matter Network and is part of the broader Movement for Black Lives (M4BL), a collective of more than 150 organizations including Black Youth Project 100 (BYP100), Dream Defenders, Ella Baker Center for Human Rights, and others that are fighting for Black liberation.

BLM5280 core members meet regularly to discuss policy initiatives, review current and future campaigns, and direct members' actions during campaigns. I was not invited to core meetings and, recognizing my identity as a white man, I did not ask whether I could attend; consequently, I attended public community meetings and other demonstrations I knew BLM5280 members would be participating in. Community meetings, typically, are held monthly to update members and allies on the work in which core organizers are engaged, and they are announced prior to the meeting date through public Facebook and Twitter posts, as well as via an email announcement to the organization's mailing list. On August 26, 2015, I attended my first BLM5280 community meeting, where I met co-founder Bianca Williams and discussed my work as a filmmaker and my interest in contributing to the movement's media strategy. I learned that Dr. Williams was a professor at the University of Colorado Boulder, where I was enrolled as a graduate student, and we scheduled a meeting on campus to talk more about what I could bring to the organization and my intentions as a community organizer.

I attended four community meetings between August 2015 and July 2016, after which time BLM5280 changed its policy and created meeting spaces for people of color only. BLM5280 explained this decision in a Facebook announcement prior to the July 27, 2016, community meeting:

> During our #135AndCounting action, we made so many inspiring and soul filling connections with folx from our beautiful communities of color. As we talked with POC [people of color] family during those hours, it became clear that communities of color need safe spaces in which we can just BE. BLM5280 wants to continue to create spaces in which POC can build relationships, heal, and strategize. We hope that you'll join us this Wednesday, as we continue discussions started at the BLM5280 tree, work on healing, building community, and planning for the work ahead of us.[26]

In July 2016, BLM5280 decided to make its community meetings spaces for people of color only. BLM5280 justified this decision by sharing blogs and news articles that discussed the importance of these spaces for Black people, but some organizers questioned the decision by noting the demographics of Denver. According to 2019 data from the U.S. Census Bureau, only 10 percent of Denver residents identify as Black or African American, whereas 81 percent identify as white.[27] Some organizers I spoke with worried that the decision would significantly limit BLM5280's ability to build local power and collaborate with other grassroots community organizations. BLM5280's decision to close its meetings and how the decision affected my activist media practices are explored further in the next chapter.

Despite not having access to community meeting spaces, I found other avenues through which to continue learning about how BLM5280 frames its struggle for justice. When I began community organizing in 2011, an organizer in Philadelphia said something to me that has stuck: "Get in where you fit in." This maxim has proved valuable for me throughout my activist media making. I continued to "get in" with BLM5280 by attending community meetings hosted by Showing Up for Racial Justice (SURJ) Denver, and by attending webinars hosted by the Movement for Black Lives.

ENTERING THE FIGHT FOR LABOR AND RACIAL JUSTICE

My activist media project gained momentum at a community meeting jointly hosted by SEIU Local 105 and BLM5280 on October 21, 2015, at the First Unitarian Society in Denver. Amy Brown worked for a brief time as a union organizer with SEIU Local 105, and she facilitated the meeting between the two groups. The meeting focused on organized labor's history of fighting for workers' rights and racial justice. During the meeting, I met Andy Jacob, the political director of Local 105, and I explained my work as a documentary filmmaker and media researcher. I expressed my interest in producing short films featuring union members, with the intention of conveying their stories and humanizing the labor movement. Jacob was excited about the idea and, after a follow-up email, he put me in contact with María Corral, the communications coordinator at Local 105. Corral facilitated the majority of my work with the union, notifying me about upcoming actions and introducing me to a home health care worker, Melissa Benjamin, who agreed to be profiled in a short film. This film was the first story I produced with Local 105, and it was done at no charge. Melissa and the union's leadership were impressed with the film's quality, and, subsequently, they commissioned me for future media projects. Although accepting payment from SEIU may be viewed as an ethical conflict for a researcher, creating the risk that I would be hesitant to critique Local 105's organizing strategies, I offer this detail to provide transparency and self-reflexivity and to acknowledge my role as a partner whose political commitments were aligned with the organizations that I studied.

I produced five short documentaries with Local 105 over the course of two and a half years: a four-minute profile of Melissa and four stories featuring rallies in downtown Denver. This series of short films culminated in a twenty-three-minute documentary, *Radical Labor: Aligning Unions with the Streets* (2018). This film expanded on the short films, which were episodic in nature and presented information only about specific rallies, and included in-depth interviews with the leadership and staff of Local 105, community organizers who had worked with the SEIU, and politicians. The twenty-three-minute film explored in greater depth the networking efforts of labor unions in Colorado and the challenges with bridging racial and economic justice, something that a three-minute film covering a demonstration cannot necessarily accomplish. Working with union leadership and community organizers, I organized a screening in Boulder, Colorado, which included a question-and-answer session with community organizers, students, and residents.

More than thirty interviews with organizers and activists were conducted for this project. Formal interviews for *Radical Labor* lasted between thirty and sixty minutes, but others, conducted spontaneously during rallies, lasted only a few minutes. Interviews and select meetings were audio-recorded, with interviewees' permission, and transcribed. I reviewed these transcripts, alongside my field notes taken during and after public demonstrations, as well as social media from BLM5280, SEIU Local 105, and affiliated organizations that promoted the Fight for $15 and racial justice. Many of the people interviewed were suggested by Corral, the communications coordinator at Local 105, and I asked interviewees at the end of interviews to suggest people I should speak with for the film. Thus, my collaborative research relied on the community partners who were involved in the research to guide the trajectory of the project. Interviewing organizers who were unaffiliated with SEIU, but who partnered with the union on campaigns and actions, broadened the scope beyond Local 105 and provided context about networking effects in Colorado and how unions, in partnership with grassroots community organizations, are fighting for justice.

My documentary productions with SEIU and BLM5280 grew out of attending community meetings, where I met key organizers and members and received

invitations to document their actions and events. Through observing public meetings and talking with organizers, I investigated how grassroots networks are created
and strengthened through media and how these networks leverage multimedia in
their pursuit of justice. The 2016 presidential election of Donald Trump created
urgency among organizers; the election compelled a racial reckoning in America
and revived left politics, as organizers debated how to respond, bridge various struggles, and combat systemic injustices. This book and the associated documentary
films, therefore, focus on the day-to-day work of organizing and detail how labor
unions and activists frame narratives of racial and economic justice. I analyze the
micro-practices of democracy and offer thoughts about the possibilities and limitations of building, through media, a broad-based left movement. Activists and
organizers referred to throughout this book performed their activism publicly by
participating in rallies, publishing social media posts and blog essays, and giving
speeches at public meetings. These very public acts sought to influence public discourse about people and places, and these activists were aware that speaking out
carried significant risks, such as being ostracized from family and friends or being
labeled as an agitator by current and possible future employers. Despite these risks,
organizers were passionate about sharing their stories with public audiences through
film and this research, and, therefore, they are identified here by name.

   I had limited access to BLM5280's organizing spaces as a result of the organization's mission to create spaces for Black people. Therefore, I rely more on public social media activity and online essays and statements from the organization
and less on my direct involvement with the group and its members. As an outsider attempting to understand this organization's mission, I drew on a November 2015 essay published by BLM5280 co-founder Bianca Williams, "Making Black
Lives Matter: Reflections on the Declaration of the Movement." In the essay,
Williams describes the movement's "four concepts of resistance": disruption,
voice, life, and collaboration.[28] The essay was shared on BLM5280's social media
accounts and spread throughout its online networks, and it informs my analysis
of the movement. Despite these limitations, I produced three short films with
BLM5280. Documenting protests and direct actions as a community-engaged
researcher and filmmaker and studying the networking efforts of grassroots organizations demands additional reflections on the evolution of activists' media practices. The legacy of radical alternative media provides important historical context
about the evolution of activist media.

THE EVOLUTION OF DOCUMENTARY: ACTIVIST
PRACTICES AND VIDEO ETHNOGRAPHY

Documentary filmmaking requires engaging in practices that are necessarily close
and intimate. Asking probing questions and placing cameras and microphones
in front of people can be uncomfortable at times; but these practices can also

foster understanding and mutual respect among the participants. Investigating these practices, in relation to how scholars have viewed ethnographic filmmaking, is crucial for understanding the social relations embedded within documentary. Scholars have discussed how ethnographic filmmaking has evolved from the classical Chicago School model, which favored a positivist approach to documentary, to *new ethnography*, which "requires the researcher to possess an extensive knowledge and expertise of the culture." [29] Distinctions between old and new approaches to ethnographic filmmaking often reflect the distinction researchers have made between emic and etic knowledge. Emic knowledge is the understanding of life and culture by those who live it; and etic knowledge is the understanding of life and culture by observers of other people's lives and cultures.

Activists' media practices have similarly evolved along this distinction between old and new ethnography. The "analog era" of video ethnography, for example, often used Chicago School methods, in which researchers documented public behaviors and then rated or coded the footage at a later time in a controlled environment. Popular documentary films of this era, such as Robert Flaherty's *Nanook of the North* (1922), used a cinema verité style that favored wide and medium shots, minimal editing, and ambient sound as opposed to music. This aesthetic gives viewers the impression that the film depicts events "as they happened." Films of the analog era share some characteristics of early radical film projects. As detailed by Angela J. Aguayo, filmmakers in the early 1900s produced "sociological films" that provided "precious historical evidence" of everyday life.[30] Although radical filmmakers did not rate or code behaviors in their footage, they often used an aesthetic of distance to communicate authenticity.

Despite any perceived distance between the filmmakers and the people represented in their films, these films paved the way for an emerging working-class film culture in the United States. Documentaries of this period coincided with the era of 1930s militant labor organizing in the United States, and Aguayo argued that radical filmmakers moved beyond social realism by highlighting strikes and labor actions and by distributing their media in real time and in concert with organizing campaigns in order to catalyze change.

Although methods from the analog era had benefits for researchers and grassroots media makers—data could be stored easily, intercoder reliability could be achieved, and later generations could access the footage in archives—contemporary activist media practices resemble the *digital era* of video ethnography, which has three distinct characteristics: (1) the technology is lighter and inexpensive, and, thus, it is more accessible to the hobbyist, traveler, and researcher; (2) in contrast to film, digital recordings can be copied to computer hard drives indefinitely without loss of picture or audio quality; and (3) nonlinear computer editing systems do not destroy the original media and allow editors to "cut, paste and modify media for analysis."[31] As video replaced film and new technologies became more widely available in the 1960s and 1970s, the barriers to media production lowered, spawning numerous community video collectives. These collectives, however, often reflected the racial, gendered, and class inequalities of the broader society. Oral histories of this era describe how media makers within these video collectives parachuted in to marginalized communities to document injustices.[32] In addition, the commune movement's libertarian ideology was reflected in these collectives; rather than use media to promote "shared political principles," participants created "alternative lifestyle communities around video production."[33]

Indymedia is notable for examining the analog-to-digital transition within radical alternative media. Founded in 1999 to document the World Trade Organization (WTO) conference in Seattle, Washington, Indymedia is a network of grassroots videographers, journalists, and activists. It sought to challenge mainstream media framings of global inequality and neoliberalism. Researchers credit Indymedia with inflecting Occupy Wall Street and the Arab Spring uprisings with discourses that bridge struggles in the global justice movement across space and time. Chris Robé and Todd Wolfson argued that Indymedia, by creating its own digital infrastructure and using it to amplify a critique of neoliberal globalization, "facilitated our imagination of a wider world of struggle." Rather than using independent networks, contemporary movements, such as Black Lives Matter and #MeToo, instead rely primarily on social media to communicate with and mobilize their supporters. Therefore, these movements struggle to link shared struggles across space and time, Robé and Wolfson argued, because the surveillance mechanisms and commercial logics embedded in social media conflict with several core features of democracy: deliberation, transparency, and accountability.[34]

The evolution from analog to digital within video ethnography is helpful for exploring my activist media practices in Colorado. Considering the lessons learned from Indymedia and past video collectives, I documented rallies and carefully edited short films and photographs in ways that linked labor and racial justice with broader communal values of equality, peace, and justice. Although activists and grassroots media makers are reluctant to use social media for reasons that I discuss throughout this book, these platforms have considerable reach, which allowed me and my community partners to identify targeted audiences of supporters and share bite-sized, emotional stories about activist campaigns and union members with them. Despite Indymedia's successes, its interface was not user-friendly or accessible for people with limited technical proficiency. Facebook, Instagram, and Twitter, although highly problematic, are fairly intuitive and have billions of users worldwide. Activists I worked with valued these sites as practical complements to their local organizing. However, it is important to note that we did not rely solely on social media as a distribution strategy; we organized community screenings and media workshops and used our films to bring organizers and community members into conversation.

Producing visual storytelling to persuade audiences, and collapsing the distance between myself and my community partners, presented additional ethical considerations for me as a researcher-filmmaker. Removing the distance that characterized the analog era allowed me to evaluate whose voices were included during the production and distribution of our activist media and who was benefiting from the outcomes. Moving between media production, writing, reflecting, and theorizing provided me with opportunities to re-examine my research questions and revise the activist media practices that I used in collaboration with SEIU and BLM5280.

Another binary within video ethnography that is helpful to review is *presentation* versus *research practice*. "Presentation" refers to filmmaker-researchers as detached observers who "portray reality on film as truthfully as possible."[35] Research practice, on the other hand, aligns closely with my activist media practices, as it contends that the camera is not a "fourth wall" that divides filmmakers and audiences from those represented in the film, but, rather, is a "fluid wall . . . [that] recognizes the mutual benefits of open communication and adaptable interactions."[36] Anthropologist and filmmaker Paul Henley believed that interpreting the meaning of filmed events requires "active engagement on the part of the filmmaker . . . and this is bound to involve some measure of subjectivity."[37] The camera, for Henley, presents filmmakers with opportunities to become intimately engaged in people's lives and to achieve an understanding that is inaccessible to filmmakers who insist on remaining neutral and distant. As Henley explained, "the implicit theory of knowledge underlying this approach is that true social reality is not to be found in the superficial observable details of everyday life but rather in the underlying relationships, sentiments, and attitudes which sustain them."[38]

Indeed, introducing cameras changed the relational dynamics between me and the organizers featured in our media. During one-on-one interviews, for example, some participants became nervous in the presence of a camera and were thus reluctant to share intimate details of their lives. In contrast, cameras are nearly ubiquitous at protests, rallies, and public demonstrations. In these instances, participants either ignored the cameras and took their presence for granted or exaggerated their behaviors in an attempt to perform for the cameras. Occasionally setting the camera down during conversations and planning meetings with community activists, or leaving it home altogether, allowed me to engage with participants on a deeper human level and understand the underlying relationships and sentiments that animated their organizing. These relationships took considerable time to develop, but they helped our productions go beyond superficial details about protest and media. Acknowledging our shared humanity during documentary's in-between moments—while setting up lights and microphones or while repositioning the camera—allowed me to remove the distance between myself and the film's participants and to create empathic spaces in which to document movement moments as unobtrusively as possible.

My filmmaking recognized the varying approaches to video ethnography and aimed for what Luke E. Lassiter called "collaborative ethnography"—a method that encourages the organizations or groups being filmed and studied to become involved in the research through consultation and critique of the practices and products.[39] The purpose of this project was not to teach community organizers and activists technical skills so that they can produce media, but, instead, to involve them in production and distribution decisions, so that our projects reflect the shared authorship and ownership that is necessary for a truly democratic partnership. None of the projects completed with SEIU Local 105 and BLM5280 was produced with a contract or licensing agreement. Although professional filmmakers may be alarmed by this fact and recommend that filmmakers always secure a contract that, at least, defines copyright ownership, I had candid conversations with my collaborators throughout every stage of the filmmaking process—from conception to production to distribution—to ensure that they were aware of and agreed with the decisions being made. Being connected with many of the community organizers on Facebook and having their phone numbers and email addresses allowed me to contact the organizers prior to the publication of a photograph, film, or research article. These brief exchanges ensured that I reflected them, their organizations, and their campaigns fairly and in accordance with their mission statements. Interviewees for the twenty-three-minute documentary, however, were asked to sign a release form, to make the project eligible for screenings on public television and at film festivals.

Such an approach to authorship aligns with the field of "participatory video."[40] Beginning in the 1970s with the National Film Board of Canada's Challenge for Change initiative, this field follows the definition of participation set forth at the outset of this chapter: democratic citizenship is grounded in people's agency over the things that affect their lives and communal values and responsibilities. Participatory video argues against making films *about* social issues and instead encourages filmmakers to use visual storytelling "as a *form* of social change."[41]

Partnering with community organizers on documentaries exploring issues of labor, race, and inequality meant centering voices of labor leaders and community organizers. Telling the history of labor, and describing the challenges to building a multiracial, multigenerational coalition of working people, meant highlighting the voices of those at the center of these struggles.

Despite not having large budgets, activists are using inexpensive camera equipment, smartphones, and free video-editing software to produce compelling films that advocate for social change. I purchased professional camera and audio equipment, lights, and editing software after leaving my staff position as a video journalist with a U.S. broadcast television station. Having a basic camera kit allowed me to make low- and no-budget films without worrying about satisfying a funding source. Activist media that radically critique capitalism are unlikely to receive grants from foundations or wealthy donors; therefore, activists must strategize about how they will sustain their media and communication initiatives without compromising their principles.[42] I am fortunate that I currently have a full-time salaried job, and I am commissioned regularly for commercial projects that "pay the bills." I view the short films that I produced with SEIU and BLM5280 as "passion projects" or "labors of love," but I critique this discourse and offer reflections on the labor of co-creative research in the book's conclusion.

CONCLUSION

Stating my political and ideological orientations, as an activist filmmaker, media researcher, and social justice advocate, places additional scrutiny on the methods and procedures that I use. Some readers may immediately discredit my analyses of activist media, perhaps because I have a "bias" or an agenda. I flatly reject these criticisms and offer, instead, media and research produced in solidarity with the communities with which I worked. These groups' missions are grounded in communal responsibility, protecting and redistributing public resources, and defending the rights and lives of society's most vulnerable people. Because immigrants and communities of color are increasingly targeted by state violence and political rhetoric that demonizes and criminalizes them, researchers have a responsibility to build partnerships with communities that have been most affected by these dynamics and to work with them to challenge dominant narratives, claim symbolic and political power, and promote new political imaginations.

This chapter has detailed how debates over structure, and over how activists navigate distance and network struggles across space and time, are not new issues for social movements. Although community organizers have done considerable work highlighting the commonalities among working people and building sustainable communication and media infrastructures that allow organizers to speak directly with supporters and publics, challenges remain. With numerous grassroots groups fighting simultaneously for Black lives, trans lives, Native lives, environmental justice, immigration reform, access to health care, and economic justice (among many other issues), how do activists produce media that capture the essence of these struggles? Learning how to share SEIU and BLM5280's stories, for me, involved navigating and embracing tensions within diverse organizing spaces, building trust with movement leaders, and understanding how and where I "fit in."

3 · PRE-PRODUCTION
Embracing Confrontation and Difference

Producing media in partnership with activists and social movements demands that filmmakers acknowledge their position to the movements with which they work and be sensitive to the racial, gendered, and class differences among all participants. Prior to documenting protests or producing films about activists' personal stories, filmmakers must spend significant time in *pre-production*. This includes, for example, engaging in various forms of political education in which organizers reflect on their political orientations, strengthen their interpersonal relationships, and recognize how their perspectives influence their communication strategies and editorial decisions. My political education as a filmmaker-researcher occurred by attending public community meetings, following key activists and community organizations on social media, and reading about the history and complexity of social movement struggles in the United States. Before I could portray adequately community organizers and activists' stories in media, I first needed to understand how activists discuss the intersections of labor, gender, citizenship, and race and recognize how these discourses inform the material and social relationships among movement members.

As a white filmmaker producing short films for Black Lives Matter 5280, a Black-led social movement, and for Service Employees International Union Local 105, a labor union with many monolingual, Spanish-speaking Hispanic members, I confronted my personal identities by acknowledging what Teju Cole called the "white-savior industrial complex."[1] In his critique of *Kony 2012*—a YouTube documentary about Uganda's Joseph Kony, the leader of the Lord's Resistance Army, and his recruitment and use of child soldiers—Cole argued that the problem with white, Western filmmakers who make social justice films is that these filmmakers do not seek justice or wish to challenge the status quo; rather, they want "a big emotional experience that validates [their] privilege."[2] As an independent filmmaker and community researcher, I regularly attended community meetings, introduced myself to organizers and volunteers working on policy reforms in Colorado, and showed up to direct actions to stand in solidarity with BLM5280 and SEIU Local 105. All of these activities are part of the "due diligence" that Cole argued is required of organizers who work with, or on behalf of, groups whose members have diverse geographic, gender-identifying, and racial characteristics.

This chapter explores my efforts as an allied filmmaker to navigate the differences between myself and the members of the two organizations with which I worked. These efforts, discussed as the pre-production of activist media, encourage researchers to confront and embrace the tensions and emotions inherent to community organizing. I review the community meetings I attended to examine how earning trust is essential to activist media. Community meetings often challenge participants to practice what anthropologist and BLM5280 co-founder Bianca Williams calls "radical honesty," a Black-feminist approach to education and organizing that embraces emotion in the service of truth-telling.[3]

Radical honesty means sharing individual and collective truths and identifying to whom you are accountable. Throughout the project, I solicited feedback from BLM5280 and SEIU and flattened the filmmaking hierarchy by sharing editorial control and authorship with my community partners. This chapter explores the behind-the-scenes practices I conducted prior to making and publishing media. Reviewing my pre-production with community organizers reveals how activist media are not about technical expertise, camera equipment, or narrative strategies per se; fundamentally, activist media are about how the material social conditions in which movements operate inform how they relate to each other and frame their demands.

COMMUNITY MEETINGS AND BUILDING COLLABORATIONS

I attended numerous community meetings, events, and rallies that were either hosted by or participated in by BLM5280. Initially, walking into these spaces brought me some discomfort. Because I was fairly inexperienced with community organizing and the language of racial justice at the outset of this project, I was reluctant to put myself in vulnerable situations where organizers might call me out for saying the wrong things, challenge me about my identities or privilege, or question my commitment to the movement for Black liberation.

I attended my first BLM5280 community meeting in August 2015, and I was unsure whether my presence as a white ally was welcome. Upon arriving, I stood near the entrance as people mingled prior to the meeting, and I was quickly and warmly welcomed into the room by an organizer who encouraged me to make a plate of food for myself (Figure 3.1). BLM5280 often offered food, prepared buffet style, for participants prior to its public community meetings. People are invited to gather around dinner and have informal conversations with those seated next to them before the "official" start of each meeting. Food may seem like an insignificant detail, but Amy Brown told me that this offering reinforces two of

FIGURE 3.1. BLM5280 community meeting in Denver, Colorado, on August 26, 2015. (Photo by Gino Canella.)

BLM5280's "community commitments" listed in its mission statement: community and love. "Our community meetings are really based on how can we actively love on our community in this time," she said. "And, yeah, when you ask someone to come out at night, what feels like love? Hot food feels like love. To me, if I got home and there's hot food, that is loving."

Because BLM5280 is also committed to honoring Black women's labor, it provides free childcare at meetings. "Childcare is hugely important, especially because we're centered around women and Black women," Brown told me. "We want them to know we see you. We see the work you're putting in. We know childcare is more expensive than rent. Let us carry that for you for a couple hours, it's the least we can do."

This particular meeting focused on BLM5280's #ChangeTheNameStapleton campaign, an effort that sought to change the name of a neighborhood in northeast Denver that was named for the former mayor of Denver, Benjamin Stapleton, who had known ties to the Ku Klux Klan. Organizers announced an upcoming forum hosted by Stapleton United Neighbors (SUN) that would discuss the name change, and they encouraged attendees to show up and voice their support for changing the neighborhood's name.

Knowing I wanted to build a partnership with BLM5280 and contribute to its organizing, I attended the SUN meeting in September and listened as residents argued overwhelmingly in favor of changing the neighborhood's name. At the conclusion of the meeting, I stood next to Vince Bowen, an organizer with BLM5280, as he discussed the meeting with a friend. Bowen's friend introduced himself to me and asked me, "Are you with them [BLM5280]?" Because, at that point, I had attended only one BLM5280 meeting, and because I did not consider myself "with" the movement, I did not know what to say. I fumbled through my reply: "Well, no, not really." I should have been more articulate and stated that, although I am not an official BLM5280 member, I strongly support its mission of racial justice, and I am willing to do what I can to advance its goals and communicate its story through media. My familiarity with BLM5280 and the etiquette around membership versus allyship was low in this moment, but I continued listening to BLM5280's organizers, learning about systemic and institutional racism, and gaining the vocabulary necessary to offer more thoughtful responses when asked about my position with respect to the movement in the future.

Continuing to observe and educate myself about the movement, I attended my next BLM5280 community meeting in June 2016. This meeting included a presentation by two speakers who were featured in future documentary films I produced, Roshan Bliss and Alex Landau of the Denver Justice Project (DJP). They gave a forty-minute presentation that focused on the Denver district attorney (DA) race in the November 2016 election, and the role the DA plays in the criminal justice system—an issue that is central to BLM's organizing against incarceration and policing. Bliss and Landau emphasized the DA's extraordinary role in negotiating plea deals, setting mandatory minimum sentences, and prosecuting police misconduct. Denver Justice Project organizers, along with BLM5280 organizers, encouraged attendees to appear at Denver City Hall the following month to speak in favor of including the Office of the Independent Monitor (OIM), which reviews police misconduct cases, into the Denver city charter.[4]

Again responding to organizers' calls, I attended this Denver City Council session on August 15, 2016. Prior to the session, organizers held a small rally on the steps of City Hall, and I talked with organizers and made a few photographs with my phone to document and promote DJP's campaign about the OIM. I posted one of my photos to my personal Instagram account that featured Landau speaking through a bullhorn on the steps of City Hall, backed by a group of allies holding a large black banner that read, in bold white lettering, "Unite against police terror!" (figure 3.2). I captioned the post: "Alex Landau speaking on the need for the Independent Monitor to be in the #Denver city charter. #DenverDeservesJustice."

The City Council session proceeded with a number of agenda items for discussion prior to the hearing on the OIM (Figure 3.3). During a break in the session, and prior to the OIM hearing, Bliss approached me and asked if I would sign up to speak in favor of the OIM. I had met Bliss at several meetings and interviewed him several months earlier at a public demonstration hosted by BLM5280, for a short documentary that I was making (discussed in more detail in chapter 4). Because speaking at a public forum was not something that I felt comfortable doing, I politely declined the invitation. I regretted not speaking, as it was a missed opportunity to build credibility, trust, and solidarity with community organizers.

FIGURE 3.2. Alex Landau on the steps of Denver City Hall, August 15, 2016. (Photo by Gino Canella.)

Filmmaking and photography suit my soft-spoken personality and provide a medium through which I am able to express my social justice commitments and amplify activists' voices at the center of these struggles. Thus, activist media provide organizers who are uncomfortable with public speaking additional avenues through which to communicate with one another and with publics in various formats. Activist media open up new possibilities for voices who have historically been excluded from the public sphere to enter democratic debates.

FIGURE 3.3. City Council session discussing the Office of the Independent Monitor, August 15, 2016. (Photo by Gino Canella.)

Defining "media" broadly recognizes speaking at city council meetings, recording interviews, and holding signs as forms of media. None is more effective than another; they each have their affordances and limitations. Activist media makers leverage the medium that best complements the story they wish to tell, and publish it on the platform that best connects it to their organizing. Although I did not speak at the city council meeting, posting a photograph to Instagram, tagging the location of the post, and using hashtags to link the DJP rally to conversations about police reform in Denver were mediated practices that let Landau and Bliss know that I showed up and supported their efforts.

Although producing photographs and videos and sharing them on social media may be criticized as voyeuristically participating in online activism, I used social media to express myself in the mediums in which I am most confident speaking— film, video, and photography—and found opportunities to have conversations with friends and family about the stories represented in my media. After posting my documentaries and photography online, I engaged people in my immediate social networks in substantive conversations about protest and community organizing, why I participate in these events, and how they might get involved. In one-on-one and small group settings, I use the language that I learned at community meetings about justice and discuss how we can create social change. The importance of meaningful dialogues during the distribution and exhibition of activist media is discussed further in chapter 5.

During the course of attending community meetings, I made it clear to organizers that I wanted to use my experiences working with their organizations to illuminate the importance of their campaigns and to understand the role media play in mobilizing people for social change. I referred organizers to my website and social media profiles so they could view samples of my creative work, but it was not until I produced media for these organizations that I began to earn their trust. The first project I produced with BLM5280 was a series of short videos in October 2015, after which organizers became more receptive to me and welcomed me into spaces where I did not expect to be invited. For example, prior to a demonstration on January 18, 2016, in which BLM5280 took over the city of Denver's planned parade route for the city's Martin Luther King Jr. Day celebration under the banner "#ReclaimMLK," I was invited to a planning meeting to discuss the group's strategy for the march. Members at this meeting discussed logistics, such as the meeting time and location of the march, where protesters were to be positioned during it, and a brief explanation about what to do if police detained someone. I documented the march the following day and, within a few hours, I uploaded to Facebook a collection of photographs and a three-minute short documentary.

Because live-streaming video and social media operate at such a rapid speed, it is difficult to separate pre-production from production and distribution. These interconnected and overlapping processes reveal one of activist media's contradictions—on the one hand, media circulation in contemporary media ecosystems is instantaneous and immediate; conversely, campaign planning, community meetings, and deliberation (the pre-production of activist media) can be quite slow. As these processes are essential for developing relationships with movement leaders, and for understanding how best to represent their stories to various audiences through media, activist media makers and community researchers must practice patience.

Patience means asking for feedback from your collaborators. I produced videos and photos at the 2016 MLK Day rally and subsequently posted this media to my personal Facebook page, tagging BLM5280's account and key organizers of the movement. Members and supporters of BLM5280 "liked," commented on, and shared this content with their online networks, which let me know they approved of how my media depicted the event and the movement. In another instance, BLM5280 reused an image that I produced at the 2016 MLK Day rally to promote its 2017 MLK Day events. The image featured a young Black man with his right hand at his side in a fist, mouth opened mid-chant, and wearing an "I Can't Breathe" T-shirt. He was marching slightly ahead of a group of protesters who were holding a sign that read, "Which Side Are You On?" BLM5280 captioned the post, "#ReclaimMLK 2017 in 9 . . ." It was part of a series of images that BLM5280 posted to Facebook to count down to the 2017 demonstration and build anticipation among BLM5280's followers.[5] I followed BLM5280's lead and posted to Facebook the short documentary I produced of the 2016 rally, with the caption: "In 2016, Amy Brown and Black Lives Matter 5280 demanded 'resources not retribution' from Denver Mayor Michael Hancock. Join activists and organizers tomorrow to again #ReclaimMLK and declare that #BlackLivesMatter."[6]

Attending community meetings and producing and sharing media with BLM5280 reveals not only the fluidity of pre-production, production, and distribution but also how the social relationships among activist media practitioners and researchers evolve through these processes. Patricia A. Adler and Peter Adler discussed researchers' "membership" with regard to groups that the researchers work with and study. My position to BLM5280 has changed over the course of my time working with the organization.[7] During the first few meetings, I was in what Adler and Adler called "peripheral membership," in which researchers observe and do not participate in group activities. By the time that I attended planning meetings and began documenting, through photography and video, the MLK Day rally, I was an "active member" of the group. As a white organizer, I never attended BLM5280's core meetings, in which organizing strategies and campaigns were discussed in greater detail; hence, I never reached what Adler and Adler referred to as "full membership." My membership categories as a researcher and media maker with BLM5280 were constantly evolving, and as my involvement with the organization progressed and my confidence as an organizer grew, I was able to better recognize my membership status and respond with the appropriate level of support.

Pre-production, therefore, provides filmmakers, organizers, and scholars with opportunities to recognize and reflect on their positionality with respect to the groups with which they work. Although pre-production often does not provide filmmakers with compelling or dramatic footage, it is essential for identifying the networks in which activist media are being produced and understanding how these networks influence the distribution of media. Networks built on trust and rooted in democracy require feedback and active listening. These provide organizers and grassroots media makers with additional perspectives through which to examine how publics, counterpublics, and institutions compete for power within networked society. In addition, active listening offers organizers opportunities to learn about your opposition and to strategize about how best to disrupt institutional power structures. By maintaining open dialogues with my community partners and actively soliciting feedback throughout pre-production, activist media promoted a subjectivity in me based on solidarity and mutual respect.

Black Lives Matter 5280 Joins with Service Employees International Union

Connecting BLM5280 and SEIU Local 105's stories began for me at a public community meeting on October 21, 2015, at the First Unitarian Society of Denver. The meeting was jointly hosted by BLM5280 and SEIU Local 105, and organizers from both groups used the event to explore how racial, gendered, and economic injustices are interrelated. Group activities and invited speakers emphasized how peoples' identities are often related to the sociopolitical and material conditions in which people live.[8] Although the U.S. labor movement has had a troubled history supporting efforts for racial justice in the workplace and organizing diverse workers, this meeting confronted this history and aimed to build a multiracial coalition grounded in shared struggles and communal values. Fostering relationships through community meetings, organizers hoped, would create a network of activists capable of claiming political power.

Organizers at this meeting emphasized cross-racial solidarity by relying on language used by the national Black Lives Matter movement, showing how contemporary movements build and strengthen their networks through communication. Opal Tometi, co-founder of BLM, wrote in *Time* magazine in December 2015 that BLM is not a civil rights movement but, rather, a human rights movement. "This period in history is a celebration of intersectionality, which mandates that the breadth of our humanity be acknowledged and embraced," Tometi wrote. "This means that queer, trans, migrant, formerly incarcerated, disabled and all of us who find ourselves unapologetic about our complexities are more committed than ever to champion the scope of the human rights agenda that we deserve."[9]

BLM5280 brought Tometi's declaration to the local level by partnering with members of the labor movement who are fighting for higher wages, benefits, and fairness in the workplace. By bringing these groups together, BLM5280 sought to educate residents and community leaders about the racial inequalities that underpin economic equalities. Although these community meetings do not appear in the activist media that I produced with BLM5280, the labor that occurred in these spaces was essential to informing the narrative strategies I used in our films.

Monthly community meetings, according to Amy Brown, former co-lead of BLM5280, provide participants with a space to speak freely and discuss the status of current and future campaigns. More important, though, the meetings create venues for people to discuss openly race, socioeconomic conditions within the Black community, and identity. These venues are crucial to the pre-production of activist media because they provide opportunities for allied media makers to educate themselves about the movement and confront what Eduardo Bonilla-Silva called "whites' racial ambivalence."[10] Following the 2008 election of Barack Obama as the first African American president of the United States, many people demonstrated racial ambivalence by declaring that the United States had entered a post-racial era. Post-racial analyses are based on color blindness, which argues that inequalities can be understood best by going "beyond race." The challenge, therefore, for Black Lives Matter and other movements fighting for racial justice is understanding how to confront racial injustices while also celebrating and complicating individual success stories of high-profile Black people (e.g., Oprah Winfrey, President Obama, LeBron

James, and Beyoncé). Of course, color blindness and post-racial discourses are inadequate for examining structural inequities. White backlash and elevated racial tensions in the United States since 2016 demand a racial reckoning among people committed to justice. Bonilla-Silva also studied the physical and verbal discomfort people have when talking about race, and he found that white people use incoherent speech when discussing issues such as affirmative action, mixed-race couples, and racial discrimination. Bonilla-Silva's research reveals the importance of pre-production and the socialization it provides. During public meetings and community gatherings, organizers gain the social skills needed to confront their discomfort with and ambivalence about race, and they develop the trusting relationships that are needed to embrace that discomfort within a collective.

Another issue that community meetings address is the "racial empathy gap." This theory argues that participants in experiments—regardless of their race—perceive that Black people feel less physical pain than white people and, therefore, are able to tolerate more pain.[11] This gap has important implications for the medical care that African Americans receive and for how African American defendants are treated in the criminal justice system. One strategy for overcoming the racial empathy gap is perspective taking, which BLM5280 practiced at its community meetings through small group discussions and presentations from community leaders. BLM5280 offers opportunities for allies and organizers working on immigrant justice, gender justice, environmental justice, and workers' rights to examine structural inequalities from Black perspectives—encouraging activist media makers to zoom out and adjust their focus.

The October 21 meeting between BLM5280 and Local 105 was similar to other community meetings hosted by BLM5280, in that the room was arranged so that open space was provided at the front of the room for speakers and core members to address the crowd (Figure 3.4). Brown opened the October 21 meeting with a brief speech that detailed BLM5280's partnership with Local 105 and discussed campaigns the union was currently pursuing in Colorado. "Whether it is calling for immigration reform, whether it is actively registering new voters . . . that should be known about the labor movement, and that should be known about Local 105," she said. "Regardless of your history or where you come from, your experience, most of us know the oldest trick in the book, and one of the most effective tricks in the book by those on top to stay on top, is to limit our ability to control our own lives—to limit our ability to control our destinies."

With these comments, Brown refuted how journalists, politicians, and even some progressive activists have framed BLM as a divisive and polarizing movement; instead, Brown highlighted the historical connections between labor and movements for racial justice in the United States. These connections were highlighted in the twenty-three-minute film *Radical Labor: Aligning Unions with the Streets* (discussed further in chapter 4). Brown welcomed new opportunities to

FIGURE 3.4. BLM5280 community meeting jointly hosted by BLM5280 and SEIU
Local 105, October 21, 2015. (Photo by Gino Canella.)

work with labor unions and other community groups to create partnerships based
on solidarity with all working people.

At the conclusion of her opening remarks, Brown introduced Ric Urrutia, an
organizer with Colorado Jobs with Justice, who gave a passionate eight-minute
speech about the history of the labor movement and how, historically, its mission
of fighting for economic justice has been linked to fights for racial and immigrant
justice. Urrutia connected the Great Migration in the United States—in which
African Americans fled racism in the Jim Crow South and sought economic opportunities in the industrial North and Midwest, from 1916 to 1970—with migrations
in the early 2000s, in which Latin Americans moved to the United States, seeking jobs and economic stability for their families. Urrutia explained how both
groups faced (and continue to face) racial discrimination at their destination, and
he concluded with a call to unity: "When we band together, no matter what kind
of worker it is, when we band together, we have the power to control production
in the workplace, in the community, in the nation, and that's our power: To stop
revenues, to stop profits, 'cause that's the something they care about."

I spoke with Urrutia after the meeting about the importance of connecting
movements for racial justice with the labor movement and how these conversations should inform activists' communication strategies. "We have to unite," he
said. "Dust off labor, too, man, 'cause labor is in a very conservative space, where
its political activity is all at the legislature. Strikes aren't a consideration. So, yeah,
I guess I was trying to agitate both groups."

After Urrutia's speech, Brown explained a group exercise that participants were
asked to perform with those sitting at their table. Each table was given two sheets

of poster board. The first sheet was divided vertically with a line drawn down the middle; one column was titled "Race," and the second column heading was titled "Money." The second poster board was blank. Each table of approximately five to ten people was given several magazines and asked to cut out advertisements and articles to determine whether the content should be glued to the "Race" column, the "Money" column, or the blank poster, which represented both race and money. Brown acknowledged the discomfort that an activity such as this would elicit for participants. "These are things people hate, hate, hate to talk about. Right? It's an important first step, but it's just a first step."

At the conclusion of the exercise, tables chose a representative to present each group's findings at the front of the room. A meeting facilitator from BLM5280's core team led a review of the posters and encouraged participants to explain their choices. He asked teams to rethink their decisions that divided products, advertisements, and photographs into race *or* money, and he explained how advertisements for items such as makeup, jewelry, and cars are connected intricately to *both* race and money. His comments challenged those at the meeting to consider the capitalist ideologies that allow low-cost products to be made at the expense of low-wage work and how media institutions market these products through the commodification of race, gender, and citizenship. Critiquing commercial mainstream media by remixing magazines represented a lo-fi activist media practice that visualized new ways of seeing race, class, and consumerism.

Although the meeting was designed purposely by BLM5280 organizers to be a safe space, Urrutia thought that this particular exercise was *too* safe. "We made some good observations, but it never felt uncomfortable," he said. "I think that these conversations are uncomfortable, and I think that's when growth happens, when you become uncomfortable." Andy Jacob, political director of SEIU Local 105, agreed that union organizers need to aggressively confront their discomfort talking about race, but he said he was grateful for the conversations that the meeting elicited. Race, he said, is "a tough topic to broach, and so we really wanted to make this as accessible to folks as possible." Jacob continued: "I think the plan is that [we] have a series of these [conversations] to continue to get deeper and deeper every time. . . . Hopefully, [the meeting] was able to help people to have a better understanding of the way that race and economics collide, and how they're really intertwined in our society."

At the conclusion of the meeting, I asked Jacob about the labor movement and its history in the United States working with the civil rights movement. He explained that labor is strongest when unions focus on community issues and engage with grassroots activists.

"We've seen that whenever the labor movement has started to work on the 'isms' [e.g., racism and sexism] throughout our country's history, it's not only done a lot to help the people affected by those 'isms,' but it's really helped the labor movement," Jacob said. "We here at the Local, I think, really intimately understand that.

That doesn't mean that we're doing all the work we should or can on it, and so, I think, we're trying to make the steps in the right direction to start doing that." Championing police reform, immigration justice, and LGBTQ rights—issues that are central to BLM5280's platform—while simultaneously negotiating labor contracts reveals how Local 105 is not concerned simply with its members' economic status but also advocates for their human rights.

Following my interview with Jacob, I explained my intentions to make short documentaries that highlight the personal stories of union members and connect them with broader systemic inequalities. Several days after the meeting, Jacob introduced me via email to María Corral, communications coordinator of SEIU Local 105, and she agreed to meet for coffee, learn more about the project, and identify members who might be willing to participate in a documentary.

As an informational and educational forum that included speeches from core members and guests and a group exercise, BLM5280's community meeting with Local 105 addressed the intersections of race and class and revealed the importance of pre-production. The conversations at this meeting sparked a working relationship between myself and local organizers and provided opportunities for the emotions embedded in radical antagonistic democracy—love, discomfort, care, and tension—to be expressed and embraced. Doing so was essential for communicating and visualizing these emotions through media.

As I moved my filmmaking with SEIU into production, I continued attending BLM5280 community meetings and other public demonstrations that the organization promoted via its Facebook page. By showing up at those events, I hoped to make it known to organizers that I was committed to contributing to the movement. I also was responding to Brown's comment at the first BLM5280 meeting I attended on August 26, 2015, when she said that new members earn the trust of core leaders when they "put in the work and have shown that with radical activism comes responsibility." I continued putting in work for the next eight months to learn more about how BLM5280 discussed Black life, love, and liberation; then, in July 2016, BLM5280 announced a policy change. Following its #135HoursAndCounting demonstration outside the Colorado State Capitol—where BLM5280 sat in solidarity with the 135 Black people killed by police in the United States in the first six months of 2016—the organization decided that its community meetings would be held for people of color (POC) only. BLM5280's decision to create spaces for POC only led me, again, to confront my discomfort with race and seek out alternative venues where I could continue to contribute to the movement.

CLOSED MEETINGS AND FINDING OTHER VENUES

Attending BLM5280 community meetings and standing in solidarity with the movement by filming events and highlighting Black activists' voices in media has been exciting and challenging. My activist media projects have provided me with numerous opportunities for personal reflection and growth and have shaped my subjectivity as an anti-racist organizer and media practitioner.[12] My views about racial justice have evolved throughout my life, and have been shaped by the social and political contexts in which I have lived. I grew up the great-grandchild of Italian immigrants in Weirton, West Virginia, a small city about forty miles west of Pittsburgh that is 93 percent white. I often encountered race as a child through racist stereotypes in the media and in conversations at home and in school. Racial slurs and epithets about Black people were not uncommon for me to hear, reinforcing how groups seek status and privilege through their proximity to whiteness—and their distance from Blackness.[13] With a slightly darker complexion than many white people, I often am asked, "What are you?"—or, more sensitively, "How do you identify?" I struggle to offer a thoughtful response, relying, typically, on, "Umm, I'm white." My physical appearance has led strangers to speak to me in Spanish, assuming that, perhaps, I am Latino.

During the 1980s, Weirton was a blue-collar union town where the middle class was within reach. With Weirton Steel at its economic and social core, the city thrived during the postwar industrial boom in the United States. After several mergers and acquisitions in the early 2000s, however, the plant now sits shuttered and rusted out. My dad owned a family grocery store that was passed down from his father; but it, too, closed in the early 1990s as a result of pressure from national chains and big-box stores. The confluence of rapidly changing global economics, neoliberal policies, and shifting U.S. demographics were exploited in 2015 when candidate Donald Trump vowed to fight for the "forgotten men and women of our country." His campaign pitch—which was loaded with racist and xenophobic language about Mexican immigrants stealing jobs and included claims to revive manufacturing by bringing back "clean coal"—was effective in West Virginia and across much of the industrial Midwest.

My identities and personal history informed my activist filmmaking and were, at times, assets during my work with SEIU Local 105. For example, after a planning meeting with Corral, the communications coordinator, to discuss the structure of the twenty-three-minute documentary, she asked about my plans after completing my graduate studies. I said that I would pursue a position within higher education, to which she responded, "You'll do great. I'm happy and excited for you, but also you kinda look like us. Mi hijo [my son]."

I hesitate to embrace comments about my racial ambiguity, because I know that my privileges as a white man afford me opportunities that are not granted to Black and brown people. These privileges include having access to spaces—for example, within education and media—that, historically, have excluded people of color. Because I was using my privileges to make films that critique racial injustice and social and economic inequality, initially, I reacted to BLM5280's decision to create POC-only meetings with frustration and confusion. I had never been told that I could not access a space because of my race. Experiencing exclusion on such a personal level—something people of color have historically faced and continue to experience in the United States—was disorienting.

To deal with these emotions, I talked with white friends and anti-racist organizers, read articles that justified Black organizers' need for Black spaces, and read BLM5280's social media posts, in which the group shared status updates that explained its policy decision. I read through the comments shared on BLM5280's Facebook page to understand how other community organizers were reacting to its decision to create meeting spaces for POC only. Some of the comments asked BLM5280 for clarification, whereas others did not know what "POC" meant. A comment on a post about the meeting policy on BLM5280's Facebook page following the #135HoursAndCounting vigil read: "I love the idea but I don't prefer to participate in events that are geared toward one race only. Especially when the only race is the human race, I don't like to participate in events that exclude others on the basis of race as we understand it now."

The comment received a few "likes" and was met with this response from a BLM5280 supporter: "POC aren't only black people. They're everyone that identifies as such. We have Asian, Latin, Mexican, Native, etc. people in the room because they identify as persons of color. It's not exclusionary. It's a focused space for safe healing. What we've seen as a community is that it's not always safe for POC to grieve and heal in spaces that include other Non-POC."[14]

BLM5280 organizers, typically, do not wade into the comments on the organization's Facebook page to moderate offensive or abusive language, but on August 16, 2016, BLM5280 addressed the animosity that was being directed at the group because of this decision. BLM5280 posted a Facebook status update that read:

> We have reached a point in the movement where certain actions and specific behaviors will no longer be tolerated. BLM5280 is dedicated to supporting Black life in the greater Denver metro area. We have neither the capacity, patience, nor time to educate current and potential allies on the struggle that black folx have endured; we encourage those looking for their genuine questions to be answered to contact their local SURJ [Showing Up for Racial Justice] organization. Racist comments and blatant internet trolling have no place on our comment section. This is a safe place for POC and we will delete and ban inappropriate comments and commenters.[15]

The decision to create POC-only spaces at BLM5280's community meetings, organizers stated, was done to create safe and healing spaces for people of color. Research has shown that social media and online discussion forums are often filled with toxic rhetoric, making them difficult venues in which to promote healing or political education.[16] Because activist media focus on the connections between online and off-line spaces, it's important to examine how several in-person incidents likely contributed to BLM5280's policy change.

The first incident occurred at a BLM5280 community meeting I attended on June 22, 2016. BLM5280 meetings, typically, begin when a core member reads BLM5280's mission statement and states that all visitors are invited guests in a space that was created by Black women and is primarily for Black people. At this particular meeting, a white lady interjected her thoughts and comments on each agenda item throughout the meeting. At the conclusion of the meeting, Amy Brown delivered a pointed message to those in the room about self-awareness. "Really do some self-checking of privilege, whether that's class, race, gender, sexuality," she said. "Honor our space and our presenters. Remind yourself that BLM was started by Black women, and that you're guests."

The second incident occurred at the #135HoursAndCounting vigil. BLM5280 had posted, repeatedly, on its Facebook page that the vigil was designed as a POC-only space, but community members ignored this request. At one point during the vigil, BLM5280 posted a video of a white man berating organizers at the vigil for excluding white allies. The man claimed to have attended BLM5280 community meetings and be "all with you guys" and told a BLM5280 organizer that the movement should "be trying to broaden democracy."[17] He claimed to be a member of the International Socialist Organizers and was offended that BLM5280 did not allow him to collect signatures for a petition at the vigil.

Such rhetoric, unfortunately, has become a common critique of the broader BLM network, as people who seek to discredit the movement chastise it for exclusionary tactics that favor Black people at the expense of "all lives." These perceptions, however, are uninformed and often lodged by people who do not engage with the movement in any meaningful way. POC-only community meetings should not define BLM5280; rather, filmmakers, journalists, and researchers must understand the messiness and unevenness of radical pluralist democracy. I continue to have mixed feelings about BLM5280's decision. Although I understand the importance of having POC-only spaces, I also recognize how these policies have the potential to fuel white resentment. BLM5280 collaborates in numerous ways with progressive community groups in Colorado and around the country. Rather than spend energy coddling hurt feelings, I identified alternative venues that allowed me to continue collaborating with the movement for Black liberation. One of these venues was Showing Up for Racial Justice.

Showing Up for Racial Justice

As mentioned earlier, BLM5280 organizers often encouraged white allies at its community meetings to get involved with Showing Up for Racial Justice (SURJ; pronounced "Surge"). SURJ, founded in 2009, is a national network of organizers fighting for racial justice, with about 150 local chapters in the United States and one in Canada. According to SURJ's website, "SURJ's role as part of a multi-racial movement is to undermine white support for white supremacy and help build a racially just society. That work cannot be done in isolation from or disconnected

FIGURE 3.5. SURJ Denver emergency community meeting following 2016 U.S. presidential election, November 14, 2016. (Photo by Gino Canella.)

from the powerful leadership of communities of color. It is one part of a multi-racial, cross-class movement centering people of color leadership."

SURJ has seven core values that guide its organizing: (1) call people in, not out; (2) accountability through collective action; (3) take risks, make mistakes, learn, and keep going; (4) organize out of mutual interest; (5) there is enough for all; (6) growing is good; and (7) center class.

SURJ has chapters in Boulder and Denver, Colorado, and I attended several SURJ Denver meetings to continue my political education and remain engaged in local organizing efforts aimed at racial justice. The SURJ Denver community meetings that I attended drew between 40 and 80 people, except for the November 14, 2016 "emergency" meeting that was held the week following the election of President Donald Trump, which drew roughly 400 people (Figure 3.5). Attending my first SURJ Denver meeting did not elicit the same hesitation or anxiety that I felt at my first BLM5280 meeting, primarily for two reasons: first, after studying, reading, and talking about race for more than a year with BLM5280, I was much more familiar with and well-versed in the language of anti-racist organizing; second, I knew that I could blend in easily in a room full of white people.

SURJ Denver community meetings are organized similarly to BLM5280's, in that core organizers or invited guests present briefly on a topic related to racial justice (e.g., police reform, criminal justice, white wealth, and gentrification) and then engage attendees in small group activities and discussions. SURJ Denver, how-ever, differs from BLM5280 in how it champions racial justice. SURJ often emphasizes the importance of redistributing white wealth to communities of color. For example, donation baskets were passed around during SURJ's November 14, 2016 emergency meeting, which raised $4,563 for POC-led organizations. Analysis by the Economic Policy Institute in 2017 showed that white wealth in the United States is seven times greater than Black wealth.[18] Hence, the generosity of white allies, it is argued, is crucial for providing POC organizers with the resources they need to fight for justice.

However, this approach to organizing stands in stark contrast to that of BLM5280, which argues for direct action, mutual aid, and a radical reorganization of our social and political economic systems. Although Black Lives Matter also solicits donations, it does not combat the disparity between white and Black wealth by injecting more capital into an unjust system. Instead, organizers critique the explicitly racist political and economic institutions that enable these disparities to exist and provide community members with creative solutions for building new systems. For example, one BLM5280 community meeting featured speakers from the cooperative and sustainable agriculture movement in Colorado. The discussion challenged taken-for-granted approaches to food, housing, and transportation, and organizers asked participants to think about how food co-ops could be a first step toward reclaiming the commons. By promoting activists' individual and collective agency and advocating for programs that compel people to think structurally about power, BLM5280's organizing operates fundamentally through the lens of justice, rather than charity.

Another common critique of SURJ and other white-led organizations that discuss race and racial justice is that these organizations create spaces where white people can feel comfortable talking about race. As mentioned earlier, these conversations should be uncomfortable. Didi Delgado, an organizer with BLM Cambridge, wrote in 2017: "By creating bubbles within white supremacy where it's 'safe' to practice anti-racism, we're implying there are places where racism can remain unchallenged. In many ways, white anti-racism spaces serve as safety nets protecting allies from their own uncertainty and fear of failure, while simultaneously keeping people of color at a distance."[19] Delgado's critique rang true in my experience, as SURJ Denver meetings did not require me to confront my identities with the same level of self-reflection that BLM5280 meetings required. After attending several SURJ Denver meetings following BLM5280's policy change, I missed the energy and radical spirit of BLM5280's meetings. These spaces forced me to confront my discomfort with race, and, however awkward or difficult that was, navigating this discomfort should be an obligatory exercise for all activist media makers.

Organizers from SURJ Denver responded to Delgado's blog by taking time off as an organization to reflect, talk with POC organizers, and decide the best approaches for being accountable to POC-led organizations. When SURJ Denver resumed its organizing, it hosted a public community meeting on February 18, 2017, to parse the meanings of the terms "observer," "ally," and "accomplice." Following the presentation by one of SURJ Denver's core organizers, attendees were asked to form small groups and discuss these terms. I began by defining "observer" as someone who stands by and passively watches as events occur, but, before I could offer a definition for "ally" or "accomplice," a member of our group interrupted me to offer references to French philosopher Michel Foucault and remind the group of his identities as a queer Indian American man. I am transparent and honest when I enter organizing circles about my identities as a white, cisgender, able-bodied man, but, in that moment, I was unsure what these comments had to do with the exercise. When attendees declare their gender, racial, or ethnic identities and do not connect these identities to their *political* or *ideological* identities, community meetings can feel frustrating. Small group discussions have the potential to steer SURJ off its core values—specifically, its value of calling people in and not calling them out—and alienating potential allies seeking to thoughtfully engage in community organizing.[20] BLM5280, following in the legacy of the Combahee River Collective, understands that identities are central to political organizing; the group also acknowledges, however, that identities must also be understood in relation to larger systems of power. The pre-production of activist media creates time and space for organizers to work through their political strategies, embrace their differences, and identify their common interests. Through active listening and honest dialogues, pre-production develops an ethic of care that creates opportunities for organizers to navigate structural constraints and provides the language needed to narrate individual experiences in relation to collective struggles.

I approached SURJ Denver organizers at community meetings and invited them to participate in the twenty-three-minute documentary *Radical Labor,* which was commissioned by SEIU Local 105. I hoped they could discuss in the film their role advocating for racial justice. I also sent numerous emails and Facebook messages to the group explaining the project in more detail, but these went unanswered. I also contacted Sasha Ramirez, co-lead of BLM5280, by email, described the documentary, and offered to meet with her to discuss including a voice from BLM5280 in the film, but those messages were also not returned. When SEIU Local 105 commissioned me to produce a documentary highlighting union members' stories and its work collaborating with progressive organizations in Colorado, I was confident that—thanks to the patience and due diligence I spent in pre-production—I had the political education I needed to craft a radical narrative that connected race, labor, and power.

CRAFTING NARRATIVES ABOUT RACE, LABOR, AND POWER

I did not want simply to observe how organizers talked at community meetings about race, labor, and social justice. I wanted to intervene in the fight for justice by creating a film about unions, workers' rights, and the tensions between revolutionary and reformist approaches to social change (as discussed in chapter 1). My interviews with grassroots organizers in Colorado formed the structure of the twenty-three-minute documentary and placed members' personal stories in broader historical and social contexts. Importantly, these interviews helped me understand how I, as a documentarian and researcher, could participate in the struggle for justice. Felicia Griffin, then executive director of FRESC: Good Jobs, Strong Communities, an organization that works on community initiatives and campaigns with labor unions in Colorado, offered me powerful advice when I asked her about incorporating a racial justice lens in a film about the labor movement.

"I think there is a beautiful story, so I hope that you tell the story of labor and the good that it does and has done," Griffin said. "I mean, this is your opportunity, right, to be a white male, and to make a stand. . . . It's important that your stand doesn't kill the good things about labor, because there are very good things. I think there's this balance that's going to be hard for you, definitely, to get in the editing room to find a balance, but I think this can be your voice and your stand personally."

Griffin's comments speak to an important point about how researchers navigate their relationships with community organizations. At the outset of this project, I wanted to show my commitment to BLM5280 and SEIU Local 105 and to support and contribute to their organizing efforts in whatever ways they asked. However, after two and a half years of studying these organizations and producing films covering public actions and members' stories, I became more willing to offer critiques about some of their organizing strategies. I tried to offer these critiques in thoughtful and constructive ways and to avoid contributing to the toxic political discourse that occurs often among activists on social media. My social media activities, consequently, were tempered throughout this work, and I instead expressed my concerns during one-on-one planning meetings or conversations with organizers.

Griffin also echoed the advice that SURJ and BLM5280 organizers, typically, offer white allies in the fight against anti-Black racism: Find your voice and speak with folks in your social circles. Organizing requires engaging allies, and, sometimes, perceived enemies, in difficult conversations. Although social media and activist filmmaking are important venues through which organizers can make emotional appeals for their causes and seek support in the public sphere, talking with family and friends who do not understand how racism has functioned historically in the United States, or who do not empathize with calls for racial justice, is important work. Taking a stand, as Griffin called it, is something I am increasingly comfortable doing after this project with BLM5280 and SEIU. Whether I am correcting racist language in a conversation with friends or challenging offensive comments on social media, activist media created important opportunities for me to engage in political education about systemic inequalities and then find the language needed—whether through film, interpersonal communication, or writing—to communicate these issues to others.

Many organizers I talked with, including Griffin, spoke with sensitivity about the connection between racial and economic justice and often waited for me to raise the topic of race in our interviews. Other organizers, however, brought up race with me early. For example, Josh Downey, President of the Denver Area Labor Federation, an umbrella organization that represents 114 local unions, highlighted how historical tensions between white and Black workers continue to affect labor organizing today. Downey said there is a perception—rightfully, in many cases—that labor is "pale, male, and stale." He explained the need to unite the labor movement with other grassroots movements, because the labor movement has been strongest throughout its history when it has aligned with social justice movements. Referencing the labor movement's solidarity with the civil rights movement and Martin Luther King Jr.'s assassination while advocating for striking sanitation workers in Memphis, Tennessee, Downey critiqued the concept of diversity. "Just having a person of color in the room, or having a woman of color in the room, doesn't quite solve the problem," he said. "It's recognizing that we need women and people of color in leadership positions and helping to move the needle."

In a leadership position as the first Black woman director of FRESC, Griffin acknowledged that "the race stuff is risky." She said that, although SEIU Local 105 is a progressive union that champions racial and immigration justice, navigating race with management, which is often white and male, is challenging. "You don't want to be the one calling out race every time. There's some other reputation that you get for doing that," she said. "But what I've come to is to really move and push, and change the places that I can and to let go of the places where I can't make any change. . . . That probably sounds like copping out, but it's actually self-protection."

Ron Ruggiero, president of SEIU Local 105, said that although the union can do more to diversify its management, the senior team is "actually very diverse in terms of men and women, Latino, white, etcetera." Ruggiero acknowledged the "long struggle in labor in terms of issues around diversity" but said that the labor movement needs to have "diverse leadership in a real way and not in some sort of token way."

A plurality of voices, Ruggiero explained, is truly heard when workers join the executive board meetings. "We have, really I would say for the most part, the diversity of America in that room," Ruggiero told me. "We have racial diversity, gender, LGBTQ folks; we have immigrant, nonimmigrant; we have people whose native language is English versus Spanish; economic diversity is in that room. . . . What we're able to do is, that body, which is about twenty-five folks, all rank-and-file members, they're the highest decision-making body in the organization, and they do . . . practicing democracy, debate, exchange. You know, back-and-forth; we have translation happening simultaneously, and it's just been kind of beautiful to see that."

Lizeth Chacón, executive director of Colorado People's Alliance (COPA), a "racial justice, member-driven organization dedicated to advancing and winning progressive social change locally, statewide and nationally," told me that difficult conversations about race are imperative if multiracial coalitions of progressive organizers are to be successful.[21] "At this moment, there is a need for white people to talk to other races," she said, "and I think that we have to be conscious about not putting the burden on folks of color to engage in conversations about race with white folks."

Chacón explained that because the political Right in the United States has been so successful at leveraging racial resentment to advance its policies, movements must be deliberate when framing justice through the lens of race. COPA conducts trainings regularly with mostly white activist organizations to advance their political education. Chacón described a workshop that she conducted with an environmental justice organization in Colorado. "We talked about structural racism. We talked about a culture of whiteness that exists in this country and what that means. Then we challenge those folks, 'What role are you going to take and how are you going to support folks of color in leading the fight?'" she said. Addressing during these workshops how communities of color are disproportionately impacted by air pollution, for example, and strategizing with attendees about potential actions, is one way COPA connects racial and environmental justice.[22]

Like Griffin, Chacón challenges white allies to listen, center the voices of those at the center of the struggle for justice, and then find a way to act. Chacón discussed with me the labor movement's capacity to promote social justice unionism by explaining what she has seen from SEIU Local 105 in her time as a community organizer. "Even before COPA started, when one of our legacy organizations existed, it did immigrant rights organizing, and SEIU was always there by our side fighting on our issues and fighting by our side and fighting for immigrant rights," she said. "That's a really good example of a union that has really looked at who are our workers, and not just looked at them as the employee, but looked at them as who are you outside your job?"

Local 105 realizes that workers have needs beyond their jobs by practicing what Ruggiero called "whole person unionism." For the labor movement to be successful, he argued, SEIU must prioritize all of the above: contract negotiations, workplace safety, broad policy reform, and issue-based advocacy for social change. "It is just a fundamental recognition that our membership doesn't just exist at work," Ruggiero said. "They exist in the communities they live. They exist in the schools their children go to. They exist on the roads they have to travel down."

"Whole person unionism," therefore, provides a framework that situates race and labor alongside power. Several interviewees discussed the need to build collective and communal power, but whenever interviewees mentioned "building power," I asked them to define what they meant. Ruggiero explained that Local 105 focuses on three key areas when building power: work sites, political arenas, and what he called "industry power or strength." SEIU builds power in these arenas by organizing new members; registering members to vote; encouraging them to volunteer in the community; and asking them to share their personal stories about work and life at rallies, with the news media, or at organizing meetings. The *place* of media power, therefore, occurs online and off-line through a series of networked communication practices.

Ruggiero offered the example of health care workers in Los Angeles in the mid-1990s to explain how industry power, media, and storytelling are connected. During the 1990s, only about 25 percent of workers in the health care industry in Los Angeles were unionized, according to Ruggiero. SEIU entered the market, organized workers, and, within a few years, the health care industry reached 50 percent union density, which raised wages and improved working conditions in Los Angeles for both unionized and nonunionized workers. Sharing these stories, Ruggiero said, is an easy way to emphasize workers' collective power. "The conversation we have with folks is, 'What's happened in this country for the last forty years?' People can make those connections that as unions have declined, so have their paychecks across the board." Activist media create empathic spaces where organizers can communicate stories about collective struggles and connect them to workers' personal experiences. Deconstructing power through media means telling stories that emphasize people's agency and their ability to effect change.

Griffin noted that although power begins at the individual level, individual power must be organized through political education, informational workshops, and media publicity. From an individual perspective, she said, power is "about any person, no matter where they live, being able to take part in the decisions that impact their lives." Organizers, Griffin said, conduct one-on-one sessions with their neighbors and allies to help them navigate bureaucratic institutions and reform local laws and policies. This work, she said, is done alongside direct actions that raise people's awareness on a broader scale.

Building power, therefore, means promoting individuals' agency, while simultaneously recognizing their limitations. It also requires being deliberate about how you activate publics through targeted communication—in the streets, and on social media. Following Ruggiero and Griffin's advice, I highlighted the personal stories of union members and community organizers in the twenty-three-minute documentary *Radical Labor* and placed them in conversation with the public demonstrations in which the publicity of these groups was most visible. The documentary, discussed further in chapter 4, connected mobilizing—short bursts of energy from already committed activists—with the long-term organizing needed to build collective power. Although activist media may be a powerful tool for mobilizing supporters, many organizers I spoke with stressed the importance of deep organizing and channeling the affect and emotions within activist media into building durable infrastructures.

Chacón said COPA was founded in 2015 because there was a "desire to really create and build power for folks in the state of Colorado . . . [and] radically change the level of organizing . . . to make sure that we mobilized a lot more people." She said that her organization defines *power* as "being able to mobilize people and mobilize money . . . so we can have a large group of folks and a large base to work on the issues." Soliciting donations is important to sustain organizing, Chacón said, but financial resources must be channeled into building "governing power" that moves policies through legislative bodies.

Having a dialectical analysis of power that incorporates its symbolic, economic, and political dimensions was crucial for producing activist media about rallies and demonstrations and exhibiting them at community screenings and publishing them online. Capturing the attention of publics immersed in online spectacles is a challenge for activist media makers. The activist media I produced with BLM5280 and SEIU complemented organizers' campaigns by creating additional online and offline spaces in which organizers could dialogue with prospective members and broader publics. Although media constitute the space where power is decided, pre-production helps organizers analyze power structures and strategize about how to challenge them. Attending meetings; having in-depth conversations about race, labor, and citizenship; and thinking deliberately about how best to craft narratives about justice are essential practices that inform organizers' messaging and campaign strategies.

CONCLUSION

Producing activist media through an intersectional lens requires spending a significant amount of time engaged in political education—attending community meetings and direct actions and having conversations with organizers about how to frame stories about social justice, labor, and race. Through community meetings and candid dialogues, organizers are able to identify one another's political sensibilities and commitments to justice. My efforts navigating difference as a white filmmaker may not be immediately applicable to Black filmmakers producing media about racial justice or to undocumented filmmakers producing media about immigration justice; however, I hope my reflections encourage all grassroots media makers to do the due diligence needed to understand the breadth and depth of the issues they are documenting and visualizing.

Although I have referred to the practices in this chapter as pre-production, activist media blur the lines among pre-production, production, and distribution. Throughout the production and distribution of our media, I continued attending community meetings, talking with organizers, interacting with my partners on social media, and gathering feedback—all to improve on what worked, understand what did not, and make adjustments as needed.

Pre-production may seem tedious or unimportant to first-time filmmakers. Media practitioners may become impatient with political education and workshop trainings and not care to inform their films with critical theoretical approaches to democracy, race, and power. These practices, however, provide the antiracist language and personal relationships that are needed to produce radical media; most important, they force participants to confront the uncomfortable emotions inherent to organizing. Embracing discomfort and reflecting on your political and ideological orientations, in relation to the people with whom you work, certainly is challenging but, ultimately, is a necessary step in creating social change. Although navigating personal identities can be precarious terrain, organizers and activist media makers must distinguish between *identities* and *identification*. Identities are superficial characteristics that often do not reveal much about people's political commitments; identification, on the other hand, is an active social process in which organizers define their shared interests and narrate their political goals. Identification lets organizers know with whom they are aligned politically and strategically.

Slowing down to reflect on your personal experiences—and understanding how these experiences have been shaped by the material conditions in which they occurred—runs counter to the speed of contemporary media. Filmmakers may feel compelled to keep up with digital media's rapid pace and to produce and share media quickly to obtain the instant gratification that social media views, likes, and comments provide. Media that are produced hastily by filmmakers who do not value or have time to participate in the labor of pre-production, however, often offer simplistic narratives about movements and justice. My collaborations with BLM5280 and Local 105 highlight how activist filmmakers and community researchers must commit to struggles for justice for the long term. Pre-production requires time, a luxury that many working people cannot afford, which highlights another class contradiction within activist media. However, through these practices, organizers create new alliances and script passionate narratives that elevate radical demands for justice.

4 · PRODUCTION
Scripting Solidarity and Radical Storytelling

Participating in ongoing political education by attending community meetings and protests, engaging in conversations with organizers, and interacting online with grassroots groups helped me to better understand how Black Lives Matter 5280 and Service Employees International Union Local 105 promote racial and economic justice and talk about their work. This understanding, in turn, aided my ability to produce compelling, radical visual storytelling about the organizations' values and campaigns. Intervening in public discourses through critiques of systemic inequalities and demands for justice is central to the communication strategy of most progressive movements. Through textual and narrative analyses of the short documentary films that I produced with BLM5280 and with SEIU Local 105, this chapter examines my documentary films as activist media that scripted solidarity among grassroots groups fighting for justice. I review a series of short films I made with these organizations and a twenty-three-minute film, *Radical Labor: Aligning Unions and the Streets* (2018), and focus on four key aspects of my activist media: (1) their narrative structures; (2) the ways images and audio were edited together to reinforce these narratives; (3) my collaborations with these organizations during pre-production and production of the films, which allowed me to document the personal stories of members and key moments that occurred during our collaboration; and (4) the politics that informed the films' aesthetics.

The documentaries were created by paying careful attention to whose voices were featured and how these voices are often underrepresented, misrepresented, or erased in mainstream commercial news media and in popular culture. Thoughtful editing that juxtaposed interview excerpts with compelling imagery and the natural sound of protest marches reinforced a narrative of a networked movement in collective struggle. These narratives were produced, primarily, to encourage empathic listening, elicit an emotional response in viewers, mobilize members and community allies to join these campaigns, and assist the groups' organizing efforts. Following a self-reflective review of our films, three themes emerged from our activist media: (1) the collective agency of working people organizing for justice; (2) the connections between the personal stories of movement members and structural constraints; and (3) moral arguments about communal responsibility.

Depending on the scope of the production, documentary filmmaking requires various levels of collaboration among those involved in the project (for example, director, producer, camera operator, audio technician, and interviewees). Coordinating shoots and locations, discussing technical logistics, and conducting interviews are documentary practices that demand teamwork and communication among crew members. Video editing, however, is a much more solitary task. I demonstrate in this chapter how I navigated the varying levels of collaboration in pre-production, production, and post-production by working with organizers to plan shoots, providing organizers with early drafts of our films, and co-editing media with them. Sharing editorial control with SEIU Local 105 and BLM5280, and co-producing narratives that aligned with the core values and missions of these groups, reflect activist media's fundamental characteristic—media production and distribution are relational practices that organize and animate the social and democratize knowledge production. By staying true to these groups' radical messaging, I did not seek to produce films about multicultural inclusion or diversity, and I avoided placating polite liberal conceptions of justice; rather, these films are movement media, made for us and by us. As a researcher, documentarian, and visual storyteller, however, I hoped that audiences beyond the choir could also view these films and be compelled by their stories of shared communal values and collective responsibility. Therefore, I relied on my expertise as a researcher and journalist and complemented the affective elements of these films with empirical evidence and historical context, in the hope of persuading even the most unsympathetic audiences. Narrating compelling personal stories that resonate with viewers is key to engaging audiences inside and outside of movement circles in conversations about justice and calling them in to the work. I begin with the story of Melissa Benjamin, a home health care worker in Colorado. I show how I connected her efforts in the Fight for $15 with broader discourses of union organizing and social and economic inequalities.

NARRATING STORIES ABOUT ACTIVIST LABOR UNIONS

The first documentary I made with SEIU Local 105, as mentioned in chapter 3, featured Melissa Benjamin, a home health care worker in Denver, Colorado.[1] The documentary focused on her personal story as a home health care worker, with the goal of humanizing unions and working people and connecting labor organizing in Denver with the Fight for $15 campaign (which, as discussed in chapter 2, SEIU helped to launch in 2012, to unionize and raise the working standards of workers across the service industries). Her film and others I produced with SEIU Local 105 sought to highlight the precarity of service-sector work and stress the intersectionality of care work, which is often done by women and people of color. Following the BLM5280 community meeting where I met Andy Jacob, political director of Local 105, and explained my intention to produce documentaries with grassroots groups in Colorado, Jacob connected me with María Corral, then communications coordinator with Local 105. After a few brief emails and a telephone call in which I explained my professional video production experience and my research as a doctoral student at the University of Colorado Boulder, Corral agreed to identify a Local 105 member who would be willing to be featured in a short film about union organizing. About a week after our initial conversation, Corral introduced me via email to Melissa. I explained to Melissa in several emails how she would be depicted in the film, and I answered her questions and concerns regarding the shoot and interview.

One concern that Melissa expressed was related to the public-facing nature of her activism with Local 105; specifically, she had reservations about being labeled an "agitator" by her friends, family, and current and future employers. I eased this concern by explaining that, prior to distributing the film publicly online, or sharing it with Local 105 staff, she would receive a password-protected link to view the first cut of the film and have an opportunity to suggest any revisions of it. Providing those who appear in films with this level of editorial oversight, certainly, goes against professional journalistic norms, but collaborative filmmaking with community organizers and social movements demands that media practitioners flatten the production hierarchy and situate their media making in ethical values based on collective responsibility and democratic participation. Producer, director, and crew should be equal participants throughout the production and postproduction processes. Melissa and SEIU Local 105 were full-fledged partners on this project, not "subjects" or "clients." As an activist filmmaker, I recognized my partnership with Local 105 as an opportunity to contribute to a resurgent activist labor movement in the United States, rather than viewing Melissa or Local 105 staff as obstacles to my creative vision.

I explained to Melissa before filming that I envisioned her short documentary as a day-in-the-life story that showed her at home with her family and at work. Films about labor often feature on-the-job aspects of workers' stories, such as poor workplace conditions; however, to truly humanize labor, the Fight for $15 movement, and working people's lives, I wanted to depict Melissa in an intimate setting that highlighted her agency and humanity. Explaining the shoot to Melissa and organizing the logistics of her appearance (pre-production) was more time-intensive than filming her working and conducting her interview. I remained patient throughout these initial conversations and relied on my partners with Local 105 to move the project forward. One logistical hurdle that Melissa handled for me was identifying and securing permission from a client to film in that person's home.

FIGURE 4.1. Melissa Benjamin at home eating dinner with her daughters. (Photo by Gino Canella.)

After several weeks of discussions about the film with Melissa and staff at Local 105, production on the four-minute film was fairly brief. I spent one full day with Melissa, filming her at home making dinner and eating with her two daughters (Figure 4.1), driving to a client's home, and providing medical care to that client in his home. Prior to leaving for the client's home, I conducted a forty-minute interview with Melissa; because the film did not use a reporter's voiceover, her interview narrated the documentary. Melissa responded to many of my questions similarly to how politicians answer questions posed by journalists, repeating, in a public relations style, talking points about workers' rights and Local 105's efforts to raise the minimum wage. Although I appreciated Melissa's passion for organizing, I encouraged her to be more conversational in her responses to avoid appearing overly scripted.

"Coaching" interviewees presents another key difference between activist media and other documentary films that use a traditional journalistic approach. Coaching also poses an ethical challenge for ethnographic researchers who attempt to convey the essence of their subjects and the authenticity of the research site without manipulating the data. As a social justice partner with SEIU Local 105, I was committed to documenting and presenting service workers' stories ethically, which meant that I respected the dignity of their labor and embraced their humanity; as a visual storyteller and filmmaker, I understand that activists and community organizers might not be comfortable appearing on camera or familiar with what footage or sound bites are needed to produce an emotionally compelling narrative to audiences. Thus, it is my responsibility to direct certain aspects of the

FIGURE 4.2. Melissa Benjamin providing home care in Denver, Colorado. (Photo by Gino Canella.)

filmmaking process to ensure that I have what I need for editing. At the conclusion of my interview with Melissa, I asked her to continue wearing the wireless lavalier microphone, which allowed me to record additional natural sound of her at work, to ask follow-up questions, and to record spontaneous and impromptu moments that occurred between her and her client.

I could tell immediately that Melissa was passionate about her work as a home health care provider, and, consequently, I decided to open the film with her love for home care, prior to transitioning into her organizing efforts with SEIU. The film began with soft piano music and onscreen text that describes the state health care program that Melissa contracts through, Consumer-Directed Attendant Support Services (CDASS). Following this brief explanation of the program, the film cut to images of Melissa assisting her client with changing his shoes and cleaning his intravenous (IV) drip. Short, natural sound clips were interspersed throughout this section to emphasize Melissa's upbeat nature and the relationships she has with her clients. For example, as she wiped the client's shirt and repositioned his wheelchair, Melissa asked him, "You alright?" A few moments later, after he said that he would share his water with her, Melissa told him, "That's 'cause you're awesome!" By showing Melissa performing her duties as a home care aide, I visualized care work, and I emphasized women's labor in this sector (Figure 4.2).

Portions of the interview in which Melissa talked about her love for home care were included to develop her character as a health care professional who is passionate about her work. For instance, she said, "I like home care because it's one-on-one work, and I find that people are happier, they're a lot happier in their homes." To avoid romanticizing work or contributing to "labor of love" discourses, these sentiments were juxtaposed with structural problems that are endemic to Colorado's state health care system. "You have health care agencies that oversee a group of home care workers," Melissa said, as she was shown in the film brushing the client's teeth, "and they take a large percentage of the money allotted for the disabled person." Her statement addressed how public money is siphoned off by private, for-profit companies and connected Melissa's personal story with state and national health care policies that affect nurses' pay and, consequently, the quality of care that patients receive.

In addition to the emotional sound bites connecting Melissa's love for home care with problems that characterize CDASS, I made a conscious effort to incorporate fact-based and informational quotes from Melissa. Comments from Melissa describing the rapid increase in the cost of living in Denver were edited to footage of her driving to the client's home. "The cost of living has gone up so drastically, and wages have stayed the same, that 43 percent of people in Denver do not make a wage where they can sustain a life," she said, as images of the Denver skyline were seen in the distance across the highway. I considered showing close-up images of new condominiums and office high-rise buildings in downtown Denver, but I decided that drive-by shots conveyed more effectively the income and wealth disparities between service workers and the businesspeople and residents occupying those buildings. *Physical* distance from the city's economic and political centers of power, thus, highlighted the widening space between those who are rich and poor.

The film highlighted Melissa's involvement with the union, because this documentary was intended to function as an organizing tool for SEIU Local 105, as well as to encourage other workers to get involved in labor actions. Melissa explained in the film how she signed an online petition pledging support for the Fight for $15 and then, subsequently, was contacted by an SEIU Local 105 representative, who asked if she would volunteer with organizations in Colorado working to raise the minimum wage of health care workers in Denver. She agreed and, in her time as a volunteer, has distributed flyers throughout the city, telephoned health care workers to ask them to join this effort, and spoken at public rallies (Figure 4.3). Paging through names of potential volunteers listed in a binder, Melissa told me, "People think that getting online and signing a petition is enough. We really we have to stand in a group."

Melissa's comment spoke to the limitations of social media and online petitions and it also transitioned the film to a scene in which protesters marched with signs in front of the Colorado State Capitol. The Reverend Dr. Dawn Riley Duval, co-founder of BLM5280, shouted through a bullhorn at the demonstration, "This is what the people standing up for $15 feels like!" Although that protest occurred prior to my involvement with SEIU Local 105, videographers working with the

FIGURE 4.3. Melissa Benjamin working the phones to organize home care workers. (Photo by Gino Canella.)

union filmed the event, and Corral shared the footage with me via Google Drive. At first, I was reluctant to use the footage, because, compared with my footage, which was filmed with a digital single-lens reflex camera and high-quality lenses, the images were grainy, not composed properly, and shaky. However, I realized that the union's footage could be an asset to our production, as it emphasized what Mary Bock called an "aesthetic of authenticity."[2] Low-quality images produced with smartphones, tablets, and other "prosumer" devices highlight "the object of observation rather than traditional aesthetic concerns."[3] Although images produced by activists may be dark, shaky, or poorly composed, these "low-grade image[s]" can be a "privileged form of TV 'truth telling', signifying authenticity and an index-ical reproduction of the real world."[4] As claims to "the truth" are increasingly elusive—amid fake news, misinformation, and conspiracy theories that spread on social media—visual storytelling may be one way through which activists can frame "the truth" and compete for epistemic authority.

In addition to highlighting the collaborative nature of my work with Local 105, using the photographs and videos that were produced by SEIU Local 105 show-cased the importance of racial justice in service-sector union organizing and the "whole person unionism" noted by Ron Ruggiero, president of Local 105 (see chapter 2); hence, it was essential to include those clips. Showing Rev. Dr. Duval shouting through a bullhorn at the Colorado State Capitol and raising her fist, as the film cut to video of a sign that read, "Black Lives Matter," reinforced the intersectionality of service-sector union organizing. In addition, including this footage avoided depicting Melissa in the film as exceptional or positioning her as the lone hero championing workers' rights. Footage of the public demonstration

FIGURE 4.4. Melissa Benjamin speaking out at a Fight for $15 rally in Denver, Colorado. (Photo courtesy SEIU Local 105.)

networked her story and connected it to working people across the service industry, including fast-food workers, janitors, and airport staff. After this brief interlude featuring protest footage, Melissa re-entered the film and said, "That's why I'm for unions, so that the worker has a say and we can have rights." (In the first draft of the film, a comment from Melissa about collective bargaining was included here, but Ruggiero asked for that comment be edited out, because it misrepresented union negotiations.) The film continued with a montage of still images showing union members protesting and holding signs, with upbeat music added to bring the film to an energetic conclusion. Before the film ended, however, a cautionary sound bite from Melissa was included to let union members and potential community allies know that this fight is "going to take time." She said, "Change does not happen overnight. We are actually talking about getting laws changed." This quote, I believed, balanced the revolutionary demands of protest movements with the reformist nature of SEIU Local 105 and the interdependent relationship between the labor movement and political institutions.

Photographs of Melissa speaking at rallies were included near the conclusion of the film to show her publicly advocating for change (Figure 4.4). During the interview that I conducted with her, I asked why she agreed to participate in a documentary film about her work and organizing efforts, and her response, which was used to conclude the film, was a call to action:

"I knew people would see it [the film]," she said, "and it might create a spark in them to stand up and say, 'This isn't right. This isn't gonna happen to me anymore. I'm gonna do whatever I can about it.' If that's speaking out, attending actions, signing petitions, telling people that there's a Fight for $15 going on in Colorado,

I want people to see that, and I want people to join in, because together, we can make a change."

Melissa, currently, is a full-time organizer with Local 105 who speaks with nurses, janitors, and other service industry workers about the collective strength of united workers. It was crucial that the film concluded by showing Melissa in a hopeful light that emphasized her agency, rather than as a helpless victim complaining about her circumstances.[5] I shared a draft of the film with Melissa via a password-protected Vimeo link, and she emailed back within a few hours with a glowing review. "I just viewed the video, and it's fantastic, Gino," she wrote, "awesome job. I'm sure my client's mother will be pleased." Her desire to mobilize allies and engage supporters, through compelling and affective visual storytelling, acknowledges the role of media and culture in claiming symbolic power—challenging representations of working people as lazy or unmotivated and resisting rhetoric that pits working people against one another. Shifting the narrative of working people, through protest and creative media, as described next, was also a focal point in the Justice 4 Janitors docuseries.

The Justice 4 Janitors Series

I produced two short documentaries for SEIU Local 105 that covered rallies held on April 15 and June 15, 2016, for the Justice 4 Janitors (J4J) campaign.[6] Both films used interviews conducted with protesters marching through downtown Denver, and the documentaries are discussed together in this section to show the ongoing nature of that campaign and reveal how serialized activist media mirror the temporal nature of the current media environment. In the J4J campaign, Local 105 organizers were demanding a new master contract for 2,400 janitors working under twenty-seven contracts with businesses in the Denver metro area. After months of negotiations and public demonstrations, in July 2016, the union agreed to a four-year contract that included a pathway to $15 per hour by 2020, expanded child health care coverage, and no increases in the cost of health care premiums.[7]

I interviewed numerous janitors and Local 105 staff at the rallies, asking people why they were demonstrating in the streets. Jesus Cervantes, an organizer with Local 105, said that the union was demonstrating in the downtown business district to let members of the public, and the companies with which the janitors were in negotiations, witness the janitors physically in the streets. Because janitors often work overnight or early in the morning before office buildings open, Cervantes said, their labor is often obscured or invisible. "We wanted to put an actual face to those members, to that movement," he told me at the June 15 rally. "We want them to see that they are real people, that they have families, and that they want their kids to go to college."[8] Several clips of young children were edited to Cervantes's interview audio to emphasize his comments and make a moral argument that janitors are "real people" who are aspiring to create a good life for their families. During the short film produced about the April 15 rally, several quotes were

edited together to argue that Denver's increased cost of living is making it difficult for workers to achieve and maintain a basic quality of life. A woman janitor
and Local 105 member spoke to the assembly in Spanish, saying, "Estamos luchando
por la justicia! Declaramos que queremos llegar a quince dólares la hora. Respé-
tanos y páganos un salario digno que alcance para vivir." (We are fighting for justice! We demand a pathway to $15 per hour. Respect us and pay us a living wage
that is enough to live.")

Luis Castillo, a security worker at Denver International Airport, was included
next in this film, and he connected the J4J campaign to the local socioeconomic
context in which Local 105 is organizing. "Denver is very crucial, because the cost
of living in the past one or two years went up extremely high, so it's very hard for
the families to stay with only one job and be able to survive," he said. "They are
forced to have two jobs or, maybe, work seven days a week."

Ruggiero also emphasized Denver's cost of living at the June 15 rally, saying,
"These workers make anywhere from $9 to $12.60 an hour, so we think it's vitally
important that in these negotiations, we create a pathway to $15 an hour. There's
no question enormous wealth is being created in our economy, and, yes, we absolutely have to share it more broadly."

Ruggiero's comment addressed the massive disparity between U.S. management and worker pay (discussed in chapter 2), and how this gap has grown wider
in the past thirty years. The J4J films asked viewers to recognize the value of service work and attempted to disrupt characterizations that diminish the dignity of
janitors, fast-food workers, and health care professionals, among other workers.
Felicia Griffin, then executive director of FRESC: Good Jobs, Strong Communities, highlighted at the July 15 rally how the recent population growth in Denver
was affecting working people's living standards. "I think we're trying to build a thriv-
ing Denver, not a Denver where people are living on poverty wages and barely
able to get by," she said. "Every single worker in our city is important."

Both short films included Spanish subtitles and short, natural sound clips of
organizers speaking in Spanish to the assembly. A majority of Local 105's members are Spanish-only speaking Mexican immigrants and Latinos, and we therefore
made films that reflected those members and that spoke to the union's core audience. Because I have only basic proficiency speaking Spanish, Corral provided subtitles and reviewed first drafts of the J4J films to ensure the accuracy of those subtitles. Corral's assistance with the translations highlights the collaborative nature
of my activist media and shows how Local 105 engaged the broader Latino community in Denver through bilingual media. These efforts also reveal how activist
media has the potential to decolonize knowledge through research that is produced
in various formats and that uses the language of grassroots activists.

Another important aspect of the J4J films was incorporating music performed
by a marching band that was protesting with the union. These sounds were cut to
images of organizers marching, with quick, one-second edits to match the tim-

FIGURE 4.5. Janitors, union members, and organizers march on the Colorado State Capitol during a Justice 4 Janitors rally. (Photo by Gino Canella.)

ing and rhythm of the beat. This editing style generated a sense of the campaign's urgency and emphasized how union members were prepared to strike if a new contract was not agreed to by the deadline. Cultivating viewers' enthusiasm and showing Local 105 members as "really excited," Cervantes's words from the April 15 rally, was important for portraying the positive energy of union workers rallying together (Figure 4.5). As in the film about Melissa, which showed her love of home care, creating an upbeat and festive atmosphere in the film reinforced workers' solidarity and hopefulness, rather than portraying them as disgruntled employees complaining about their situations.

Also contributing to the positive energy of the J4J film about the April 15 rally was a short clip of Valerie Long's speech to the assembly near the Colorado State Capitol. Long, the international executive vice president of property services with SEIU, said, "You are joining with three hundred cities that are fighting for 15 today!" Her comment, coupled with images of workers cheering, jumping, and signing their names on a large J4J banner, played a dual role: it pointed to the structure of SEIU as an international organization comprising local chapters fighting for collective change and also challenged news media narratives that depict protest participants as violent or angry. To strike a balance between the festive environment that was elicited by the marching and mariachi bands that performed at the rally and the seriousness of the campaign, I filmed footage of janitors chanting, "¡Huelga! ¡Huelga!" (Strike! Strike!), and I spoke to Cervantes about the looming July 2 contract deadline. "We want them [management] to know that we're not putting up with this anymore," he said. "We're going to be radical. This is not the end, this is the beginning. Next time it might be a little more, and they should be prepared for that."

FIGURE 4.6. BLM5280 organizers Amy Brown and Sasha Ramirez march with SEIU Local 105 at a J4J rally in Denver, Colorado. (Photo by Gino Canella.)

To highlight the networking efforts of grassroots organizations in Denver and the intersectional nature of labor, I interviewed Sasha Ramirez, co-lead of BLM5280, prior to her speech at the April 15 assembly. She addressed the significance of connecting organized labor with racial justice, saying that it was crucial that BLM5280 showed up publicly to stand in solidarity with SEIU Local 105 janitors, who, primarily, are women, Mexican immigrants, and Hispanic. "Economic justice, the ability or the inability to live successfully on a minimum wage affects mostly Black and brown communities," Ramirez said. "Racial justice and economic justice are inextricably linked in that way." Video of Ramirez and Amy Brown, co-lead of BLM5280, was shown over this comment, to highlight the shared struggles of working people and the multifaceted organizing strategy of BLM5280 (Figure 4.6).

Producing the J4J series allowed me to continue building relationships with members of Local 105 and the activist community in Denver. Melissa Benjamin attended both J4J rallies; she told me at the April 15 march, "It's time that we get what we deserve, which is fair pay for being the people who maintain the very fabric of this society." Showing up regularly to Local 105 rallies and speaking with members on-camera and off-camera provided me with opportunities to strengthen the trust and credibility that I had earned with my community partners during pre-production. Denver City council member Paul Lopez, with whom I conducted an in-depth interview for the twenty-three-minute documentary, spoke at the April 15 march and addressed the assembly in Spanish. His speech was edited to audio from a mariachi band that played there.

"Aumentar el sueldo mínimo a quince. No menos de quince. ¡Quince!" Lopez proclaimed through a bullhorn. "En esta ciudad que es carísima para vivir, en Denver, la renta es super alta, el costo de vida es alto, el costo de la comida es alto. ¡Nuestro salario también debería ser alto!" (Raise the minimum to $15. Not less than 15. Fifteen! In the city of Denver, where it is so expensive to live, the rent is super high, the cost of living is high, the cost of food is high. Our wages should be high, too!)

Both short films were distributed, primarily, on social media, and the films concluded with hashtags, details about future actions and events, and websites where viewers could obtain more information about these campaigns. Rather than persuade audiences about fine details of a campaign, activist media should utilize visuals and audio to generate affective responses in viewers and then direct them to additional background and context regarding campaign issues. Our media accomplished this by animating union members and supporters with fast-paced films that were set to music and that concluded with on-screen text (in Spanish and English) that included Local 105's website, its Facebook and Twitter accounts, a phone number that viewers could text to obtain more information about the campaign, and the hashtags #Fightfor15 and #J4JDenver.

A secondary goal of the J4J film series was to put pressure on businesses that contract with SEIU Local 105 and on government officials who implement policies that affect working people. As discussed in the next section, I continued my filmmaking in 2017 by documenting rallies with Local 105 that focused on the fight for health care and workers' rights.

Staying Connected with Local 105 as an Activist Filmmaker

Following my work producing the short films featuring Melissa's story and the J4J campaign, SEIU Local 105 commissioned me to produce a twenty-three-minute documentary about organized labor and the networking efforts of grassroots organizations in Denver. The narrative and visual frameworks of that project are discussed at the end of this chapter, but I knew that I needed to gather additional footage from various events to better depict SEIU's social justice unionism. Because the union does not focus solely on negotiating janitorial contracts or advocating for health care workers, the twenty-three-minute documentary needed to reflect Local 105's broader community work. Following Local 105 on Facebook allowed me to remain up-to-date on events and demonstrations. Although trying to keep up with every scheduled protest can be overwhelming, I attended two rallies and produced impromptu videos for Local 105: the first was held in downtown Denver on #MayDay2017; the second was a #ProtectOurCare march to Republican senator Cory Gardner's Denver office on June 13, 2017, in which organizers protested a proposed Republican health care bill.[9] These projects helped me to stay in touch with Local 105 organizers and with allied community organizations that showed up to these rallies, to continue building on our partnership, and to gather additional footage for the twenty-three-minute film.

The first of these two short documentaries was produced on May Day, also known as International Worker's Day, which commemorates economic and

FIGURE 4.7. Workers raise fists in solidarity with #MayDay2017, May 1, 2017. (Photo by Gino Canella.)

workplace gains that the U.S. labor movement has secured. The date also marks the 1886 Haymarket affair, when workers in Chicago went on strike to obtain an eight-hour workday; several workers were eventually killed in a violent clash with police.[10] Because the fifty-second video that I produced on May Day 2017 could not reflect this history adequately, I sought to reinforce workers' solidarity amid continuing attacks against organized labor.

The video began with an organizer saying, "It's not about any of us here; it's about our families; it's about those who are working today and can't be with us; it's about your neighbor who is afraid to come outside."[11] Images of about fifty demonstrators holding signs that read, "¡Vamos Adelante!" (We go forward!), "No Muslim Ban. No Border Wall," reinforced the organizer's speech by depicting the range of issues working people are championing. May Day 2017 occurred at a time when the Trump administration was proposing a travel ban restricting travel to and from seven Muslim-majority countries, and was using rhetoric that criminalized Mexican immigrants; consequently, the film highlighted Local 105's support for Latino and Muslim people. The organizer who was featured at the beginning of the film, a Black woman, continued, "It doesn't end here. It continues to go. All of our organizations care about the same thing." An image of two organizers raising fists—one Black and one white—was shown to signify multiracial solidarity (Figure 4.7).

Similar to the May Day film, the #ProtectOurCare film was not commissioned by SEIU Local 105, but I received a Facebook notification about the event at the last minute, so I decided to attend with my camera to support the union, foster my relationships with organizers, document the event, and add to my video library for the twenty-three-minute film. Unlike the J4J rallies, which relied on the energetic music of marching bands, the health care demonstration was a silent "death march." Local 105 utilized attention-grabbing stunts, such as an organizer dressed as the grim reaper who marched through the streets holding a sickle, and demonstrators carrying foldout caskets to represent people who, under the Republican proposal, would lose health care coverage and die without it. These props were juxtaposed with emotional comments from Local 105 organizers and members.

Corletta Hithon-Davis, a home health care worker, spoke at the rally, backed by Melissa Benjamin and other health care workers, and provided data about the number of people who will lose coverage if the Affordable Care Act is repealed. Hithon-Davis issued a call for solidarity in her comments that opened the film: "271,000 Coloradoans will lose care with the replacement. People such as myself, home care workers, thousands across the state, are paid through funding provided by Medicare. If we are forced to get other jobs, who is left to care for the elderly, the sick, the disabled? Let's stand and march in solidarity today."

I spoke with Cervantes, the Local 105 organizer, during this march, and he connected the issue of health care with the temporary and precarious work that is common in the service industry: "A lot of members don't have health insurance because they work part-time, so the companies are not required to pay for health insurance." This film made a moral argument, similar to the narrative strategy that was used in the J4J series, that, regardless of employment status, health care is a human right. Following President Trump's campaign promise to "repeal and replace Obamacare," several Republican health care bills were put forward in 2017. However, despite Republican majorities in the U.S. House and Senate, Congress was unable to pass a bill that reformed or replaced the Affordable Care Act.

I asked organizers about the symbolic power of protest and how marching in the streets puts pressure on elected officials, such as Senator Gardner, who are concerned with remaining in office in the face of an angry constituency. "We want our elected officials here in Colorado to hear our voices," Juan Gallegos, an organizer with the Colorado Immigrant Rights Coalition, told me. He continued: "We're gonna stand up and hold up a sign, and, then, later on, in the elections, we're going to go out and vote, and we're going to remember those people who voted against our health care, those people who voted against working families, those people who voted against immigrants."

Following his comment, the film cut to a black screen, with white text that read: "Call Senator Gardner and tell him a YES vote is a death sentence for Colorado. #ProtectOurCare (202) 224–5941." The text was enlarged to the beat of a drum, played during the rally as a death knell. Recognizing how access to health care, janitorial contracts, and fighting to increase the minimum wage affect "mostly Black and brown people," as Ramirez said in the J4J film, I collaborated with BLM5280 to produce videos and films that centered Black voices in the fight for social justice.

DOCUMENTING THE MOVEMENT FOR BLACK LIVES

My filmmaking with BLM5280 began with a series of short videos that I filmed for a #BLMDebate challenge. Bianca Williams, co-lead of BLM5280, emailed me prior to the October 21, 2015 community meeting, to ask whether I would be attending and would be able to film BLM5280 organizers speaking into the camera and posing questions to the 2016 U.S. presidential candidates. BLM national headquarters requested short videos from local chapters, with the goal of pressuring the Democratic Party into hosting a debate that focused solely on racial justice. The Democratic National Committee agreed to discuss racial justice in a town hall, rather than a debate, but neither a town hall nor a debate occurred. The video series consisted of three short videos about health care, education, and reparations. The videos began and ended with the hashtag #BLMDebate appearing in plain white text on a black screen.

Like BLM's street demonstrations, the debate questions were meant to be provocative. The reparations video, for example, consisted of six short clips of BLM5280 core members and organizers asking presidential candidates for the Democratic Party to address the exploitation of Black labor and lack of public resources in African American communities. Some organizers were sarcastic or used a mocking tone. "So, ummm, what's this check gonna look like?!" a core member asked. A white organizer affiliated with the movement said, "My friends were talking about this thing the other day. I think it rhymed with preparations. Reparations?"

Williams, however, used a more serious tone in her speech. Looking directly into the camera, she said: "In the past, my people were promised forty acres and a mule. Now, that is the name of Spike Lee's production company. What I would like to know from our presidential candidates is: When are we going to get our reparations? We need equity in education, in housing, and in job opportunities. When are we going to get our reparations?!"[12]

I shared the videos with Williams the following day via Google Drive, and BLM5280 posted them to its Facebook page. Williams complimented me on the videos' high production value, and she thanked me for assisting with the project on short notice. Although the videos were produced easily and quickly, they helped me gain trust with BLM5280, and they connected the movement to political debates about reparations. Most important, by showing up to make the videos and sharing them without expecting payment or credit, I demonstrated to BLM5280 that

I was committed to the fight for justice, which, as explained later, led to future opportunities with the movement.

#JamarClark and #4thPrecinctShutdown

Following the #BLMDebate series, I produced a two-minute video with BLM5280 that focused on a demonstration the group organized near the Colorado State Capitol on November 24, 2015.[13] I spoke with BLM5280 supporters and organizers at the demonstration and recorded natural sounds of participants using a bullhorn to express their frustration with events that had occurred in Minneapolis on November 18, 2015, when two Minneapolis police officers shot and killed Jamar Clark, an unarmed, twenty-four-year-old Black man. Protesters subsequently sat outside Minneapolis's 4th Precinct, demanding the release of surveillance video of the incident. Eight days into the sit-in, five protesters were shot near the precinct, allegedly by a group of white supremacists attempting to intimidate protesters and those associated with the BLM movement. Alex Landau, a supporter of BLM5280, told me during an interview at the rally that the events in Minneapolis were intended to elicit fear among BLM organizers and supporters, and the assembly was needed so organizers could "stand together stronger than ever in a time like this."

During the rally in Denver, organizers asked that only people of color address the crowd, and the video adhered to that request. Because BLM5280 was established by and for Black people, I reflected on my identities as a white filmmaker and avoided using voiceover narration in any of BLM5280's films, producing, instead, media that reflected the movement's mission of centering the voices of Black women. BLM5280 announced the vigil a few hours prior to the demonstration on its Facebook page, which has more than thirteen thousand followers, and about sixty people attended. Because of the evolving nature of this networked movement, and the sense of urgency about combating state violence against Black people, this video was shot, produced, and distributed on Facebook within a total of four hours. Despite criticism that social media provoke outrage and produce knowledge paralysis as a result of information overload, social media allowed BLM5280 in this instance to visualize its support for another chapter—through photography, video, and a public demonstration—and to quickly mobilize supporters and community organizations.[14]

The two-minute video featuring the vigil began with Roshan Bliss, a former organizer with BLM5280, saying, "This is terrorism. It is an act that's aimed at a civilian population to make them fearful for their safety." Bliss used the state's language of national security and terrorism to reveal how the silencing of Black activism occurs not simply online but through on-the-ground intimidation of and violence directed toward activists. Bliss's comments were edited to visual images of attendees holding signs that read, "White ppl Against White Terror," "End White Supremacy," and "I Reject White Supremacy," and showed them lighting candles

FIGURE 4.8. BLM5280 organizes vigil to stand in solidarity with BLM Minneapolis. November 24, 2015. (Photo by Gino Canella.)

near the Colorado State Capitol. In his interview conducted for the film, Bliss connected the shooting outside the police precinct to law enforcement's refusal to release video of the shooting: "Those protesters in Minneapolis have simply been demanding the release of a videotape, and if they hadn't forced those protesters to sit out front of their police station for so long while demanding the simple release of this tape, this never would have even had an opportunity to even happen."

Ending police violence and releasing the video of the shooting were the central foci of the event, and, thus, became the narrative focus of the short film. In addition to demanding video evidence of the shooting, Bliss shouted a systemic critique of police reform to the crowd, with many joining the chorus: "The whole damn system is guilty as hell. Indict! Convict! Send those killer cops to jail!" Organizers encouraged participants to gather in a circle as Black attendees were asked to speak to the crowd (Figure 4.8). Many expressed sadness and frustration with the shooting death of another unarmed Black man by police and the subsequent intimidation by alleged white supremacists. In the short film, somber comments were juxtaposed with protesters' fiery comments, including a BLM5280 organizer chanting, "We can't be silent while our friends are gunned down!" Videos from protests in Minneapolis were crowdsourced via Twitter and Facebook and were included in the film with permission. Within two hours of the event, our film was edited and posted to YouTube and Twitter, using the hashtags #JamarClark and #4thPrecinctShutdown, to encourage viewers to gather more information and background about the events in Minneapolis and to engage in this important conversation. Sharing this film on social media allowed BLM5280 to speak across geographic boundaries, stand in solidarity with people in Minneapolis, and thereby elevate the movement's discourse about the need for police reform.

Although gathering in public space was essential for community members to express their frustrations concerning the events in Minneapolis, filming the rally and distributing it on social media expanded the space through which activists could dialogue with allies and stand in solidarity with the Minneapolis chapter. One woman's comments at the rally expressed powerfully the importance of holding physical spaces: "I came out here tonight because I'm hurting, and I wanted to be with community while I hurt. I have to go to work and pretend that everything is okay, and not necessarily having the space to talk about these things as a person of color, as a Black woman, as a queer Black woman. I'm hurting and it's hard; it's really hard."

Whereas this comment provided the film with a sensitive tone and reinforced the movement's attempts to center the voices of Black women and queer and trans people of color, earlier portions of the film highlighted BLM's commitment to radical dissent. In one scene, a Black woman speaking to the assembly through the bullhorn said: "It is not time for you to sit here and pacify your hearts, because anger is what gets shit done, and we are upset. I am pissed the hell off! I have to . . . sit here and worry about every single child who I look at as some next target for some next cop, for some next white supremacist."

Part of her comments were edited to images of the crowd, one of which showed a young Black boy listening to her, which put a visible face to the concerns that had brought many people to the rally. Used together, the narration and image reinforced one of BLM's central arguments: an end to state violence that is inflicted disproportionately upon communities of color. Through the use of upbeat music, quick edits, and chants, the film created a sense of immediacy about and outrage with the events that had occurred in Minneapolis.

For organizations and movements that lack large financial resources and rely, primarily on volunteer support, activist media shared online help these movements to remain visible through daily updates, calls to action, and consciousness-raising. Prior to attending the Denver solidarity rally for BLM Minneapolis, I viewed a significant amount of user-generated content about protests in Minneapolis, primarily on Twitter, posted with the hashtags #JamarClark #4thPrecinctShutdown. Our video concluded with a black screen that contained these hashtags to encourage viewers to link to existing conversations, to gather more information about the protest and shootings, and to share the video of the Denver rally.

Crowdsourcing material quickly from social media is another example of the participatory and collaborative nature of activist media. When movements organize for justice across national and international borders, they often need to communicate instantly, sharing information and connecting with others who are fighting for similar issues under the same banner. As evidenced by BLM5280's

FIGURE 4.9. Amy Brown marching to #ReclaimMLK during the Marade, January 18, 2016. (Photo by Gino Canella.)

mobilization of more than sixty community allies to a rally in several hours, as well as my filming of that rally and connecting the Denver and Minneapolis chapters through media, social media played an important role in allowing us to connect the emotional personal stories told at the Denver rally with actions across the country.

The Hennepin County attorney eventually released video footage of the shooting, but, following an internal investigation, Minneapolis police chief Janeé Harteau did not discipline the two officers involved in the shooting.[15] Thus, our short film reveals some of activist media's strengths and limitations. The documentary successfully leveraged social media to raise public consciousness about the shooting death of Jamar Clark and connect BLM5280 with BLM Minneapolis; but the refusal to prosecute the officers involved shows that seeking justice through video evidence is insufficient. BLM5280, however, continued its demands for police accountability during an organized disruption of Denver's 2016 Martin Luther King Jr. Day parade.

The "Marade" and #ReclaimMLK

The second film I produced with BLM5280 featured a demonstration that was held on January 18, 2016, during the Martin Luther King Jr. Day parade (Figure 4.9).[16] The night prior to the MLK Day protest, BLM5280 hosted a planning meeting for a small group of organizers and supporters. Williams invited me to this meeting as an allied media maker who had produced several videos with BLM5280 to date. Organizers discussed the positioning of Black and white supporters at vari-

FIGURE 4.10. A witness documents the Marade with a smartphone near the Colorado State Capitol, January 18, 2016. (Photo by Gino Canella.)

ous locations during the demonstration, and they offered advice about what to do if protesters were confronted or detained by police. Before the meeting began, participants were asked to place their smartphones in a box outside the room, as Black activists are aware of the digital and state surveillance that is used disproportionately against them, and they took additional precautions in this instance to avoid being monitored. Organizers at the planning meeting decided that white allies and leaders of Denver's faith community would form a protest circle surrounding BLM5280's core members. This tactic recognized how white activists are not policed in the same ways as Black activists are; thus, allies could create a barrier for BLM5280 organizers to voice their demands to the crowd and elected officials.

The film was narrated by a speech given at Civic Center Park by Brown, co-lead of BLM5280. Her speech issued demands for justice and equity from Denver mayor Michael Hancock, and audio of her speech was juxtaposed with video of protesters marching the three-mile parade route down Colfax Avenue, a major east–west corridor through Denver that wraps around the Colorado State Capitol (Figure 4.10). When the demonstration reached Civic Center Park, Brown stood behind a podium and used a public address system that had been set up by city organizers to deliver her message to the mayor. She was backed by BLM5280 core members, including Williams, Ramirez, and several other Black women. Their positioning at the front of the stage and in the documentary centered the voices of Black women who had been instrumental in founding and organizing the BLM movement. "We did not ask permission," Brown said in the opening line of the film. "We did not get permits. We were not invited." Refusing to get permission or permits for its march showed that BLM5280 was intent on "reclaiming" MLK

Day and King's message of radical democracy. BLM5280 members expressed repeatedly their displeasure with Mayor Hancock and his administration, chanting, "If you refuse to lead, we refuse to follow!" By marching outside of designated, preapproved areas (often called "non-free-speech zones"), and repeating the mantra "Reclaim MLK," BLM5280 rejected soft-force protest policing tactics, disrupted a sanitized collective memory of King, and practiced antagonistic democracy. [17] As Brown said in her speech, "When you reclaim this day, and when you reclaim the truth of this day, it's scary as hell."

On a day that City of Denver officials likely hoped would be celebrated by the Black community, BLM5280 seized the opportunity to highlight local issues, including affordable housing and criminal justice reform. I asked a protester why BLM5280 took the streets and rerouted the parade from the city's planned route; his comments, which were not included in this film for the sake of time, but were used in the twenty-three-minute documentary, confronted the sterilized narrative of MLK as a pastor and leader in the civil rights movement:

> I'm here because justice hasn't been served. The dream hasn't been fulfilled, and we need to get people away from this dream they got us in. They have politicians that we've been marching and protesting against all day, every day last year, coming here to speak for us on a day that's supposed to be ours. Martin Luther King wasn't a man of peace; he was a man of civil disruption by nonviolence. That does not mean he was peaceful. We are not here to try to keep this dream a lullaby. We are here to wake these people up, let 'em know this dream has not been fulfilled. We got people being murdered by police every single day, and this President [Obama], this Governor [of Colorado, John Hickenlooper], this Mayor [of Denver, Michael Hancock] have done nothing! We are here to wake them up, and let them know it's time to keep fighting. This dream needs to become a reality.

Some attendees at the city's official event in City Park viewed BLM5280's demonstration as divisive and polarizing. People shouted, "Let him speak," when BLM5280 organizers disrupted Mayor Hancock's speech at the foot of Dr. King's statue. The protest and repeated interruptions by BLM5280, however, connected King's radical politics with a critique of democracy and access to public resources. Demonstrating without permits and "shouting truth to power," a common refrain from BLM activists, showed their commitment to claiming public space and challenging institutional politics and the elected officials who lead these institutions. Brown's speech was edited to quick-cut images of demonstrators marching down Colfax Avenue, chanting "Show me what democracy looks like," through a bullhorn, and carrying signs that read, "#BlackLivesMatter," "Which Side Are You On?" and "We Are Baltimore" (Figure 4.11).

Images were shown of demonstrators marching, raising their fists, and singing to the beat of a marching band (Figure 4.12). These messages, grounded in

FIGURE 4.11. Protesters ask "Which Side Are You On?" at the MLK Day Marade. (Photo by Gino Canella.)

collective Black resistance and love, highlighted commonalities among the struggles for Black liberation. Documenting them in video and photography, depicted BLM5280 in solidarity with oppressed people and amplified and visualized its mission to chapters across the United States. As BLM5280 critiqued the local political economy of Denver and Colorado, images that referenced national issues related to the BLM movement were shown. Thus, our media connected local struggles to broader demands for justice and accountability.

Brown shouted the movement's demands to Mayor Hancock at the rally, which included calls for affordable housing and criminal justice reform. Brown also demanded the release of surveillance video that showed the murder of Michael Marshall, a Black man who was mentally ill and was killed in 2015 while being restrained by law enforcement during a psychotic episode that he experienced in the downtown Denver jail.[18] To highlight the Marshall case and raise public

FIGURE 4.12. Alex Landau marches down Colfax Avenue in the Marade, January 18, 2016. (Photo by Gino Canella.)

consciousness about police violence against Black people, activists set up head-stones with the names Mike Brown, Walter Scott, and Freddie Gray, among others, and they erected a cemetery in Civic Center Park. These images were edited to a portion of Brown's speech, in which she said, "Honor Dr. King's commitment to community by diverting 12 million of our dollars to rehabilitation programs aimed at reducing, *reducing* our prison population, and providing mental health resources to our brothers and sisters in jail." Protesters cheered this critique of militarized policing and incarceration, and they followed Brown's speech by chanting, "Resources, not retribution!"

. Brown raised public awareness about the death of Marshall and addressed Mayor Hancock directly when she called for releasing the video evidence of the incident. "Mayor Hancock, will you honor Dr. King beyond your poetic words this morning?" she began. "Will you honor Dr. King by immediately releasing the tapes showing the Denver sheriff's deputies brutally murdering Michael Mar-shall?!" The crowd cheered and shouted in unison, "Release the tapes! Release the tapes!" Calling out Mayor Hancock again, Brown demanded that the City of Denver invest in rehabilitation programs and community resources, critiquing the city's increased spending on law enforcement. "You gave 24 million of our tax dol-lars to the Denver sheriff's department—24 million dollars!" she shouted. "The police department does not need to be further militarized! Our communities are already in terror. Demilitarize the police!" The assembly joined with BLM5280 organizers, shouting, "Resources, not retribution!" The figure referred to the may-or's decision in 2016 to spend $24 million of the city's $1.8 billion budget on

FIGURE 4.13. Holding a fist and a phone in Denver's Civic Center Park, January 18, 2016. (Photo by Gino Canella.)

hiring sheriff's deputies, updating law enforcement computer systems, and improving training for inmate care and use of force—which, potentially, are all useful expenditures for improving police officers' on-the-job conduct but fail to address the root problems of police-community relations.[19]

The protest and associated documentary, which was distributed, primarily, on social media, raised awareness about Marshall's death.[20] They were also instrumental in pressuring public officials to release security footage of Marshall's death and elevated a critique of militarized local law enforcement at the expense of civic resources. But justice was not realized for the Marshall family. In November 2017, the City of Denver announced that it had reached a $4.65 million settlement with the Marshall family, which, in addition to the payment, included improving mental health services in the downtown jail and developing protocols for handling inmates who are mentally ill.[21] That settlement followed a disturbing trend evidenced in recent years: Since 2004, the City of Denver has paid more than $30 million to settle police and jail claims, revealing how demands for more body cams and the publication of video evidence of police violence on social media does little to change the neoliberal logics that underlie U.S. law enforcement.[22]

Both short documentaries produced with BLM5280—the Minneapolis vigil and the MLK Day march—utilized episodic narratives at the expense of a deeper, well-researched analysis of state violence and racial injustices. This trade-off speaks to the limitations of film as a medium (Figure 4.13). Short documentaries posted to social media can effectively communicate the emotional salience of a protest and can increase spaces for movements to voice their demands, but these short documentaries are not ideal vehicles for educating publics about detailed policy proposals or organizing strategies. Our films, however, did address broader themes of the BLM movement, such as shouting truth to power, critiquing systemic racial and economic inequalities and how they disproportionately affect communities of color, and claiming public space to stand in solidarity with allied chapters and local community organizations fighting for justice. Working closely with BLM5280 on these short films also provided me with much-needed footage for the twenty-three-minute documentary that I produced with SEIU Local 105 and allowed me to place union organizing in conversation with the fight for racial justice. More important, these films continued my political education regarding the intersection of racial and economic justice, which was invaluable as I began producing a story about one union's attempts to build a broad-based multiracial coalition within the labor movement.

CONNECTING UNIONS WITH THE STREETS

Radical Labor: Aligning Unions with the Streets was produced in collaboration with SEIU Local 105, and it stitched together the short documentaries reviewed in this chapter in an in-depth narrative that focused on three themes: (1) organized labor's checkered history fostering racial justice among workers; (2) the importance of street demonstrations for claiming and translating symbolic power into political and institutional power; and (3) the collective strength of working people engaged in multifaceted organizing campaigns. The film was commissioned in August 2016, following my work on the J4J series, and I discussed with Corral my vision for the project. She agreed to put me in touch with local community organizers and politicians with whom Local 105 had worked who could speak to the relationships the union has in the community. I explained how interviews with supporters and politicians, next to visuals from protests and members' stories, would create a compelling narrative about social movement unionism. I told Corral that the film could be a powerful organizing tool for future campaigns and membership drives.

Corral agreed to identify two or three members who would be willing to share their stories in the film and to introduce me via email to key organizers. After months of back-and-forth emails and gentle reminders for those names and introductions, I contacted community organizers whom Corral mentioned in our meetings and I introduced myself and the project. Most people I contacted were receptive to the film and agreed to participate (for sample interview requests, see the appendix). Interviews that were conducted included Ruggiero; Griffin; council members Paul Lopez and Robin Kniech; Josh Downey, president of Denver Area Labor Federation; and Lizeth Chacón, executive director of Colorado People's Alliance. As I mentioned in chapter 2, invitations were sent to Amy Brown and Sasha Ramirez of BLM5280 and organizers with SURJ Denver, but they either declined to participate or did not return my request. Because I had listened to Black organizers, particularly Black women, at community meetings describe the labor that is required to explain racial justice to white allies, I balanced my request for interviews with a sensitivity for the labor and emotional energy that these interviews require. I explained to organizers that I wished to provide a platform to illuminate their campaigns, but I also recognized when my calls and requests for interviews were too much.

In June 2017, I still had not been put in touch with members to profile for the documentary, and Corral told me that she was resigning from her position as the communications coordinator of Local 105. Andy Jacob, political director at Local 105, connected me with a Denver-based communication consultant who was working with SEIU Local 105, and I explained to her who I was, what I was doing, and my relationship with the union. Regular turnover in grassroots organizing is a frustrating reality of community-based work and activist media. As a result of limited resources and burnout, organizers and volunteers resign, forcing new members to pick up where others left off. Maintaining relationships among movement members and organizers—relationships that often take years to develop—is a challenge that activist media makers must navigate. Because the additional interviews were never confirmed, I moved forward with the project and decided to focus on Melissa's story to humanize labor and place the labor movement in conversation with allied community organizers and politicians.

The documentary opens with a quote from Rosa Luxemburg: "Democracy is indispensable to the working class, because only through the exercise of its democratic rights, in the struggle for democracy, can the proletariat become aware of its class interests and its historic task." The quote sets up the documentary by emphasizing the protagonist of the film (the proletariat) and the conflict—the struggle for democracy. The film then transitions to a scene with Melissa providing care in a client's home and describing her work. As in Melissa's short profile film discussed earlier, I began *Radical Labor* with a portrait-style, human interest story to humanize the labor movement and to update the image of a union organizer. As many factory workers and trade unions are struggling in the current economy—because of automation, antiquated labor laws that make it difficult to organize workplaces, and globalization—care and service work are emerging sectors for the labor movement. The film reflects this trend.

Following the brief introduction of Melissa's story, the film moves to a J4J rally hosted by SEIU Local 105. The transition uses music from a marching band at the rally, which conveyed the event's energy and excitement. After brief quotes from organizers and members of Local 105, Ruggiero explains Local 105's mission statement: "We are about improving the lives of our membership, but really all working people." He describes the range of issues the union is engaged in, from health care to immigration reform. Archival footage of an automobile factory is cut in next to provide historical perspective and background on the labor movement in the United States. Ruggiero talks about the auto industry providing a stable middle-class life for those in trade unions and the subsequent decline of unions. "As unions have declined, so have their paychecks across the board," he says. Downey provides further explanation for the loss of unions: "As we've been under attack, too many unions have gone insular to protect what they had." This comment foregrounds the theme of labor-community partnerships that comes later in the film and critiques the postwar U.S. labor movement as exclusive and inward-looking. Ruggiero does not lay all of the blame with unions, however; rather, he explains how violent attacks on workers by the state were also responsible for breaking radical unions. Images of police beating workers outside of a factory are shown here to highlight the state violence that has been exerted against workers who dare to challenge capital. Ruggiero describes how the "decline in unions has absolutely gone lock-step in tandem with the massive inequality that we have today, and I would even argue further . . . the degraded level of our democracy."

Downey provides further historical context in this section of the film by explaining the United Auto Workers' organizing efforts in 1937, and how "they couldn't crack the nut with Ford," because, as he says, "Henry Ford had done a masterful job of splitting the workforce, Black workers versus white workers." This quote transitions the documentary into a discussion of racial justice, and presents a key theme I sought to discuss in the film: the importance of a multiracial and multiethnic activist labor movement. "I would look to the '50s when labor was a part of the civil rights movement," Downey says, as images of Martin Luther King Jr. marching with union organizers are shown. King, notably, was assassinated in Memphis, Tennessee, while supporting the striking municipal sanitation workers. Other black-and-white still images in this section of the film include workers on picket lines holding signs referencing apartheid, the National Association for the Advancement of Colored People (NAACP), and housing discrimination, further reinforcing the legacy of radical labor activism in the United States. To connect this history to the contemporary moment and to local politics in Colorado, footage from BLM5280's rally to Reclaim MLK Day is shown next. To make the transition, I used a short clip of an activist shouting, "Show me what democracy looks like!" Upbeat music slowly rises to a crescendo, and a series of quick edits are cut to the beat, bringing viewers to the Denver march on MLK Day.

In the film's transition to the segment on BLM and racial justice, I was sensitive to whose voices had been featured in the documentary thus far. Because I had relied heavily on Ruggiero and Downey's interviews to provide historical context on the labor movement and its handling of racial justice issues, I wanted to shift the film's perspective by relying in this section primarily on interviews with people of color and women. As footage of BLM5280's protest on MLK Day is shown, a demonstrator is heard shouting, "Whose streets? Our streets!" A quote from Chacón is included next, in which she says, "Black Lives Matter has really done a lot of work to really bring the issues from the African American community to the front." Audio from BLM5280 activists at the MLK Day rally is interspersed, and viewers hear protesters' demands for "affordable housing now" and an end to police violence against communities of color—stressing the range of issues on which community activists are fighting.

Incorporating these images and quotes into the documentary seamlessly was a challenge for me as an editor. I was attempting to show these fights in the film *as* labor issues, and not as disconnected or random protests. Chacón's interview is heard again over footage of the MLK Day demonstration in order to stress the intersection between race and class. "Making sure that we tackle the issue of class and also race, because we're not going to win the economic justice fight if we don't include race in it," she says. "We have to pick bigger fights, and we have to have a long-term vision for what we want our state to look like and this country to look like if we want to change things." Chacón goes on to say that labor and community organizers need to follow the lead of activists like BLM5280 who are "bold" and willing to "call things how they are." This is an important note about strategy: SEIU, generally, is viewed (and critiqued) as approaching politics through a reformist approach to policy and contracts, while BLM is often understood as a movement that uses a radical and revolutionary approach to politics. The film depicts both methods to advocate for a multifaceted, hybrid political strategy that simultaneously attempts to seize symbolic, political, and economic power.

After the section with BLM5280 fades to black, Ruggiero transitions the film to a critique of neoliberal individualism by discussing the "right to work for less." A clip from a Walmart employee training video is shown in the film to provide viewers with a sample of how competitive individualism is framed by corporations. The employee, standing in a Walmart warehouse, explains how workers can "get ahead based on their own performance" and notes how union membership has declined in recent years. "Unions are fighting to survive," he says. Chacón describes how this coordinated rhetorical strategy by "the other side" successfully created a "1 percent economy." Framing this political economic agenda as "the other side" establishes the opposition against which unions and working people are struggling for power—namely, the capitalist class. Griffin puts the responsibility back on unions by explaining how neoliberal discourses were successful, in part, because many unions "kept a lot of segments of our population out, specifically people of color and women," she says. "But what it was is kind of a club, and you let in your family and you let in your friends. There were communities that couldn't get access to those good jobs." This comment picks up the thread started earlier by Downey, who explained how capitalists divided working people along racial identities; but the comment also confronts the labor movement's failures and calls on union organizers to do better.

Councilman Lopez challenges the "deliberate attack" on working-class solidarity by referencing the United Farm Workers in Delano, California. He discusses a moment of unity in U.S. labor history—how the Filipino workers stood up to strike for their rights, better working conditions, and higher wages and how the Spanish-speaking Mexican community joined these workers. "That movement was successful not just because of Méxicanos having their own self-determination, or Filipinos having self-determination, but because of the allied support from people who are not like them around the country."

The documentary then returns to Melissa's story and shows her caring for her children at home. She explains how she got involved in union organizing, which transitions the film to a segment on protest and the politics of visibility. An organizer with a bullhorn is shown at a rally hosted by Local 105 shouting, "What kind of power? Union power!" Jesus Cervantes, an organizer with Local 105, is shown in the film describing how being in the streets is crucial for the union's efforts because it puts "an actual face to those members, to that movement." This comment is especially true for janitorial workers who work cleaning offices on overnight shifts, which obscures their labor. Griffin says that because demonstrations are broadcast online and in news media, the movement "gains moment and support" and uplifts "a conversation about change that a lot of folks feel is needed." Lopez says, "We create a reflection. We create a surface that people can see themselves in."

As the section on protest ends, the camera moves in on the back of a man whose T-shirt reads: "We Deserve More." Councilwoman Robin Kniech appears next to transition the film to a brief interlude about the importance of infrastructure. She asks, "Who is going to carry that conversation forward beyond the streets?" Kniech makes an important point about the changing nature of labor in the contemporary economy by explaining that unions have the infrastructure that is needed for long-term policy fights and contract negotiations, but, because of U.S. legal decisions, unions do not have the membership that they once had. "What does it look like for a person who is not in a unionized workplace to be a member of the labor movement?" she asks. "What are the pathways to be a part of the infrastructure?" Kniech discusses in the film the challenge for both community activists and labor unions seeking to develop a model that balances the energy and spontaneity of protest with the organization and infrastructure that is necessary to conduct long-term political organizing. "What does membership and participation look like beyond what we were founded on, which was a workplace model that isn't applicable anymore?" she asks. These comments were edited to footage of a Local 105 year-end workshop in a hotel ballroom. This footage, although not as compelling or visually exciting as protest footage, was necessary to include in the film. It stressed the importance of bringing workers together to discuss and deliberate on communication strategies, foster their working relationships, and celebrate their successes. Kniech's comment about a "workplace model" also critiqued the trend toward precarious and temporary work in the "gig economy," and the notion that certain sectors of the economy, such as information and technology, for example, do not need unions. There are unionization efforts, in the United States and around the world, in which organizers are attempting to disrupt this logic and build union infrastructures where they do not currently exist.

The film transitions to another scene of Local 105's meeting practices, this one involving the ratification of the J4J master contract. I used footage that Corral filmed and provided to me in Google Drive, which showed Ruggiero speaking to Local 105 members with the assistance of a Spanish-language interpreter, in the union's offices. He was standing on a chair, high-fiving members, and chanting "Se puede! Se puede!" As footage of Ruggiero continued, I edited in a quote from Downey's interview, in which he said, "What we've seen is, in those places, with those affiliates, with those unions who have embraced a racial justice lens and tackled racial justice, they happen to be the affiliates that are growing the most and gaining the most power." Live music from a Latin band at the ratification event completed the transition to this scene, again stressing the diversity of Local 105's membership and complementing Downey's comment about the link between racial and economic justice. Footage of members dancing, attending information sessions about union benefits and political initiatives, and casting their votes for the J4J master contract (which was ratified by 98% of the members) was used in this segment to emphasize how Local 105 fosters comradery among its members, and how it promotes democratic unionism.

This section, however, was altered slightly from its initial version. Following completion on the film's editing, I shared the documentary with Ruggiero and Jacob on a password-protected Vimeo link. Ruggiero, overall, was happy with the first draft, but he expressed concern with the inclusion of an interview with someone who no longer worked with SEIU. I argued for keeping the interview in the film because it conveyed a powerful story. In the interview, an organizer with Local 105 spoke through tears about her experiences as a Mexican immigrant; she discussed how proud she felt empowering janitors to find their collective voice and fight for their rights. Because she described her path from janitorial work to union organizer, I thought the clip stressed the themes we sought to communicate—specifically, workers' agency and solidarity across identities. This interview, I believed, also highlighted the importance of organic leaders and member-led union organizing. Ultimately, I allowed Ruggiero to make the final decision; he asked me to interview another Local 105 organizer and use the new interview in place of the original. I struggled with my decision to concede this much editorial control to my community partners; however, after reflecting on my desire to produce a collaborative film in the spirit of democratic participation, I gave Ruggiero and SEIU editing authority and made the revisions. Another interview with a Latina organizer was conducted at Local 105 headquarters, and the section was relatively similar to the original version. This instance reveals the difficult ethical decisions that activist media makers must make when working in partnership with grassroots community groups. Practicing democracy, fundamentally, involves maximizing human agency so that people have control over the decisions and resources that affect their lives. Activist filmmakers and community-based researchers cannot simply espouse trendy concepts such as "participation" or "engagement," and then fail to follow through on these concepts' basic premises.

CONCLUSION

This chapter reviewed the narrative strategies used in a series of documentaries that I produced with SEIU Local 105 and with BLM5280. I paid particular attention to how interview excerpts, visual images, and natural sounds worked together to produce intersectional and affective narratives based on solidarity and collective responsibility. Although I filmed and edited these documentaries, my efforts to send scripts and first drafts to organizers in advance of their publication, schedule interviews in accordance with collectively agreed upon production plans, and follow these organizations' social media activities so that I could pick up my camera quickly and attend rallies all highlight activist media's democratic nature. Although this chapter briefly discussed social media as a distribution outlet and as a platform on which to crowdsource content, chapter 5 explores in further detail the potentials and limitations of online distribution. I review next how SEIU Local 105 and BLM5280 used a multifaceted distribution strategy for their activist media that complemented and enhanced their on-the-ground organizing.

5 · POST-PRODUCTION
Distribution, Exhibition, and Impact

Media makers and organizers who make films or photographs with the intent to mobilize allies and promote social justice campaigns are confronted with the question of how best to distribute their work to publics. As smartphones and inexpensive camera equipment have made media production easier and more accessible, there is an endless sea of content online. Identifying an audience and connecting that audience with the issues raised in your film to build power, therefore, is a major challenge. Although sites like Facebook, YouTube, and Twitter provide instant publishing and the ability to reach global audiences, these sites present organizers with numerous contradictions. The collecting and selling of users' personal information and social media's commercial incentives make these platforms problematic for activist media makers seeking to make radical anti-capitalist critiques about social and economic inequalities. This chapter details my efforts working with Service Employees International Union Local 105 and Black Lives Matter 5280 to exhibit our media through a multifaceted distribution strategy. Social media are discussed as a distribution outlet, but I focus also on how public screenings, community media workshops, and the visibility of protest are key distribution practices for networking solidarity among grassroots organizations. Our media amplified the networking effects of community groups in Colorado, highlighted the social nature of organizing, and reinforced the relationship-building efforts that occur in public spaces. These relationships are necessary for movement organizing.

To avoid a media-centric analysis about activist media distribution, I discuss my filmmaking with SEIU Local 105 and BLM5280 as digital storytelling that injected radical narratives of social justice into the public consciousness. Recognizing the goals of my community partners helped me identify audiences and decide where and how to best reach them. In addition to sharing our activist media online, to be viewed primarily by allies and supporters who follow these organizations' social media accounts, we used media to open physical spaces for dialogue about race, immigration, and labor. BLM5280 and SEIU Local 105 also shared articles and videos from news media outlets on their social media pages and discussed their relationship to local news outlets in Colorado. These practices recognize how activists use a variety of methods to disrupt the framing of race and labor. The politics of protest is examined to understand how the visibility and networking of movements in the streets is complemented by mediated stories. Finally, I discuss a media workshop I conducted with SEIU Local 105 and a public screening I organized in Boulder of the twenty-three-minute documentary *Radical Labor: Aligning Unions with the Streets*. The workshop and the screening fostered meaningful conversations among organizers about shared struggles, communal values, and coalition building.

RECLAIMING NARRATIVES OF RACIAL AND ECONOMIC JUSTICE

As discussed in chapter 3, community meetings, planning sessions, and interviews with Denver-area labor organizers and activists helped me to understand my partners' communication strategies. Several union organizers I spoke with for this project admitted that it is not so much that unions have communicated working people's stories poorly but that unions have not told their story at all. Josh Downey, president of the Denver Area Labor Federation, explained, "I do think that in the labor movement we have been sometimes slow to adapt to changing social media." Placing workers' personal stories at the center of our films and leveraging social media to distribute these films were essential to pushing back against negative depictions of unions and challenging mischaracterizations of organized labor. Downey discussed how stories about individual workers could humanize the labor movement and connect unions with allied community organizers fighting for change. "When we talk about getting members front and center and talking about their stories," he said, "I think things like documentaries and videos are very helpful in making sure that we're sharing our story to the masses."

Lizeth Chacón, executive director of Colorado People's Alliance, echoed Downey's concerns. She said the U.S. labor movement has largely failed to communicate the importance of unions with broader publics. Meanwhile, she explained, the Right has promoted a neoliberal discourse based on competitive individualism, free markets, and personal responsibility. She said:

You had a specific agenda that was implemented by the other side to really take control of our economy, and they did it. They implemented a four-year plan that's gotten us to today, that has won the narrative. That talks about immigrants as lazy and taking jobs from other people. That talks about African Americans as only criminals. A narrative that just says, 'If you don't work hard, you can't make it. If you would've worked hard, you would've been successful.' Those types of narratives, they won the narrative fight. They've really made a lot of policies to attack our community and win, and be in control of our economy, and that's why we have a 1 percent economy right now.

Robin Kniech, Denver city council member at large, agreed. She explained how the "folks on the Right" have built an infrastructure to promote anti-union rhetoric. This infrastructure, she said, has "seeded media. They've seeded school boards. They've seeded a whole set of institutional think tanks, and they've used that infrastructure to fuel a message that is antithetical to the values that we all stand for." The comments by Kniech and Chacón recognize several points about activist media distribution: first, the role culture plays in shaping public opinion and influencing dominant discourses; second, and perhaps more important, how the political economy of media affects media production and distribution. Filmmakers, grassroots activists, and nonprofit organizations that produce radical media are faced with an increasingly consolidated media ecosystem. Activist media makers who wish to reach broad audiences to combat negative stereotypes about unions and to organize community members to influence public policy must decide how to navigate a corporatized media infrastructure. As mobile internet (e.g., AT&T and Verizon), broadband access (e.g., Comcast and Time Warner), and online platforms (e.g., Google, Facebook, and Amazon), are controlled by fewer corporations, activist media makers must think strategically about how and where their texts are distributed and which audiences have access to digital spaces.

Thinking strategically about distribution includes recognizing whom your media is for. Ron Ruggiero, president of SEIU Local 105, explained how scale was not a priority for Local 105's media. Rather, our films were primarily movement media designed to enhance the union's ability to organize workers. Ruggiero said the affective nature of media is an incredible asset for Local 105's organizers because it gives their campaign literature increased salience and resonance among working people. "Our members and folks we're organizing with, you can show [videos] at membership meetings and with other organizations that we're working with, and people can really see directly those stories," he said. "I think [films are] just tremendously valuable because it is about power and passion, authenticity, credibility," he continued. "That comes across when workers are talking directly into a camera about the struggles they're facing every single day. They're just incredibly powerful. There's no other way to say it. That's why I would say those internal videos we've produced really do matter because you are able to then move them out to different areas."

Ruggiero's comments reveal how activist media complement union organizing by jump-starting discussions among members, organizers, and community allies about power and workers' agency.

Moving media "out to different areas," as Ruggiero said, speaks to our efforts to produce documentaries that would resonate with a core audience of union supporters and progressive groups in Colorado and also connect with broader conversations around racial and gender justice, environmental activism, and immigration reform. To achieve this broader appeal, we utilized public screenings and social media to distribute narratives that linked individual narratives, through data, evidence, and emotion, with systemic critiques of inequalities. Ruggiero said, "You have to build up those individual stories with the statistics and other data points that really show this is a much larger issue." Recognizing SEIU Local 105's organizing needs was important for me in understanding how I could counter neoliberal discourse through media and identify an audience for this work.

Organizers largely agreed that, although social media are problematic, they are a necessary component of local organizing and movement building. Chacón said social media help organizers spread working people's stories to diverse audiences and challenge individual narratives. "I think the media has played a huge role in all of this," she said. "And I think that the [Right] has been able to use [media] to their advantage. So for us, we've actually partnered with some of our labor folks here in Colorado and other folks in our community to think around what are the messages that we're using, and how do we move forward the messages that tell what we see happening, rather than the dominant narrative from the other side."

Chacón challenged progressive organizers to not cede social media to those who promote hate and division. Instead, she argued that activists must utilize storytelling to push back against narratives that criminalize and dehumanize working people, inform and educate publics about the material conditions of marginalized communities, and leverage media to disseminate messages that resonate beyond the base. She called on organizers to reach people where they are: both via social media, as this is where many people receive news, and also ideologically. She echoed Ruggiero's point about bridging the empathy gap by centering workers' voices. She said:

> I think social media is something that is exciting that we could use more as a movement. A lot of folks actually get their news from social media now, and we should make sure that we're getting the stories from our members out there. When we see a story about minimum wage, put a face to that story. And then we have someone that lives in our neighborhood talk about what it's like to be a minimum wage worker. Sharing their story, I think, could be really powerful. We just have to make sure that we're using that platform a lot more to make sure that people understand the issue, but also that we don't forget the humanity behind that issue.

Incorporating personal stories of members in our films (for example, Melissa Benjamin's story as a home health care worker), as Chacón suggests, could elicit empathy from viewers who are moved by moral arguments about fairness and communal responsibility. Chacón is also correct to say that social media is a primary source of news for people. According to a 2017 Pew Research Center report, 67 percent of U.S. adults reported getting at least some of their news from social media.[1] It is understandable, then, that activists use Facebook, Twitter, YouTube, and other social media to promote social justice, combat anti-union rhetoric, and connect with allies. It is essential, however, that these efforts serve to bridge online and off-line spaces.

THE STREETS AS DISTRIBUTION AND NETWORKING SITES

In addition to using social media to challenge neoliberal narratives presented in corporate media outlets, progressive organizers often rely on public spaces to exhibit their stories. Ruggiero referenced the Fight for $15 as one example of workers taking to the streets to demand a minimum wage increase. The use of protest, he argued, changed the narrative about fast-food jobs. Ruggiero said that Democrats were hesitant in 2015 to embrace the demand for $15 per hour and countered with a minimum wage of $10–$12 per hour. The Fight for $15, however, backed by SEIU, "threw down a pretty bold demand," Ruggiero said. While much of the Fight for $15 discourse occurred online, Ruggiero said, the visibility in the streets "matters a lot." He pointed to several historical examples of movements that relied on protest. "There's a tremendous number of examples all the way back to the beginning of this country's history from the suffrage movement, the abolitionist movement, civil rights movement," he said. "That's how progress gets made in this country, people coming together making their voices heard."

It is important to note that although the Fight for $15 has made significant progress in reconceptualizing service industry workers in the streets, detractors remain. For example, during SEIU Local 105's #ProtectOurCare march on June 13, 2017, a group eating lunch on a restaurant patio along Denver's 16th Street Mall heckled the protesters: "Get jobs!" Andy Jacob, political director of Local 105, responded saying, "We do." After the exchange, I asked Jacob about how he deals with negative comments hurled at members and staff during a protest. He said comments such as "get jobs" represent ignorance about union organizing; these attitudes are a major reason why the labor movement must be in the streets to reclaim working people's stories through public visibility. He said public perception toward the Fight for $15 was much more hostile when the movement began in 2012; but Jacob argued that, through a multimodal distribution strategy that combines public demonstrations, email newsletters, and social media, people and politicians have begun to recognize the importance of this campaign.

Greg Douros, chief of staff at Local 105, was also marching at the #ProtectOurCare rally, and he told me that engaging with people in the streets requires recognizing the heckler's intentions. Often, Douros said, the aim will be to antagonize union members and supporters in order to provoke a reaction that is then filmed and posted to social media, furthering the demonization and criminalization of protest. Douros said the streets can be a venue for sparking conversations, but orga-nizers must turn that spark into dialogue, which is essential for sustained organ-izing and social justice campaigning.

Chacón echoed this sentiment and argued that protest is a crucial component to identifying the movement's opposition and distributing its messages. "Actions are a critical component for us to be able to win on the narrative fight to win on our issues," she said. "Part of what we have to do is we have to keep our commu-nity energized and we have to keep pressure on our elected officials and the tar-gets that we have." Identifying targets is essential for using activist media as an organizing method; creating a clear opposition helps people identify with the movement and understand what is at stake. It is not enough, however, to describe what the movement is against—activist media must describe what the movement is *for.* Felicia Griffin, executive director of FRESC: Good Jobs, Strong Communi-ties, said that protest is an important tactic in which activists, through claiming public space, distribute what they are for and against to various publics. "We're trying to also bring [our issues] to the public realm, so that it becomes a conversa-tion for the public and we gain more momentum and support for the issues," she said. Griffin noted that media about the protest—live-streams, photos, videos, and blogs—make movements more accessible. "Everyone can't make it out to a direct action," Griffin said. "People are going to see that on their Facebook, on their Twit-ter, on their social media feeds. They are going to see articles in the paper about that. It's really about really uplifting a conversation about change that a lot of folks feel is needed, and trying to really gain support and momentum for that change."

Presenting a multiracial, multigenerational coalition of working people to the public in the streets *is* a distribution tactic. SEIU Local 105 and BLM5280 dissemi-nate their messages to the public and network with allies through protest and direct action. Denver city council member Paul Lopez referred to the labor movement's most iconic tactic, the picket line, as a distribution method that builds solidarity between labor and grassroots community groups.

"Our presence, our visibility is absolutely critical," Lopez said. "It's critical to our movement, it's critical to what we're talking about, and it's critical for folks to see and know this isn't just a movement by itself, this isn't some picket line, some issue that's happening that's aside from me that I'm not a part of. We do this to create a reflection. We create a surface people can see themselves in, and that's exactly why we do it. And that's exactly why we've had the support we've had."

Creating a mirror, through protest and activist media, means challenging pub-lics to empathize with the movement's demands. Protests, Lopez argued, have been a key component for the labor movement and Fight for $15, because they allow organizers to disseminate narratives about social and economic inequalities to broad audiences and foster a positive identification with service workers.

Robin Kniech, Denver city council member at large, said that protest is an important tool for visualizing and distributing the stories of workers who typically are unseen, misrepresented, or overlooked in the news media, popular culture, and everyday life—workers such as janitors, home health care aides, and fast-food workers. Kniech cautioned, however, that mobilizing via protest and direct actions must be connected to an "infrastructure" that is capable of fostering long-term organizing. "Who is actually going to carry that conversation forward beyond the streets into implementation, into school classrooms with kids who are looking at the potential for careers?" she asked. "That's where infrastructure matters, and I think unions are an example of that infrastructure that maybe some of the folks who are in the streets right now didn't know or understand." Kniech said unions have a responsibility to adapt their organizing to a twenty-first-century workforce that is heavily reliant on freelance, temporary, and gig employment and to encourage community groups to join with unions in bolstering their existing infrastructure. Kniech said unions could offer training programs for high school students so that historically disenfranchised communities (for example, women and people of color) could gain access to and network with the labor movement.

"What I'm often advising when I get emails and calls from constituents who say, 'I have this fire in the belly and I want to be a part of something that lasts,' I say to them, 'Find an existing organization, and be a part of that infrastructure and building and shoring it up,'" Kniech said. "I think the challenge for labor and for unions is to say, 'Okay, I've got a model designed to represent members, so what does it look like for a person who's not in a unionized workplace to be a member of the labor movement? What are the pathways to be a part of the infrastructure?'" Having a deliberate strategy for how and where activist media are distributed is key to building a networked movement infrastructure.

"I think there's a challenge on both sides," Kniech continued. "There's a challenge from the spontaneous movement to understand the need for infrastructure that lasts and can stand the test of time and help to do the work in between the rallies. And then there's the test of these institutions to say, 'What do membership and participation look like beyond what we were founded on, which was a workplace model that isn't applicable anymore?'"

Relating to working people's struggles, through stories and public visibility, Chacón argued, is crucial for grassroots organizers. "It's also really important that we work with our allies in the labor movement to make sure that we have different perspectives and that we show that the issue of climate is something that is supported by labor, and it's something that's important and that there are different folks supporting it," she said. "That's really important for [unions] to show that not only by strategizing on policy or by trying to advocate through campaigns, but also by being active in the streets and making sure that we're gaining support from other folks in the community."

SEIU Local 105 utilized protest to visualize its members, champion its demands, and network with community allies working on immigration justice, environmental justice, and racial justice. At the #ProtectOurCare march, organizers with Mi

Familia Vota and the Colorado Immigrant Rights Coalition joined the union to discuss the connections between access to health care and immigrant rights. Juan Gallegos, an organizer with Colorado Immigrant Rights Coalition, was featured in a short video I produced about the rally (discussed in chapter 4), and I asked him about the significance of demonstrating in front of the Colorado State Capitol.

"We know that this is an axis of power for government, especially local government, and we want our elected officials here in Colorado to hear our voices and know that anything that happens in Washington, we're going to be there to call them out on their mistakes," Gallegos said. "Mobilizing the people that show up today to walk on the streets during the electoral season to elect candidates who are going to support our issues better, who are going to support working families better and are going to represent us better as a whole."

BLM5280 also used protest to distribute its messages of solidarity with activist organizations locally and across the United States. For example, BLM5280 supported Indigenous people and Native land rights during the Dakota Access Pipeline (DAPL) protests in Standing Rock, North Dakota. The protests centered on the Sioux Tribe's demands to stop to the construction of the DAPL. Native tribes from around the world and grassroots environmental activists opposed the pipeline because, they argued, the planned route under Lake Oahe would contaminate the Native Americans' water supply, disrupt sacred lands, and violate the Fort Laramie Treaty of 1851. To connect this struggle with the fight for racial justice in Colorado, BLM5280 organizers participated in an October 8, 2016, rally in Denver that opposed Columbus Day and the settler colonial logic behind this holiday. Activists from numerous local community organizations marched from four locations in Denver—representing North, South, East, and West—and converged on the Colorado State Capitol for a rally (Figure 5.1).

Throughout the event, BLM5280 organizers kept their distance from the center of the rally, standing about fifty yards down the street and serving, primarily, as support. BLM5280, in this instance, used its name recognition and its organization's visibility to draw attention to the event. Organizers told me that environmental and racial justice are inextricably linked, and marching in the streets was an opportunity to network with local activists and reframe dominant understandings of land, environmental racism, and citizenship. Collaborations in the streets are an extension and reinforcement of the online relationships that groups such as BLM5280 and SEIU Local 105 foster regularly through event updates, live videos, and links to news articles. Documenting protests and broadcasting them online creates a bridge between physical and virtual spaces for publics to witness the movement's demands and learn how they can get involved.

BLM5280 continued its show of solidarity with Indigenous people by traveling to Standing Rock in November 2016 to support the Sioux Tribe. Organizers brought needed supplies to the camp and highlighted their trip on social media to stress the intersection of racial and colonial oppressions. Prior to traveling to

FIGURE 5.1. Community organizers gather near the Colorado State Capitol to protest Columbus Day 2017, Denver, Colorado, October 8, 2017. (Photo by Gino Canella.)

North Dakota, BLM5280 solicited supplies and donations on its Facebook page, revealing social media's utility for activists who wish to quickly call on allies for support. Jumoke Emery and Angela Maxwell, organizers with BLM5280, spoke with *Westword* magazine upon their return from Standing Rock and insisted that two members of the American Indian Movement of Colorado join the interview because, they said, "it was important to have Indigenous voices at the table."[2]

When asked how the issues at Standing Rock are connected to BLM5280's fight for racial justice in Denver, Emery said, "For us, the same law enforcement that's being employed to brutalize sovereign nations is simply an extension of the forces being used to brutalize and terrorize [Black] communities. . . . We do not believe that the history of stolen lands is separated from the history of stolen labor, so while we're not centered in this fight, it is absolutely something we are proud to be a part of, because our histories are intertwined."[3]

Although BLM5280 is often misunderstood as an organization that only focuses on "Black issues," Emery argued that BLM5280 understands the importance of connecting racial justice and Indigenous rights. The movement understands how sharing monetary and symbolic resources is essential for building a broad-based anti-capitalist and anti-colonial movement. The radical tactics of BLM, such as shutting down bridges and roads or disrupting politicians' speeches, may be polarizing and produce backlash, particularly on Twitter and cable news. But focusing on these tactics obscures the movement's on-the-ground efforts. As Emery said in the *Westword* article, the movement's visibility is rife with contradictions. "When we take the streets and disrupt traffic, when we disrupt conferences, and at that point, all of a sudden, people want to come to the table—if that's the order in which we need to move things, then we will continue to disrupt finances," he said. "Sovereignty over our lands, our bodies and our children's futures is more important than any amount of money."[4]

These comments underscore the importance of using activist media and alternative news outlets to promote a radical critique of state violence against racialized people and spaces. Understanding the connections between historical struggles of Indigenous peoples and African Americans, and how these struggles are central to the construction of race, is essential for a progressive political project. Because mainstream news media focus on spectacle and conflict, complex and nuanced historical narratives are often absent in stories about protests and public demonstrations. Therefore, BLM5280 uses activist media to disrupt popular understandings of race and citizenship, reimagine conceptions of space, and collaborate with grassroots groups.

In another example of how protest reveals the link between activist media distribution and social movement networking, SEIU Local 105 marched in the Denver Pride Parade on June 18, 2017. Along with allied labor unions in Colorado, Local 105 organizers marched the parade route, from Denver's Cheesman Park to the Colorado State Capitol, behind a rainbow-colored float decorated in balloons and a sign that read, "RESIST WITH PRIDE!" (Figure 5.2). I attended the event and took only a few images with my smartphone. I chose to march in solidarity with the LGBTQ+ community, rather than attend as a filmmaker and document the event. Thousands of residents and supporters lined the parade route and offered supportive cheers as labor's float passed, shouting "Yes! Unions!" Participating in the parade with labor and community organizers reinforced Local 105's mission of "whole person unionism" and visualized an updated profile of the contemporary labor movement.

Protest and public demonstrations, however, were only one method through which BLM5280 and Local 105 distributed their demands and connected with grassroots organizations. Documentary films and photographs from protests, social media, and mainstream news media were also used to disseminate these group's campaigns for racial and economic justice.

Although some organizers with BLM5280 have expressed a reluctance to engaging in institutional politics and collaborating with elected officials to champion legislative reform, Local 105, through social media and meetings with local politicians, uses an interdependent approach to claiming power. For example, Local 105 worked with community allies in 2016 to promote and successfully pass Amendment 70, a ballot measure that increased Colorado's state minimum wage

FIGURE 5.2. SEIU Local 105 marches in Denver Pride Parade, Denver, Colorado, June 18, 2017. (Photo by Gino Canella.)

from $8.31 to $12 per hour by 2020. Before the November 2016 election in which Amendment 70 was on the ballot, health care workers represented by Local 105 met with U.S. Secretary of Labor Tom Perez on September 14, 2016, to discuss the economic challenges health care workers in Denver were facing and how a minimum wage increase would improve the lives of working families. Local 105 posted a photo of its meeting with Secretary Perez to its Facebook page and encouraged members and supporters to vote yes on Amendment 70.

In another example of Local 105 pressuring an elected official and using protest and media to highlight these efforts, organizers at the #ProtectOurCare march delivered a "death certificate" symbolizing the death of the Affordable Care Act to Senator Cory Gardner's office in downtown Denver. As discussed in chapter 4, I documented the rally and María Corral, Local 105's communication coordinator, asked me to follow Local 105's organizers into Senator Gardner's office to film the meeting and the delivery of the death certificate. The senator's office did not allow video-recording inside the office, but prior to the meeting between Local 105 organizers and the senator's staff, I made a photograph of union members (including one dressed as the grim reaper) holding the "death certificate" in the lobby of the senator's office, and I used the image in the short documentary about the demonstration (Figure 5.3).

FIGURE 5.3. Local 105 supporters wear T-shirts that say "GOP LIE PEOPLE DIE" and deliver "Certificate of Death" to Colorado senator Cory Gardner's office in Denver, June 13, 2017. (Photo by Gino Canella.)

Promoting actions and meetings with elected officials on social media has been one distribution method Local 105 has used to engage its members and the broader community in politics and power building. Democratic participation and radical pluralistic politics are evident in BLM5280 and Local 105's various distribution tactics. Through protest, film, and face-to-face meetings, these organizations highlight injustices, identify their opposition, and recruit supporters. Viewing protest, social media, and community meetings as activist media distribution recognizes how a multifaceted distribution strategy is necessary for movements that seek to challenge mainstream journalistic accounts about protest and network with allies.

PUBLICITY'S CONTRADICTIONS: LOCAL NEWS AND SOCIAL MEDIA

The distribution of activist media, however, reveals publicity's contradictions. BLM5280 and SEIU Local 105 navigate these contradictions in several ways. A 2017 community forum on public access television is instructive. Christina Hughes, an organizer with BLM5280, participated in a panel discussion on Aurora TV (Aurora, Colorado, is a Denver suburb) to talk about Martin Luther King Jr. Day. When a panelist confronted Hughes about what policies BLM5280 has advocated for, or what reforms the group has championed, she gave this response:

It's almost an uninformed question to even ask me what policy we've changed, because by asking that you assume that our intention is to change policy. You assume that our intention is to buy-in to the system . . . there are some people in our group that absolutely divest from the system. . . . I will say that we were instrumental in Michael Marshall's family being able to see the tapes of what happened. That was one of the things we lifted at the Marade last year when we disrupted it, and we were instrumental in them being able to actually see what happened to their loved one. . . . We don't have to broadcast what we do because for us it's not about self, it's not about who we are and what it is that we're doing. We just want to love on our community and for us that looks like not always telling people what we do, but absolutely doing things that impact people directly in our community.[5]

Hughes' comments acknowledge the complexity of movement messaging in the contemporary media ecosystem. Organizers and activists who focus solely on policy reforms fail to recognize how culture influences politics. Focusing solely on policy also ignores the social relationships embedded in movement cultures and how these social relations inform organizing.

Although Aurora TV is a relatively small cable access station, local news outlets are an important distribution site for activist media. Some researchers are wary of local news, arguing that "news coverage is often unsuitable for movement proselytizing" because it "emphasize[s] action rather than context, leaving readers ignorant of the causes and goals of the movement."[6] Nevertheless, BLM5280 and SEIU Local 105 recognized the built-in audiences that local news outlets provided and leveraged these platforms to advance their campaigns. Charlotte Ryan, Kevin Carragee, and Cassie Schwerner's work with the Media Research and Action Project (MRAP) informs my analysis of how intervening in journalistic discourses is part of a multifaceted distribution strategy.[7] MRAP is an advocacy organization that works with community groups to help them frame their social justice campaigns and influence news coverage to promote change. For example, during the city council hearing about the Office of the Independent Monitor, Alex Landau of BLM5280 spoke with a local television news reporter outside of City Hall to promote the Denver Justice Project's campaign. Speaking with a journalist from local Fox affiliate KDVR-TV prior to the hearing gave Landau the opportunity to frame the issue in the news media as an issue of law enforcement accountability (Figure 5.4).[8]

Agreeing to interviews with news media outlets that may not share the movement's political orientation provides activists with opportunities to reach people beyond the base. SEIU Local 105 relied on its relationships with members of the Spanish-speaking news media to connect its campaigns with the Latino community in Colorado. During its contract negotiations and organizing efforts at Denver International Airport, for example, Local 105 shared photos and videos on its Facebook page that showed an airport worker speaking with a reporter from

FIGURE 5.4. Alex Landau speaking with local television news reporter about the Office of the Independent Monitor, Denver, Colorado, August 15, 2016. (Photo by Gino Canella.)

Telemundo (Figure 5.5). The caption read: "We're here at Denver International Airport today standing up and speaking out on behalf of airport security workers! They keep us all safe & deserve better wages & benefits. Right now, campaign coordinator Luis is talking to Telemundo Denver about the Airport Security Officers at DIA and their struggle for better wages and benefits. Sign our petition on behalf of airport workers: actionsprout.io/84C8F5. Learn more by following Airport Workers United."[9]

Shortly after sharing this post, Local 105 streamed a Facebook Live video from the airport that showed workers demonstrating throughout the airport terminal and discussing the purpose of the action.[10] The caption of the video read, in part: "Every day, airport security workers keep us safe. It's past time to honor their request for fair pay and treatment! #StrongerTogether #PovertyDoesntFly." Activist media distributed on social media, in this instance, allowed SEIU Local 105 to present its action with a confrontational frame, something journalists and local news media outlets are unlikely to do. The creative hashtag, #PovertyDoesntFly, and video of workers confronting management to demand improved health care coverage play into the spectacle of social media and represent activist media's mobilizing dimension. Conducting interviews with Telemundo, on the other hand, shows how Local 105 does not rely solely on social media to broadcast its campaigns but also

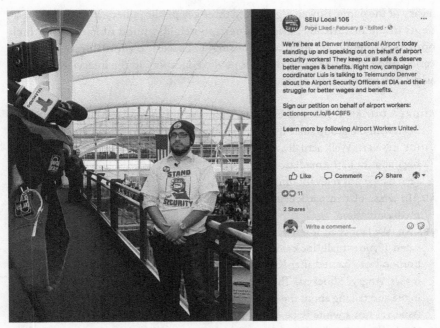

FIGURE 5.5. SEIU Local 105 Facebook update showing an airport worker speaking with Telemundo at Denver International Airport, February 9, 2018.

builds and leverages strategic partnerships with media outlets in Colorado that Spanish-speaking union members and supporters are likely watching.

BLM5280 also used local news media to frame its #ChangeTheName-Stapleton campaign. Vince Bowen appeared on Colorado Public Radio (CPR) to discuss the movement's campaign and attempted to reach an audience outside of BLM5280's base. Bowen framed the campaign through the connections between racism and historical memory. By using a discourse of communal values, Bowen argued that the name "Stapleton" signifies violence against African Americans.

#ChangeTheNameStapleton, as discussed in chapter 3, sought to change the name of Stapleton, a neighborhood in the northeast section of Denver, named for former Denver mayor Benjamin Stapleton, who had known ties to the Ku Klux Klan. BLM5280 partnered with grassroots community groups in Colorado to launch a campaign that highlighted Stapleton's membership in the Klan and sought to convince residents that a name change was needed. A commercial development firm was in the process of building housing and commercial real estate in the area, and the firm argued that a name change was not possible for financial reasons connected to the marketing and branding of the development.

Bowen, a BLM5280 core organizer, went on CPR to discuss the campaign with host Andrea Dukakis. He explained BLM5280's efforts to problematize the racist legacy of the name. Bowen highlighted three key public policy areas affecting residents in the historically African American neighborhood of Park Hill, which borders Stapleton: (1) affordable housing; (2) access to affordable, healthy groceries; and (3) increased funding for public education. In the interview, Dukakis asked Bowen about the campaign.

ANDREA DUKAKIS: Black Lives Matter 5280 was just created in May [2015]. You've been with the group since then. Why make this campaign your first big initiative?

VINCE BOWEN: Well, actually, what I would ask is why make this campaign the first big initiative in the media?

[Exchange not relevant omitted.]

AD: In terms of that particular campaign, though, did you launch it in part to get media attention?

VB: No. We launched it—if you look at our flyer, we launched it to get folks activated. If you actually look at what the flyer says, it says, 'Did you know? Your neighborhood was named after Klansman #1128, Ben Stapleton.' And then on the back it says, 'Angry? Shocked? Then Act.' So we're inviting people to start having a dialogue and talking about the implications of this because we think it is not a Black issue, it's not a white issue, it's an American issue. And we want everyone to be involved in doing the right thing and creating a community that lives up to the best that Denver has to offer.[11]

This exchange reveals several key issues related to BLM5280's use of local news media to frame and distribute its campaign. Bowen challenged Dukakis's desire to make the #ChangetheNameStapleton campaign the focus of the interview and instead emphasized communal resources. By challenging the framing of the issue from one that asks, "Why this campaign, why now?" to one about "dialogue" and "community," Bowen rejected an agitational framing of BLM5280 and challenged the implied suggestion that BLM5280 does not advocate for material change.

Bowen's responses are indicative of how movements participate in what Dietram A. Scheufele has called "frame building" and "frame setting."[12] Although researchers have paid significant attention to how the news media apply narratives to social movements, activists, and protest, I examine how movements craft and distribute campaign messages through media—from local TV and radio to self-produced multimedia—to study framing contests as social processes. Bowen's appearance on CPR reveals how BLM5280's "ability to challenge hegemony is tied directly to framing processes and to their effectiveness in influencing news discourse."[13] Following the part of the interview excerpted earlier, Bowen went on to describe how the name "Stapleton" signifies the site of the Stapleton International Airport, which served as the primary airport for Denver from 1929 until 1995; more importantly, Bowen argued, the name symbolizes the structural and institutional legacy of anti-Black racism in the United States and the fear and intim-idation perpetuated by the Klan against Black communities.

"[The name] represents a long legacy of racial exclusion, domestic terrorism, and lack of access to resources in pursuit of the full fruits of our democracy," Bowen told Dukakis. This history continues to resonate within Black communities in Denver, according to Bowen. By drawing a link between the history of racial exclusion to the lack of material resources available to the predominantly Black community living there today, Bowen connected the dots between symbolic racial injustices and material inequities.

#BlackIsBeautiful

To show how the legacy of racial injustice continues to permeate U.S. society today, BLM5280 also shares updates regularly to social media. In addition to posting original media produced by organizers, it also posts articles from mainstream publications (e.g., *The Atlantic, New York Times*), articles from alternative media outlets (e.g., *Westword* and *Liberation News*), and articles from Black media (e.g., *Essence* and *The Root*). The group's Facebook page has 36,800 followers, and its Twitter account has 8,100 followers as of May 2021. BLM5280 regularly uses Facebook to distribute campaign messages; post updates about community meetings and events; promote fundraisers; and challenge hegemonic narratives of race, class, gender, and citizenship.

Sharing news articles and opinion pieces from local, national, and international media outlets that critique racial injustices and the legacy of racist policies shows how BLM5280 builds the case for systemic change through well-researched and affective media. Although images of police shootings and videos from protests rely on episodic and "action" frames, using media to distribute visual evidence of racial injustices shows how various issues—from criminal justice to affordable hous-ing to public education—are central to BLM5280's platform. These posts also serve to foster solidarity between the local chapter in Denver and other BLM chapters.[14] Posting in-depth, historical analyses about race and racism in the United States from popular media outlets promotes BLM5280's political education, which is crit-ical to the movement's consciousness-building efforts.

In addition to sharing articles from mainstream media outlets, BLM5280 also curates its own media on its Facebook page. A notable project for exploring the multifaceted distribution strategies of activist media is BLM5280's daily photo series #BlackIsBeautiful. This project involves sharing an image each morning to its Facebook page with the caption, "Good morning #Beautiful people! #BlackIs-Beautiful." The images depict Black people in ways that challenge heteronorma-tive assumptions about family, skin color, body type and hairstyles (Figure 5.6). Black hair has "significant impacts on [Black people's] economic, social and emo-tional lives," impacts their employment prospects, and influences how Black women are perceived by Black men.[15] Therefore, #BlackIsBeautiful invites viewers to

FIGURE 5.6. Screenshots from BLM5280's #BlackIsBeautiful Facebook project.

rethink their conceptions of Black beauty, complicates accepted or limited understandings of Blackness, and strengthens the social and emotional well-being of its online and off-line communities.

To understand the radical politics of Black hair, it must be situated in its historical and socioeconomic contexts.[16] Hair is intimately and physically connected to the body; reviewing the history of Black hair provides necessary context for BLM5280's Facebook project and recognizes the Black body as a site of struggle. During the enslavement of Black people in the United States, the African diaspora in the South wore creative hairstyles to challenge the institution of slavery.[17] Following the abolition of slavery, former enslaved people wore their hair natural to contest white supremacist power structures and counter a "color complex" that privileged a Eurocentric beauty ideal of straight hair and light skin.[18]

Ayana Byrd and Lori Tharps examined the modern political history of Black hair in the United States from the 1920s to the early 2000s. The authors detailed the political organizing of Marcus Garvey, a Jamaican-born activist and member of the Harlem Renaissance who formed the United Negro Improvement Association in the 1920s, which sought to reclaim an "African-based aesthetic [as] a central tenet of his political platform."[19] Black Power activists in the 1960s built on this legacy by wearing Afros to symbolize their revolutionary struggle against white oppression, global capitalism, and imperialism. Seeking to reclaim the African diaspora during the U.S. civil rights era and eschew European aesthetics, Black Power activists viewed "conking and straightening. . . . [as] emblematic of internalized self-hatred."[20] Afros, many activists argued, signified defiance against the system and association with the movement, while straight hair represented conformity with systems of oppression.

By the 1970s, however, Byrd and Tharps noted how popular films such as *Shaft* and *Superfly* brought the Afro mainstream and "normalized the style and placed it so far out of any context of Black revolution and pride. . . . that Whites who had once felt intimidated could now relax when an Afro passed their way."[21] Although the natural hairstyles of this era challenged white supremacist culture by exhibiting outward strength that could instill fear in whites, bell hooks argued, fear can also be internalized by Black women. "The extent to which we are comfortable with our hair usually reflects our overall feelings about our bodies," hooks wrote.[22]

For Amy Brown, co-lead of BLM5280, sharing daily reminders that "Black is Beautiful" is one way the movement engages in "truth telling." She told me, "[Social media] give me a chance to create my narrative and my truth for people because the media is not going to do that for us, and I can't expect people to know what's in my heart and head as I go through this work." BLM5280's #BlackIsBeautiful project, therefore, is a disruptive rhetorical intervention in the contemporary media ecosystem that enables viewers to politically and culturally identify with the movement.

I examined #BlackIsBeautiful through feminist visual culture, which allowed me to study the power relations that are constituted and reconstituted through the gaze and the Black body. Feminist visual culture takes into account not only the images themselves but also the relationships between the subjects represented in the images, the people doing the looking, and the sites in which these images circulate. As Lisa Cartwright argues, "Understanding the ways in which desire and sexuality are not simply reflected in the content of the images or appearances, but also structure looking practices as a nexus of power, agency and the human subject's psychic life has been a fundamental aspect of visual culture studies."[23] BLM5280 structures looking on social media by amplifying the stories of Black women and girls and offering nuanced representations of gay, queer, cisgender, nonbinary, and transgender Black people. These representations seek to claim symbolic and political power and reinforce BLM5280's mission of building community through care and love.

Although bell hooks focused on film and the cinematic experience, her work is relevant for understanding BLM5280's Facebook project as the strategic distribution of activist media. By inviting the oppositional gaze to depictions of strong Black women who look deeply into the camera's lens and challenge hegemonic beauty standards, BLM5280 "open[s] up the possibility of agency" for its online community.[24]

Stuart Hall also helps us understand the caption "Black is beautiful."[25] In his description of counter-strategies that subaltern groups use, he argued that activists turn images' accepted meanings on themselves to contest a "racialized regime of representation." Hall wrote that subaltern groups substitute "a range of 'positive' images of black people, black life and culture for the 'negative' imagery which continues to dominate popular representation."[26] Using the phrase "Black is beautiful," Hall argued, inverts "the binary opposition, privileging the subordinate term, sometimes reading the negative positively." Distributing counter-hegemonic messages, through images and text, Hall wrote, challenges dominant (stereotypical) codes and "construct[s] a positive identification with what has been abjected."[27] By welcoming and encouraging looking, Hall argued that racialized people attempt to "make the stereotypes work against themselves. Instead of avoiding the dangerous terrain opened up by the interweaving of 'race,' gender and sexuality, it deliberately contests the dominant gendered and sexual definitions of racial difference by *working on* black sexuality."[28]

By wearing natural hair loudly and proudly, the images in #BlackIsBeautiful suggest that Black people not only are comfortable wearing their hair naturally but also take pride in challenging white beauty standards.[29] Although a Facebook photo series will not alone dismantle patriarchy, white supremacy, and racial capitalism, the project represents important ideological work that movements conduct through the distribution of activist media. However, #BlackIsBeautiful must be understood in relation to social media's surveillance mechanisms, which disproportionately target Black activists, and the algorithms that filter news and information and create echo chambers.[30]

Limitations of Social Media Distribution

To convey the immediacy of BLM5280 and SEIU Local 105's campaigns, many of the documentaries I produced with these organizations were uploaded to Facebook within hours or days of the rallies. This immediacy presents another challenge for activist media makers—speed and information glut. Because one hundred million hours of video are viewed each day on Facebook, media makers are tasked with trying to get users to pay attention to their content. In addition to making our films accessible to Spanish-speaking members of Local 105, the subtitles and captions on our Justice for Janitors films served a second purpose. Research from Facebook showed that captions increase video viewing time by 12 percent; hence, the Spanish subtitles may have improved our chances of standing out in a crowded media environment.[31] Although I stress the social nature of activist media and encourage scholars to complicate market-based notions of "impact" and "engagement" that focus on quantifiable metrics and audience analytics, it is essential for activists to understand and be aware of the venues in which their media are circulating and these platforms' affordances and limitations.

Because social media can be difficult venues for conducting deep political education, I discussed with Corral at a J4J rally how the union instructs members on engaging with opposing views and toxic behaviors on these platforms. Corral said Local 105 hosted a social media workshop the morning of the June 15 J4J rally to educate members about how to promote the event across social media, and she said members were met with a "Twitter storm" of negative comments about the Fight for 15 and labor unions during this training session. She explained that the response was from "people who don't support an increase in the wages" but that the union tries "to use social media as positive and educational media. Hopefully, if it can promote the campaign that we're working on with our members and help boost the need for standards to equalize the inequity of incomes, then that's what we try to do."

Corral said that Local 105 leans on the "progressive community" in Denver to neutralize online hostility directed at its the campaign. "[Our members] got on board and actually began balancing out the negative and the positive messages, which is awesome," she said. This episode speaks to how social media do not promote critical debate and democratic deliberation; rather, they are venues that silo audiences and incentivize outrage.

Keeping up with the latest updates to Facebook and Twitter's interface, and Google's search preferences is a constant challenge for activist media makers. For example, I edited the #ProtectOurCare film at SEIU Local 105's Denver office with Corral watching over my shoulder and approving the final edit. I worked with her to upload the video directly to Local 105's Facebook page, rather than posting it to my personal account. This was an opportunity for me to share with Corral what I knew about sharing video on Facebook and to optimize our content for the platform. Facebook's auto-play function instantly plays video as users scroll through the news feed; this feature incentivizes users to upload directly to the news feed and use on-screen text, rather than post videos on YouTube and share the link on Facebook. Uploading content to social media will continue presenting issues for activist media makers, because these sites constantly update their algorithms, features, and functionality. The task for activist media makers, therefore, is not so much knowing where to post content as understanding how to strategically connect the dots so that these small bits of information across various networks cohere to form a meta-narrative about justice, equality, and communal values.

COMMUNITY EXHIBITIONS AND MEDIA WORKSHOPS

Despite the contradictions discussed in this chapter, activist media present significant opportunities for organizers to engage their members and supporters in political education. The documentaries I produced with BLM5280 and SEIU Local 105 were shared repeatedly across social media over the course of several years. The profile of Melissa Benjamin, the home health care aide, for example, has been viewed in a variety of venues. I created an additional version of Melissa's story with Spanish text and captions so Local 105 could use the video during an organizing meeting with Spanish-speaking health care workers. Nearly two years after this film was first produced, Corral contacted me about uploading the film to Facebook to kick off Home Care Appreciation Month. I was happy to see the project receive new life and, of course, I agreed. Local 105 posted the film to its Facebook page with the caption: "Melissa Benjamin has been a home care worker for 16 years, and she is standing up in a powerful way to demand better wages for all home care workers. November is Home Care Appreciation Month, and we are uniting on behalf of the heroic and compassionate home care workers in our community! Join them in their #FightFor15: https://fightfor15.org/c-petition /home-care/." The caption concluded with Melissa's quote at the end of the film in which she explained her reasons for participating in the documentary. As when BLM5280 shared my 2016 MLK Day film to promote its 2017 action, these instances reveal the persistence that is needed during activist media distribution. Repeat shares over several years remind members, supporters, and publics about the ongoing and long-term nature of political organizing and activist campaigns. Distributing activist media within the current rapid-paced news cycle means movements must find creative ways to intervene in discourses and keep the movements' demands on the public agenda.

Throughout the production and post-production of the twenty-three-minute film *Radical Labor*, I also used media to share regular updates about activist campaigns in Colorado, keep in touch with my collaborators, and inform my partners about the messages I was crafting in the films. Following my interview with Denver council member Paul Lopez, for example, I posted a short excerpt of our interview to Twitter. The tweet included video of Lopez speaking in Spanish with English subtitles about the importance of unions in building solidarity, with the caption: "Councilman @PaulLopez5280 Talking about #labor and #union solidarity for my upcoming #documentary with @SEIU105 #Denver #Fightfor15."[32] Lopez retweeted the video, helping to contribute to my promotional efforts and also providing me with confirmation that he approved of the clip. I also shared a portion of my interview with Ruggiero discussing "whole person unionism" to Twitter and Facebook and tagged Ruggiero and Local 105's social media accounts.[33] Ruggiero emailed me within minutes of posting the video, writing, "Hey, just saw a clip on whole person unionism on Twitter! That was both cool and weird! .... Can't wait to see the whole thing!!" These brief online exchanges let my partners and their online networks know that the film was moving forward. These exchanges also informed Lopez and Ruggiero which portions of their interviews I was identifying as important and provided them with opportunities to give feedback.

As I was finalizing post-production on *Radical Labor* in February 2018, I worked with Local 105 staff to organize a public screening. It was important for me to bridge my online activities with in-person organizing and political education about the themes raised in the film. We identified panelists for a question-and-answer session following the screening. The panel consisted of Ruggiero, a Local 105 organizer, a labor and economics professor from the University of Denver, and an organizer with Showing Up for Racial Justice Boulder. I located an auditorium in Boulder that could accommodate a screening and worked with Local 105 organizers to promote the event. We promoted the screening primarily via email listservs, a Facebook event page, and flyers hung around Boulder.

Turning people out for events is always a challenge for local organizers, but the event drew about thirty people. I partnered with a grassroots organization in Boulder for the event, hoping the partnership could help turn people out or create new connections among progressive organizers in the area. Prior to the screening, an organizer from the Boulder group made an announcement about an environmental campaign his organization was working on and passed around a sign-up sheet to gather signatures and email addresses. Following his announcement, I introduced the film by describing my partnerships with Local 105 and BLM5280 and my intention to produce a film that linked the labor movement with the Movement for Black Lives.

Following the screening, I asked the four panelists to join me at the front of the auditorium to share their reflections about the issues raised in the documentary. I asked the panelists questions about the fight for racial and economic justice and about media's potential to bring people together. The SURJ Boulder organizer spoke powerfully about the limitations of media for social justice. She said that although media may introduce people to new concepts and ideas, face-to-face interactions are essential for developing empathy and creating an inclusive and compassionate society. She described her personal experiences as a queer person, explaining how the fight for LGBTQ+ justice occurred, in part, because members of that community and their friends and family members were forced into direct confrontation. "We were right here," she said, placing her fingers together at the tip of her nose. She went on to say that schools and cities in the United States are more segregated now than they were prior to the 1960s and that this should concern everyone fighting for justice and equality today. Her comments resonated so strongly with me then and continue to inform my approach to activist media today. Recognizing that social media, film, and art will not in themselves bring about justice cannot be stressed enough. Organizers, media practitioners, journalists, and researchers must get out of their homogenous silos—on social media and in their own neighborhoods—and identify comrades with whom to build a broad-based movement for change. Media can be a conversation starter for organizers, but people represented in media make their issues more tangible and urgent when they intervene directly in people's social lives.

After the public screening with Local 105, I secured distribution for the film, with SEIU's permission, on *Roar Magazine,* an online socialist magazine that publishes long-form essays and films. *Roar Magazine* provides international perspectives on labor, race, and activism, so I decided it was an ideal platform for connecting the local stories shown in *Radical Labor* with global justice movements. I thought the film would resonate with *Roar*'s readership, so I pitched it to the editor, Jeremy Roos, who viewed a screener and agreed to host the film on the website. In addition to using the film to promote Local 105's organizing, I also wanted the film to connect with a wider audience and to be in conversation with the international labor movement. *Roar* promoted the film on its social media accounts, and it has since been shared and viewed by people in the United States, Australia, the Czech Republic, Spain, and India.

Storytelling Workshop

Another in-person exhibition I conducted with SEIU Local 105 was a storytelling workshop on April 18, 2017. During an initial planning meeting for *Radical Labor*, Corral invited me to lead a media workshop with a small group of Local 105 members and organizers. Corral provided me with flexibility on the format of the meeting but suggested we screen Melissa's film and discuss how I connected her personal story to systemic issues facing home care workers. I suggested to Corral conducting on-camera interviews with the workshop attendees so that union members and organizers could practice communicating their personal stories to one another and to members of the news media. This exercise challenged participants to think of possible questions to pose to one another and think through how to answer these questions thoughtfully and succinctly (Figure 5.7). I provided Corral the video files of the interviews, written transcripts, and feedback about the interviewers and interviewees performances, which Corral then shared with the attendees.

Screening Melissa's film at the workshop served as a focus group for me as a grassroots filmmaker. After a brief introduction in which I explained to the workshop attendees how we coordinated filming logistics, we watched the documentary and opened the floor to general reactions and comments. There were ten Local 105 members and organizers present for the workshop, and most participants worked in health care or organized in that industry. Because many participants were familiar with the difficult and thankless work that home health care workers provide, they were sympathetic to Melissa's story and appreciated the way the film made visible the unseen labor of health care providers. Not all attendees at the workshop reacted favorably to the film, however. One home health care aide at the workshop said the film did not accurately reflect the dynamics of in-home care. By showing Melissa adjusting her client's chair and brushing his teeth, the participant argued, the film portrayed home health care work as "easy." This did not match her experiences of being spit on and cursed at while providing care to clients. Corral and other workshop participants intervened and explained that the purpose of the film was not to delve into the unfortunate aspects of home care, but rather to elevate a health care worker's personal story and connect it to dis-

FIGURE 5.7. Media workshop with SEIU Local 105. María Corral conducting practice interview with Cassandra Garcia, Denver, Colorado, April 18, 2017. (Photo by Gino Canella.)

courses about economic inequality and fairness. Another participant reflected on the film's ability to highlight the intersectional nature of Local 105 and connect labor with racial and gender justice. This was accomplished, the participant noted, through images such as a sign that read "Black Lives Matter" and still photographs of Black and Latino workers marching in rallies. I discussed with attendees my desire to include the emotional aspects of Melissa's story next to fact-based comments about Denver's cost of living. One participant responded that she did not get any facts from the film, but others contested her comment and pointed to statistics referenced by Melissa during her interview. The ability to convey statistics, such as the minimum wage or the percentage of people who can afford to live in Denver, is a challenge with visual media. Perhaps information graphics could have more effectively conveyed these points, but the exchange acknowledges the unevenness of activist media reception. In-person exhibitions offer organizers opportunities to follow up on issues raised in the film and ask participants what they thought of the messages and images presented in the film. The goal is not to persuade viewers but to recognize how meaning is contested and socially constituted.

The reaction to Melissa's film was unsurprisingly positive. Because there were a few conflicting reactions to the representation of home care workers, I asked Loree Lattik, a home care worker who has been active in Local 105's organizing campaigns, to expand on her thoughts about the film during our mock interview. "I could see and feel that Melissa was speaking from her heart, and that is her true and authentic story, very realistic," she said. "I remember in the video when she actually gave some affection to the person she was caring for, even though that person couldn't respond in kind. That's what happens, you get to know these folks and you get to care about them and you take care of the details of their life and it feels like family." In a journey similar to Melissa's path into union organizing, Loree saw a flyer promoting the Fight for $15 and contacted a Local 105 organizer to find out how she could get involved. She has attended rallies in Denver and Boulder and has spoken about her work to journalists with the *Denver Post*.

The power of film, Loree said, provided an added dimension to Melissa's story because it depicted her at home with her family and providing care at her client's home. "People have heard me talk about what I do, and tell my story about the skills that I use and the duties that I do," Loree said. "But I've never been filmed or shown actually doing that work, and I think that makes a big difference. I think that does send a message in a different way."

The media workshop provided me with an opportunity to guide Local 105 members and organizers in how to communicate effectively their stories to journalists. The most difficult aspect about the workshop as an experienced filmmaker was encouraging the attendees to be conversational in their responses to the interviewers' questions. Corral, during practice interviews, would often ask interviewees for a heartfelt, personal story about themselves or their families. For example, during one interview with a health care worker, she focused repeatedly on his passion for cycling. I told Corral in my feedback that although personal anecdotes about workers' hobbies may humanize working people, they can feel somewhat contrived. Although fun anecdotes may have the potential to go viral on social media, nothing substitutes for the tireless work of diligent and committed organizing.

CONCLUSION

This chapter has discussed the multifaceted distribution strategy BLM5280 and SEIU Local 105 used to publish and promote their campaigns—in the streets, on local news, via social media, and at public screenings. Distributing activist media strategically across various sites accomplishes two goals for organizers: (1) it reframes issues of race, space, gender, and labor, introducing new understandings of these issues into the public consciousness; and (2) it fosters social interactions among organizers to network working-class solidarity. My analysis has only briefly mentioned the reception of activist media. Studying how audiences perceive social media posts or documentary films about social justice would provide additional insights into the efficacy of activists' communication strategies.

Despite this limitation, I argue that activist filmmakers and grassroots organizers must think holistically when distributing media. Although social media offer organizers instant distribution and a built-in audience of activated supporters, "impact" cannot be quantified solely through online metrics. Rather, having an impact requires using a variety of distribution tactics simultaneously to intervene in public spaces and create room for meaningful dialogues. These dialogues realize activist media's potential as discursive bridges that network disparate constituencies and engage publics in radical political education.

CONCLUSION

> When we engage creation, we must be willing to be responsible for
> everything that we create, knowing that the world is interconnected
> and that every thought, breath, and action influences the whole.
> —Sherri Mitchell, *Sacred Instructions*

As politicians and journalists use media to sow division and fear, organizers and community-based artists are creating their own media to script solidarity, build networks of care, and promote meaningful engagement in civic life. The competing incentives and contradictions within our current media and information systems, however, demand that we approach activists' media practices through theories of democracy and networked media power. These theories recognize how contemporary networked movements that communicate and collaborate through media are influenced by the material social conditions in which they exist. Interrogating the connections between media systems and the social exposes activist media's limitations and potential. The incentives within our media systems were exploited recently by candidate Donald Trump when he announced his bid for president of the United States.[1] While many journalists and politicians dismissed Trump's racist and xenophobic rhetoric as a sideshow and media spectacle, these same institutions played a key role in amplifying and normalizing his messages. The media spectacle that gave rise to Trump's hateful ideologies has had material consequences. According to research, bias-related acts of intimidation and harassment against minority groups rose following the 2016 election. The Southern Poverty Law Center, for instance, reported 1,094 bias-related incidents in the month following the 2016 U.S. presidential election, with anti-immigrant cases (315) being the most reported, followed by anti-Black (221), anti-Muslim (112), and anti-LGBTQ (109) cases.[2]

Community organizers and grassroots media makers committed to justice, therefore, are creating media not only to uplift working people's agency but also to deconstruct the political, economic, and media institutions that have allowed hate and division to spread. Responding minute by minute to the latest Twitter outbursts and social media trends creates a sense of disorientation among activists about when and how to respond to injustices. The intense speed at which social media operate strain organizers' limited resources and make it difficult for them to pursue long-term campaigns with coherent and consistent messaging. The visibility that these platforms provide, however, make them irresistible to organizers seeking to broadcast their campaigns to national and global audiences.

The rhetorical and physical attacks against marginalized communities must also be understood in relation to the coordinated legal attacks against unions and workers' rights. In May 2018, the Supreme Court of the United States ruled in favor of employers in *National Labor Relations Board (NLRB) v. Murphy Oil*. The court concluded that employees who have signed arbitration agreements that contain class action waivers with their employers may argue workplace disputes with an arbitrator individually, rather than as part of a class, thus limiting workers' ability to pursue collective action. In June 2018, *Janus v. American Federation of State, County, and Municipal Employees (AFSCME), Council 31* was decided. In this case, the Supreme Court ruled that public sector employees should not be required to pay union dues, significantly weakening labor unions' financial strength and, thus, their organizing capacity. These rulings strengthen the argument that for the U.S. labor movement to remain relevant, social movement unionism embedded in broader community struggles is essential.

These cases also highlight the connections between culture, media, and policy. Material conditions and political ideologies are constructed and negotiated through communication, which increasingly is mediated and online. By creating media that reject and revise dominant institutional logics, community organizers are imagining new political possibilities and attempting to mold more equitable material conditions.

Activist media are intellectual and political practices that highlight *the social* in three important ways: (1) by challenging organizers to identify and embrace their political and ideological differences, activist media illuminate the risks embedded in activism; (2) by leveraging emotion, activist media create spaces for organizers to network with supporters and build durable infrastructures; (3) by centering the voices and experiences of those most affected by research and creative projects, activist media have the potential to decolonize knowledge production.

EMBRACING CONFRONTATION

Luis Guillermo Uribe and Joanne Rappaport argued that *confrontation* reveals the struggle for voice and power.[3] My activist media with Black Lives Matter 5280 and Service Employees International Union Local 105 asked me to confront my political orientation, scholarly commitments, and personal identities. This was a formative experience for me as a filmmaker, researcher, and organizer, and it revealed the risks and vulnerabilities inherent in movement organizing and community-engaged research.

Confronting differences—during pre-production, in the field, and in the edit room—asked me and my community partners to be vulnerable with our emotions and sensitive to the needs of others. Embracing confrontation required evaluating and being sensitive to risk throughout all stages of our creative projects and community-based interventions. Assessing risk forces activists to examine power— where it lies, who has it, and what strategies are needed to claim it. The risks for me, as a white male filmmaker, were different than those that Black activists and Hispanic labor organizers faced. Because these communities are disproportionately targeted by state violence and surveillance, assessing risk included evaluating our communication and media strategies and our positionality to the state and to publics. Positionality, simply put, means identifying the physical and digital spaces within the social that create intellectual gaps. Activist media practices bridge these gaps by mapping out organizers' position within the social in relation to the state and to publics; pinpointing their location within the social helps organizers determine the institutional, financial, and technical resources they need to seize power. Closeness to or distance from power and resources shapes how movements are framed and whose agency and whose voices are elevated in framing processes.

Because of my close proximity to the movements with which I worked and the personal relationships that I developed with my partners, the risks I encountered throughout this project are notable. I risked romanticizing these groups and our media in my research and writing. At a time when publics increasingly distrust institutions, specifically the news media and higher education, conducting multimodal research in collaboration with community groups put me at risk of being viewed by publics and my peers as a liberal elite who does not produce rigorous, evidence-based scholarship. By embracing confrontation, I was able to assess these risks and produce complex and dialectical analyses about activist media's potentials and problems.

As Uribe and Rappaport noted, confrontation is essential for radical scholarship that advocates for change because confrontation transforms the world and how we see it. They wrote: "It is in confrontation with people that both our knowledge and theirs will be validated, refined, and combined to produce concepts, methods, and procedures for activist research (*investigación-acción*), ways of knowing and doing that are novel, creative, and, above all, transformative of reality."[4] Transforming reality occurs during moments of rupture—what Gramsci called the "interregnum," or the gap. Activist media's creative and experimental methods help organizers navigate rupture and study rapidly evolving social and political phenomena. These methods are inherently risky because they challenge the status quo and disrupt the taken-for-granted. By creating spaces in which to theorize justice, communicate their values, and build networked infrastructures, these methods help organizers assess and mitigate risk. In the current media environment, creativity also means using experimental methods to produce and disseminate ideas across various platforms and encouraging publics to connect the dots.

Uribe and Rappaport used the term "co-writing" to describe one particular method that I used in my project with BLM5280 and SEIU Local 105. They argued that ethnography includes two forms of writing: one in which facts and data are recorded, and a second "diary format" in which "there is almost no translation, but instead the Native vocabulary, context, intonation, body language, and emphases of utterances." For the first instance of writing (the facts and data) to resonate, Uribe and Rappaport wrote, "one must be able to hear in one's head as one reads the voice of the speaker and to see in the mind's eye the image and actions of the actor."[5]

Co-writing occurred for me during post-production. Writing scripts and editing video, for example, included listening repeatedly to interviews and watching and rewatching footage from protests and demonstrations to find moments and angles that best complemented the story. Post-production is similar to dancing, in that one needs to recognize the story's rhythm and create mood through layers of sounds. By timing out scenes and finding BLM and SEIU's rhythm, I immersed myself in these groups' voices and languages; doing so allowed me to hear and see more clearly how these speakers embodied and emphasized their demands for justice. New technologies are thus updating Uribe and Rappaport's concept of co-writing. Documentaries, podcasts, and 360-degree video plunge researchers back into their data and research sites, challenging them to look closer and listen more carefully for nuance and context.

EMOTIONAL INTELLIGENCE AND AFFECTIVE BRIDGES

With a growing number of scholars conducting multimodal research, and colleges and universities increasingly promoting community engagement, it is important to recognize the link between practice and theory. By using research methods that are grounded in the principles of democracy, activist media promote grassroots epistemologies. Activist media encourage communities that have often been excluded from academic institutions to be involved directly in contextualizing their lives through media and research. During my activist filmmaking, co-creation with community groups produced a knowledge surplus that allowed me (as a filmmaker-researcher) and my partners (as grassroots organizers) to reorganize the assemblage of media, culture, and knowledge production.

Theory building with activists and organizers demands that scholars listen to those most affected by their research outcomes and give participants a say in the trajectory of that research. Rethinking our ontological positions as media and communication scholars requires practicing what Jeffrey S. Juris called "militant ethnography." Claiming to be neutral or objective during times of crisis, he argued, is unacceptable. Rather, researchers must "become entangled with complex relations of power, and live the emotions associated with direct action organizing and activist networking."[6] To investigate the emotional resonance of activism, it is essential that researchers *feel* the emotions emanating from the streets and respond according to their political and scholarly commitments. Emotional intelligence means embracing emotion in the research and creative process and viewing emotions as data. I developed my emotional intelligence throughout this project by producing passionate media that was attuned to the emotions I witnessed at community meetings, in the streets, and online. I reflected regularly on how these emotions influenced our films' narratives and the social dynamics among movement members.

Militant research that embraces emotion has a rich tradition in Latin America. Colectivo Situaciones in Buenos Aires, Argentina, for example, advocated for *militancia de investigación*—an intellectual orientation that rejects traditional academic frameworks and operates outside of institutional politics.[7] The collective argued that militant research embraces the dialectic between theory and practice by establishing "positive connections with subaltern, dispersed, and hidden knowledges," rejecting the "alienating mechanisms" of academic research, and remaining curious. Curiosity—not with the aim of confirming or rejecting hypotheses— the collective wrote, provides opportunities to identify the "emerging traces of a new sociability."

Activists and grassroots media makers are using media to theorize a radical sociability based on love and solidarity. By telling stories that challenge dominant framings of race, community, and citizenship, activists are reconstituting the social. Researchers who collaborate with activists on their communication and media strategies are better able to identify these "emerging traces" within the social. Telling stories informed by research data acknowledges the fact that data are never neutral: data emerge out of ethical commitments and the cultural and political contexts in which they are recorded.

My filmmaking could not have been possible without the cooperation and dedication of organizers and members of SEIU Local 105 and BLM5280. Both organizations, in different ways, shaped the narratives of our films. SEIU was more involved than BLM5280 in our films' production (e.g., suggesting interview subjects and revisions), but my relationship with BLM5280 was equally important. The group provided me with the radical political education that I needed to craft anti-racist, anti-capitalist, intersectional films rooted in solidarity with all oppressed people. Attending BLM5280's community meetings helped me to understand the movement's energies and emotions, which I then documented and communicated through film, photography, and writing.

Throughout this project, filmmaking was a mutually beneficial endeavor. Melissa Benjamin's organizing of health care workers in Colorado reveals how collaborative filmmaking has the potential to empower organic intellectuals to voice their agency. There is a strong legacy of organic intellectuals within the labor movement, but activist media are updating where and how organizers conduct political education. Union organizers have always hosted reading groups in the break room and displayed leaflets on the shop floor. As labor becomes more temporary and disconnected from place, however, today's organic intellectuals are getting creative about how they organize workers. Despite never seeing their colleagues at the work-site, organizers are disseminating their campaigns in various formats and reach-ing people where they get their news and information—via email newsletters, pod-casts, and social media. It is crucial, though, that organizers ground their activist media practices in workers' material conditions and within their local sociopo-litical contexts.

DECOLONIZING MEDIA (STUDIES) AND DEMOCRATIZING DOCUMENTARY

Nicholas Mirzoeff and Jack Halberstam challenged scholars to re-examine their research practices in a dossier entitled "Decolonize Media: Tactics, Manifestos, Histories."[8] The authors engaged critically with race, gender, class, and power and offered seven suggestions for scholars seeking to decolonize media studies, all of which relate to the activist media practices detailed throughout this book: "(1) Listen. To the colonized, to the historically underrepresented, to your own body; (2) Use and create open-source materials; (3) Study or learn in languages beyond English (and other colonial languages); (4) 'Text is not enough.' Produce in many forms; (5) Collaborate in your research: faculty with students, academics with the communities they serve; (6) Be 'producers not only consumers' from the outset of learning; (7) And try to live up to the injunction 'ethics above all.'"[9]

I created open-source research in multiple formats by producing films and dis-tributing them online with Creative Commons licensing. I studied and learned in languages beyond English when I worked with Spanish-language translators and produced bilingual documentaries. I fostered collaboration by involving my partners throughout all stages of production and distribution and listening to their feedback. As the boundaries between academic disciplines and fields continue to blur, scholars must invent new ways of studying media, movements, and commu-nication. Centering *the political* and *the social* acknowledges emotion and conflict in relation to digital technologies and political institutions. Activist media prac-tices decolonize media studies by forcing scholars to re-evaluate, revise, and update dominant theoretical frameworks and accepted methodologies. Co-creative research shows how writing, editing, analyzing data, and distributing cultural texts are interdependent processes that strengthen and enhance our understanding of mediated and networked society.

Reviewing the *form* of public scholarship is crucial to understanding how activ-ist media challenge dominant conceptions of race, place, gender, and citizenship and help activists curate alternative archives. Jacques Rancière argued that the form of politics represents the "distribution of the sensible."[10] Documentary is visual art that challenges viewers to witness and make sense of social life. Documenting movements and disseminating their stories in public spaces, Rancière argued, encourage viewers to reimagine the terrain of politics: "The politics of works of art. . . . plays itself out in the way in which modes of narration or new forms of visibility established by artistic practices enter into politics' own field of aesthetic possibilities. It is necessary to reverse the way in which the problem is generally formulated."[11]

BLM5280 and SEIU Local 105 used media to formulate "the problem" as racial capitalism, state violence, economic inequality, and the criminalization of immigrants and people of color. Visualizing how these groups fought back against "the problem" reversed how social and political issues are formulated and altered the field of politics. BLM5280 and SEIU Local 105's activist media show these groups use culture, language, and public spaces to challenge bourgeois conceptions of the public sphere. By shouting in the streets and raising their fists, members of these groups engage in antagonistic pluralist democracy and demand recognition.

Rancière argued that the sensible is produced and distributed through struggle. "The democratic distribution of the sensible makes the worker into a double being," he wrote. "It removes the artisan from 'his' place, the domestic space of work, and gives him 'time' to occupy the space of public discussions and take on the identity of a deliberative citizen."[12] Through co-creation, activist media create opportunities for movements to deliberate, practice solidarity, and stage the social—all of which reshapes the place of politics.

Reshaping politics through art and media contests the taken-for-granted—what Rancière called the *dispositif*. The tensions between systems (such as language, knowledge, and politics) represent points where scholars and activists can begin to decolonize media (studies). Scholars and activists must work together to study and deconstruct these systems. Narratives that center the perspectives of working people and place workers' stories in their broader historical and sociopolitical contexts ask viewers to reconsider the taken-for-granted and reimagine what else is possible.

This book set out to examine the social relations embedded in activist media and to understand what these social relations reveal about democracy. Because preproduction, production, and post-production are social practices that require deliberation, collaboration, and an ethic of care, activist media reveal the micro-practices of democracy. Democracy requires coming together in shared spaces, navigating and embracing confrontation, and engaging in vigorous political debates about how to organize society. Democracy is not a goal that can be achieved or a state in which a society arrives; rather, it is an act, a muscle that must be exercised. Activist media create opportunities for people to engage meaningfully in civic life, recognize and fulfill their agency, and make connections with their peers. As more and more people feel lonely, anxious, and depressed, activist media provide venues through which to strengthen social cohesion—encouraging people to meet their neighbors, discuss their aspirations, and identify their comrades.

I have referred often throughout this book to various *practices*—of activist media, democracy, and community organizing. I use "practice" as a verb: to repeatedly perform a skill or task in order to improve or maintain proficiency. Activists, organizers, and community-engaged researchers are using media to communicate with each another and with publics—in essence, *practicing* how to frame justice. Practicing, however, also requires critically assessing and studying the impact that these frames have on politics and power. Media's affordances and limitations have been examined in detail here because it is crucial to recognize how online platforms and telecommunications providers constrain certain frames and enable others. The incentives within our current media and communication systems raise difficult philosophical questions about privacy, language, and reality itself. Logging off and practicing political education in physical spaces demands that organizers communicate empathy, patience, and care. As I write this, however, much of the world is gripped by the COVID-19 pandemic, making activists increasingly reliant on digital media and technology to strategize and organize. Connecting online activities with peoples' material lives will be a major challenge for future movements.

Creating and distributing activist media through democratic practices invariably brings up another core feature of democracy: compromise. Organizers and scholars must consider when and how to compromise their ideas and the forms in which these ideas are expressed. Compromising an idea's form, or the venue in which it is exhibited, does not mean that the idea itself is compromised. Films, photographs, essays, and interactive multimedia are supplemental materials that activists and researchers can disseminate across a variety of platforms—in turn, spreading their ideas to diverse new audiences and complementing their on-the-ground efforts. Developing novel forms in which to package ideas helps organizers clarify their ideas, exercise their creativity, and create new spaces in which people can speak. Activists and organizers have long debated whether cultural production represents complicity with capitalist institutions that are inherently exploitative. Within the current political economic moment in which democracy is under siege and authoritarian leaders and white supremacists are emboldened, organizers must use every tactic available—including media—to promote a more compassionate, equitable and just world.

APPENDIX

LINKS TO MEDIA AND FILMS

Black Lives Matter 5280. "BLM5280 Stands With Minneapolis," November 24, 2015
https://www.youtube.com/watch?v=DddYLPiX_k8
Black Lives Matter 5280. "BLM Debate: #Reparations," October 25, 2015
https://www.facebook.com/BlackLivesMatter5280/videos/1508971816086713/
Black Lives Matter 5280. "BLM5280 on MLK Day," January 18, 2016
https://www.youtube.com/watch?v=1zhTvKNMWCE
Black Lives Matter 5280. Photo Gallery: MLK Day, January 18, 2016
https://www.facebook.com/gino.canella/posts/10153921627634365
SEIU Local 105. "Home healthcare #Fightfor15," December 9, 2015
https://www.youtube.com/watch?v=KpVzlFxPOmg
SEIU Local 105. "Justice 4 Janitors Rally," April 15, 2016
https://www.facebook.com/gino.canella/videos/10154161055684365
SEIU Local 105. "Justice 4 Janitors Rally 2," June 24, 2016
https://www.facebook.com/gino.canella/videos/10154332660324365
SEIU Local 105. "May Day 2017," May 1, 2017
https://www.facebook.com/gino.canella/videos/vb.589109364/10155319439
    504365
SEIU Local 105. "Healthcare Death," June 13, 2017
https://www.facebook.com/SEIULocal105/videos/1526350287422377
Radical Labor: Aligning Unions with the Streets, March 9, 2018
https://roarmag.org/films/radical-labor-aligning-unions-streets/

LIST OF INTERVIEWS

Andy Jacob, SEIU Local 105, political director   October 21, 2015
Amy Emery-Brown, former co-lead BLM5280   October 29, 2015
Ric Urrutia, Colorado Jobs 4 Justice   October 29, 2015
Melissa Benjamin, home health care worker   November 23, 2015
Felicia Griffin, executive director, FRESC   June 15, 2016

Ron Ruggiero, SEIU Local 105 president	June 15, 2016
David Ornelas, SEIU Local 105 member/janitor	June 15, 2016
Steve Gutierrez, SEIU Local 105, external organizer	June 15, 2016
María Corral, SEIU Local 105, communications coordinator	June 15, 2016
Jesus Cervantes, SEIU Local 105, organizer	June 15, 2016
Jesus Cervantes, SEIU Local 105, organizer	April 14, 2016
Pedro Carrillo, SEIU Local 105, property services	April 14, 2016
Luis Castillo, airport security worker, DIA	April 14, 2016
Sasha Ramirez, co-lead BLM5280	April 14, 2016
Lucia Melgarejo, SEIU Local 105, property services director	July 9, 2016
Bea Griffin, SEIU Local 105, member and union steward	April 18, 2017
John Stone, HSS, security guard	April 18, 2017
Cory Hithon, home healthcare worker	April 18, 2017
Loree Lattik, home healthcare worker	April 18, 2017
Cassandra Garcia, clinical case manager, SEIU Local 105 member	April 18, 2017
Roberto Sains, Kaiser Permanente, customer service representative	April 18, 2017
Juan Gallegos, Colorado Immigrants Rights Coalition, civic engagement director	June 13, 2017
Robin Clark, SEIU Local 105	June 13, 2017
Salvador Hernandez, Mi Familia Vota, civic engagement coordinator	June 13, 2017
Jesus Cervantes, SEIU Local 105, organizer	June 13, 2017
Josh Downey, Denver Area Labor Federation, president	June 28, 2017
Paul Lopez, City Council, District 3, City of Denver	July 19, 2017
Felicia Griffin, FRESC, executive director	July 19, 2017
Ron Ruggiero, SEIU Local 105, president	July 25, 2017
Robin Kniech, City Council, at large, City of Denver	August 24, 2017
Lizeth Chacón, Colorado People's Alliance, executive director	August 30, 2017

SAMPLE INTERVIEW REQUEST FOR DOCUMENTARY FILMS AND DISSERTATION

Dear [organizer/representative],

My name is Gino Canella, and I am a PhD candidate in media studies at CU Boulder and an independent filmmaker. I have been working closely with the SEIU Local 105 producing videos on rallies and profiles of members. I am currently working with María Corral, the communications coordinator at the Local 105, to create a documentary that will cover a brief of history of labor unions in Colorado, the current fight for workers' rights, and how the labor movement is collaborating with other progressive grassroots organizations in Denver.

María mentioned you would be a great person to speak with, and I'd like to ask if we could schedule a time for an interview. My schedule is fairly flexible as I am in the midst of summer break, but feel free to contact me via email or on my cell with any questions or concerns you might have about the project.

Thanks in advance for considering, and I look forward to hearing from you soon.

Solidarity,
Gino Canella
PhD Candidate, Media Studies
University of Colorado Boulder

SAMPLE LIST OF INTERVIEW QUESTIONS

What is Black Lives Matter 5280/SEIU Local 105?

Who can participate in the movement?

How long has BLM5280 been active?

What do you see as your primary objectives as a social movement?

How do you encourage others to join and learn about the organization?

How are participants given leadership status within the movement?

What is your relationship to the national movement/other chapters around the country/world?

Tell me about the history of labor, particularly with regard to white/Black workers.

How does SEIU/BLM5280 convey its messages of racial and economic justice?

How are racial and economic justice connected?

What do you hope to accomplish with demonstrations in the streets?

What do you think the perception of Black Lives Matter is? Does perception matter?

Do you see documentary films as a good opportunity to explore social justice campaigns and present them to larger publics online and at community screenings? If so, why?

Has the Fight for $15 campaign been successful in your opinion? If so, in what ways?

How does the SEIU network with other activist organizations and grassroots groups in Denver and across the country?

What is the value of personal stories and documentary films for persuading people to back this campaign?

Why is the contract negotiation between the janitors and the contractors crucial for your members?

How do you celebrate wins and remain focused on larger systemic fights ahead?

PHOTO/INTERVIEW RELEASE FORM

I hereby give permission to:

Name: <u>Gino Canella</u>

Organization/publication: <u>SEIU Local 105</u>

Address: <u>2525 W. Alameda Ave., Denver, CO</u>

Phone: <u>(303) 698-7963</u>
Email: <u>gino.canella@colorado.edu</u>

1. to interview me / photograph me (still or moving images) / record my voice,
2. and to use, reuse, publish and republish the same in whole or in part for any lawful purposes in any and all media whether now known or hereafter existing, including print, broadcast, and the World Wide Web,
3. and to use my full name in connection therewith. I will make no monetary or other claim, including any and all claims for libel, for the use of the interview and/or the photograph(s)/video/recording of my voice.

This authorization and release also applies to the organization(s) / publication(s) for which the photographer/interviewer took the photos/ video, recorded my voice, and/or conducted the interview, and to their legal representatives, licensees and assignees.

Note exceptions here by crossing out points above to which the photo/interview subject does not agree. Subject reserves the right to decline to answer certain questions and to stop the interview if he/she becomes uncomfortable. He/she may refuse the use of his/her full name and may refuse to have his/her full face photographed.

Name of person(s) to be interviewed/photographed:

Print name: _____

Signature: _____Date: _____

ACKNOWLEDGMENTS

This book, like the documentary films discussed here, was a collaborative effort that could not have been possible without the tremendous support of community organizers, academic peers and mentors, friends, and family. This project was transformational for me—intellectually, personally, and creatively. I have struggled, grown, and learned how to be a thoughtful and caring filmmaker, scholar, and social justice ally. The reflections and analyses offered here are equally informed by my doctoral studies at the University of Colorado Boulder and by conversations and interactions with community organizers in Colorado to whom I am forever grateful. Organizers who shared their time and knowledge provided me with a critical lens through which to investigate media, power, race, and democracy; their voices are as central to this work as the social and political theorists cited throughout this text.

Thank you to my dissertation supervisor, Nabil Echchaibi, for being a tireless advocate for my work and for encouraging me to pursue documentary filmmaking as creative research. Our graduate seminars and conversations about culture and politics shaped the way I think about activism and publicity. Thank you to Bianca Williams for showing me how to *be political* as a scholar and for imparting the lesson that academics have a responsibility to pursue justice. Thank you to Larry Frey for your endless suggestions, edits, and conversations. I am incredibly appreciative for your guidance, and I acknowledge that the quality of my writing would not be possible without your reviews. Andrew Calabrese, thank you for introducing me to concepts of the public and theories of democracy. Kathleen Ryan, thank you for showing me the value of visual analysis; I hope to emulate your work as a filmmaker-scholar. Thank you, Seema Sohi, for helping me find "my project." You had a profound impact on how I think about diversity and multicultural inclusion; when I analyze unions, I will forever be cautious to avoid reinforcing the notion of a "more perfect union."

To all the brilliant and inspiring researchers, artists, and organizers I have had the pleasure of working with, a humble thank-you: Deborah Cai, Jan Fernback, Barry Vacker, Nancy Morris, Matthew Lombard, Andrew Mendelson, Mary Bock, Ever Figueroa, Krishnan Vasudevan, Jennifer Midberry, Urszula Pruchniewska, Janice Peck, J. Richard Stevens, Paul Voakes, Michela Ardizzoni, Brian Valente-Quinn, Patrick Ferrucci, Jeff Browne, Bryan Mercer, Hannah Sassaman, Todd Wolfson, Kevin Carragee, Janet Kolodzy, Lina Giraldo, Azeta Hatef, Paul Mihailidis, Eric Gordon, Cindy Rodríguez, and so many others.

To the Colorado Commune: Thank you. I would especially like to extend my endless gratitude to Amy Brown and María Corral. Your patience and support throughout my work with BLM5280 and SEIU Local 105 were invaluable, and I cannot begin to tell you how much I have learned through our interactions. Our conversations about racial justice, workers' rights, immigration, and systemic inequality have forever changed my perspectives on life, love, and community. I hope my writing and films did your stories justice. To the other labor leaders, activists, and community organizers who made this work possible, I offer my sincere appreciation: Melissa Benjamin, Jesus Cervantes, Lizeth Chacón, Greg Douros, Josh Downey, Felicia Griffin, Andy Jacob, Robin Kniech, Alex Landau, Paul Lopez, Sasha Ramirez, and Ron Ruggiero.

To my graduate school colleagues, thank you for your friendship. Rianne Subijanto, Tyler Rollins, Kristin Peterson, Alexis de Coning, and Christopher Barnes, you made PhD life bearable and, at times, even fun. A special thanks to Kevan Feshami and Patrick Johnson. I never knew my cohort would consist of so many Steelers fans. Kevan, I especially valued our chats at No Name about Marx, labor, and reification. To my extended Colorado family—Stephen, Ana, Mandy, Katie Ray, TJay, and Bradley—your kindness made the Rocky Mountain scenery that much more beautiful.

Thank you to Nicole Solano, Angela Piliouras, and the team at Rutgers University Press for your thoughtful comments and edits and for shepherding this project through the production process.

Elen, I enjoy so much our spirited discussions about politics, culture, and life. You challenge me to think harder about justice and equality, and I am a better person with you in my life. *Te quiero mucho. Eres mi corazón, siempre, querida.*

Finally, thank you to my family: Mom, Dad, Nicholas, Ciara, Rob, Giada, Giuliana, Michael, and Nonne. You are my biggest fans, and I endlessly thank you for your unconditional love and care. Every project I have done would not have been possible without your support.

I love you all.

Peace and solidarity,
Gino
Boston, Massachusetts, October 2021

NOTES

INTRODUCTION

1. Scott, 2019; Brenan, 2020.
2. Martin, 2019.
3. Lopez, 2019.
4. For an example of a legal decision that has contributed to declining union membership, see *Janus v. American Federation of State, County, and Municipal Employees*, 585 U.S. __, 2018.
5. Jaffe, 2019.
6. Scholars often assume that activism and social change are progressive or left projects, but activist media practices can be and are being used by the far Right and white supremacists around the world. For a discussion of extremist right-wing uses of digital media, see Schradie, 2019.
7. Della Porta, 2011, 815.
8. Wolfson, 2014.
9. Wolfson, 2014, 18, 33.
10. Downing, 2001.
11. Aguayo, 2019, 12.
12. Robé, 2017.
13. Robé, 2017, 66.
14. Harvey, 2005.
15. According to the U.S. Department of Labor (2017a), union membership declined by 240,000 from 2015 to 2016. Research has connected this declining trend in unionization to growing income inequality, with "between one-fifth and one-third of wage inequality . . . due to the drop in union membership" (Windham, 2017, para. 12).
16. Frank, 2016.

CHAPTER 1   ACTIVIST MEDIA, POWER, AND NETWORKED PUBLICS

1. Downing, 1984.
2. Downing, 2001, ix.
3. Downing, 2008, ix.
4. Rodriguez, Ferron, & Shamas, 2014.
5. Grierson, 1939, 122.
6. Atton, 2002, 24.
7. Atton, 2002, 30.
8. Funke, Robé, & Wolfson, 2012, 17.
9. Wolfson, 2014.
10. Wolfson, 2014, 185.
11. Habermas, 1989.
12. Fraser, 1990, 69, 68.
13. Butler, 1997; see also Castells, 2010.
14. Castells, 2010, 36–37.
15. Althusser, 1971.
16. Butler, 1997, 43.

17. Habermas, 1992, 1998.
18. Habermas, 1996, 381.
19. Downey &Fenton, 2003.
20. Downey & Fenton, 2003, 195.
21. Jenkins, 2006.
22. Pateman, 1970.
23. Pateman, 1970, 43.
24. Pateman, 2012, 10.
25. Williams, 1977; Nielsen, 2016.
26. Nielsen, 2016, 86, 87.
27. Nielsen, 2016, 87.
28. Mouffe, 1989, 41.
29. Mouffe, 1999.
30. Mouffe, 1999, 754.
31. Dean, 2009b, 26.
32. Dean, 2009b, 25.
33. Dean, 2009a, 21.
34. Dean, 2009a, 2.
35. Žižek, 1998, 2002.
36. Dean, 2012.
37. Dean, 2012, 66.
38. Dean, 2012, 67.
39. Singh, 2004.
40. Frazier, 1962.
41. Frazier, 1962, 271–272, 272.
42. Cited in Shawki, 2017, para. 26.
43. Shawki, 2017, para. 24.
44. Singh, 2004, 25.
45. Singh, 2004, 223.
46. Lopez, 2014.
47. West, 1993, 29.
48. West, 1993, 29.
49. West, 1993, 43.
50. West, 1993, 44.
51. Singh, 2004, 28.
52. Singh, 2004, 224.
53. Davis, 1984.
54. Davis, 1984, 24.
55. Davis, 1984, 43.
56. Eisenstein, 1979.
57. Cited in CBS News, 2017.
58. See, e.g., Daum, 2017.
59. Lorde, 1984, 116.
60. Lorde, 1984, 116.
61. Lorde, 1984, 119.
62. Gramsci, 1971; Castells, 2011.
63. Goffman, 1974.
64. Carragee & Roefs, 2004, 215.
65. Carragee & Roefs, 2004, 775.

66. Carragee & Roefs, 2004, 779.
67. Hall, 1977, 333.
68. Hall, 1980, 143.
69. Williams, 1977, 112.
70. Couldry, 2015b, 42.
71. Couldry, 2008, 42.
72. Lambert, 2006, xxi.
73. Couldry, 2011, 47.
74. Gitlin, 1980.
75. See, e.g., Juris, 2012; Shirky, 2008.
76. Papacharissi, 2016.
77. Papacharissi, 2016, 310.
78. Wahl-Jorgensen, 2019.
79. Ferree & Merrill, 2000, 457.
80. Lorde, 1981.
81. Lorde, 1981, 242, 244.
82. Lorde, 1981, 248.
83. Couldry, 2015a, 611.
84. Couldry, 2015a, 620
85. Couldry, 2015a, 614.
86. Bennett & Segerberg, 2012.
87. Bennett & Segerberg, 2012, 742.
88. Bennett & Segerberg, 2012, 742, 743.
89. Bennett & Segerberg, 2012, 748.
90. Bayat, 2010.
91. Bayat, 2010, 24.
92. Piven, 2008.
93. Piven, 2008, 5.
94. See, e.g., Frey & Carragee, 2007.
95. Frey, Pearce, et al., 1996, 111.
96. Carragee & Frey, 2012, 7.
97. Gramsci, 1971.
98. See, e.g., Frey & SunWolf, 2009.
99. Cissna, 2000, 169–170.
100. McHale, 2007.
101. McHale, 2007, 199.
102. McHale, 2007, 200.
103. Kraidy, 2016.
104. Kraidy, 2016, 17, 16.
105. Freedman, 2017, 1.
106. Freedman, 2017, 7.
107. Said, 1993.
108. Freedman, 2017, 8.

CHAPTER 2　MOVEMENTS AND MEDIA

1. Chau, 2010; Jenkins, 2006.
2. Fuchs, 2014, 14.
3. Rose, 2014, 203.

4. Murdock, 1999, 8.

5. Service Employees International Union, n.d., para. 1.

6. Cited in Edsall, 2005, para. 5.

7. Unlike New York, New Jersey, and Michigan, Colorado is not known as a union stronghold. Colorado has 9 percent union density, meaning fewer than one in ten workers are unionized, placing it just below the national average of 10.7 percent. Colorado is not a right-to-work state and is unique in that it has a Labor Peace Law, a compromise between the right-to-work idea and unions that requires two elections and 75 percent approval from workers before a shop can become unionized.

8. Hendee, 2016.

9. U.S. Department of Labor, 2016.

10. Mayer, 2004.

11. U.S. Department of Labor, 2017b.

12. AFL-CIO, 2016.

13. Fight for $15, n.d.

14. National Employment Law Project, 2015.

15. Aronowitz, 2014.

16. Polletta, 2002.

17. Ngai, 2004.

18. Moody, 2000.

19. "#BlackLivesMatter," when used as a hashtag, refers to the organization's social-media-related activities, such as calls to action; announcements; and posts of photos, videos, and news articles showing solidarity with other chapters by supporting their campaigns. "Black Lives Matter," on the other hand, refers to the movement as a whole and its offline organizing efforts and campaigns. Making this distinction is somewhat difficult, as social media are connected intimately to the movement's outreach and messaging strategies.

20. Mouffe, 1989, 14.

21. Funke & Wolfson, 2017; Laclau & Mouffe, 2001.

22. It's Time for Accountability, 2020.

23. Garza, n.d., para. 11.

24. Who We Are, n.d.

25. Kilgo & Harlow, 2019.

26. Black Lives Matter 5280, 2016a.

27. U.S. Census Bureau, 2019.

28. Williams, 2015.

29. Ambert, Adler, et al., 1995, 3.

30. Aguayo, 2019, 32.

31. Schrum, Duque, & Brown, 2005, 4.

32. Nigg, 2018.

33. Aguayo, 2019, 45.

34. Robé & Wolfson, 2020.

35. Schrum, Duque, & Brown, 2005, 5.

36. Schrum, Duque, & Brown, 2005, 8.

37. Henley, 1998, 6.

38. Henley, 1998, 43.

39. Lassiter, 2005.

40. Milne, Mitchell, & De Lange, 2012; White, 2003.

41. Sandercock & Attili, 2010, 24.

42. Incite! Women of Color against Violence, 2007.

CHAPTER 3   PRE-PRODUCTION

1. Cole, 2012b.
2. Cole, 2012a.
3. Williams, 2017
4. The Office of the Independent Monitor (OIM) was created under a 2005 city ordinance. The Denver Justice Project argued that moving the OIM into the city charter would prevent Denver mayor Michael Hancock and future mayors from removing the office and that the move would strengthen OIM's ability independently to oversee police and sheriff departments in the City and County of Denver (Carter, 2016). Following the hearing on August 15, 2016, City Council unanimously voted, 9–0, to allow the issue as a ballot measure in the November 2016 election. The measure passed, with 72 percent of Denver voters agreeing to enshrine the OIM into the city charter (Roberts, 2016).
5. Black Lives Matter 5280, 2017b.
6. Canella, 2017a.
7. Adler & Adler, 1987.
8. Crenshaw, 1991.
9. Tometi & Lenoir, 2015, para. 6.
10. Bonilla-Silva, 2002, 41.
11. Trawalter, Hoffman, & Waytz, 2012; Silverstein, 2013.
12. Frey & Castro, 2016.
13. Roediger, 1991.
14. Black Lives Matter 5280, 2016b.
15. Black Lives Matter 5280, 2016c.
16. Coe, Kenski, & Rains, 2014; Santana, 2014.
17. Black Lives Matter 5280, 2016d.
18. Jones, 2017.
19. Delgado, 2017.
20. Lee, 2017.
21. Colorado People's Alliance, n.d., para. 2.
22. Mikati et. al, 2018.

CHAPTER 4   PRODUCTION

1. Canella, 2015b.
2. Bock, 2016, 5; see also Murray, 2008, and Schroeder, 2008.
3. Ross, 2014, 2.
4. Dovey, 2000, 55.
5. See Funke, Robé, & Wolfson, 2012.
6. Canella, 2016b, 2016c.
7. Corral, 2016.
8. Canella, 2016c.
9. Canella, 2017b; SEIU Local 105, 2017a.
10. Rothman, 2017.
11. Canella, 2017b.
12. Black Lives Matter 5280, 2015a.
13. Canella, 2015a.
14. Dean, 2009b; Tufecki, 2017.
15. Hennepin Attorney, 2016; McLaughlin & Sanchez, 2016.

16. Canella, 2016a. The term "Marade" is used for Denver's MLK Day celebration to describe an event that is both a parade and a march. The parade celebrates the victories won in the fight against injustice; the march promotes nonviolent demonstration against injustice.

17. Elmer & Opel, 2008; Canella, 2018b

18. Sylte, 2017.

19. Murray, 2015.

20. The #MLKDay film was posted to my YouTube and Facebook accounts on January 18, 2016, and was again shared on my Facebook page on January 15, 2017 to promote the 2017 Marade and celebrate BLM5280's action at the 2016 rally. Total views across all platforms are more than 2,000 at the time of this writing. The 2017 Facebook post has received about 1,000 views, nearly as many as the original YouTube (1,200) and Facebook (200) posts combined. This viewership suggests that activist media makers should continue distributing their creative projects months and years after their initial publication to continue the conversations that those projects intended to highlight.

21. Sylte, 2017.

22. Murray, 2017.

CHAPTER 5   POST-PRODUCTION

1. Shearer & Gottfried, 2017.

2. Walker, 2016, para. 9.

3. Cited in Walker, 2016, para. 11.

4. Cited in Walker, 2016, para. 47.

5. Aurora TV, 2017.

6. Jenkins, 1983, 546.

7. Ryan, Carragee, & Schwerner,1998.

8. Zitzman, 2016.

9. SEIU Local 105, 2018a.

10. SEIU Local 105, 2018b.

11. Wolf, 2015.

12. Scheufele, 2009.

13. Carragee & Roefs, 2004, 224.

14. See Jenkins, 1983.

15. Jacobs-Huey, 2006, 213; Thompson, 2008; Ashe, 1995.

16. Byrd & Tharps, 2001.

17. Dash, 2006.

18. Robinson, 2011.

19. Byrd & Tharps, 2001, 38.

20. Dash, 2006, 31.

21. Dash, 2006, 68.

22. Hooks, 2007, para. 8.

23. Cartwright, 2012, 315.

24. Cartwright, 2012, 116.

25. Hall, 1997.

26. Hall, 1997, 272.

27. Hall, 1997, 272.

28. Hall, 1997, emphasis in original, 274.

29. Thompson, 2008.

30. Sears & Freedman, 1967.

31. Facebook Business, 2016.
32. Canella, 2017c.
33. Canella, 2017d.

CONCLUSION

1. Cited in Reilly, 2016, para. 1.
2. Hatewatch Staff, 2016.
3. Uribe & Rappaport, 2011.
4. Uribe & Rappaport, 2011, 28–29.
5. Uribe & Rappaport, 2011, 58–59.
6. Juris, 2007, 167.
7. Colectivo Situaciones, 2020.
8. Mirzoeff & Halberstam, 2018.
9. Mirzoeff & Halberstam, 2018, 123.
10. Rancière, 2000.
11. Rancière, 1977, 65.
12. Rancière, 1977, 43.

REFERENCES

Adler, P. A., & Adler, P. (1987). *Membership roles in field research*. Thousand Oaks, CA: Sage.

AFL-CIO. (2016). Executive paywatch. Retrieved from https://aflcio.org/paywatch

Aguayo, A. J. (2019). *Documentary resistance: Social change and participatory media*. New York, NY: Oxford University Press.

Althusser, L. (1971). *Lenin and philosophy, and other essays* (B. Brewster, Trans.). New York, NY: Monthly Review Press.

Ambert, A.-M., Adler, P. A., Adler, P., & Detzner, D. (1995). Understanding and evaluating qualitative research. *Journal of Marriage and Family, 57,* 879–893. doi:10.2307/353409

American Presidency Project. (2017). Voter turnout in presidential elections: 1828–2012. Retrieved from http://www.presidency.ucsb.edu/data/turnout.php

Andrejevic, M. (2009). The body, torture, and the decline of symbolic efficiency. *Politics and Culture, 1,* Article 8. Retrieved from https://politicsandculture.org/home

Aronowitz, S. (2014). *The death and life of American labor: Towards a new workers' movement.* New York, NY: Verso.

Ashe, B.A. (1995). "Why don't he like my hair?": Constructing African-American standards of beauty in Toni Morrison's *Song of Solomon* and Zora Neale Hurston's *Their Eyes Were Watching God. African American Review, 29,* 579–592. doi:10.2307/3042151

Atton, C. (2002). *Alternative media.* Thousand Oaks, CA: Sage.

Aurora TV. (2017, January 12). Freedom of speech: 2017 MLK Jr. Forum. Retrieved from https://www.auroratv.org/mlkjr/mlkjr.html?show=4346

Bayat, A. (2010). *Life as politics: How ordinary people change the Middle East.* Stanford, CA: Stanford University Press.

Benkler, Y., Faris, R., & Roberts, H. (2018). *Network propaganda: Manipulation, disinformation, and radicalization in American politics.* New York, NY: Oxford University Press.

Bennett, W. L. & Segerberg, A. (2012). "The logic of connective action." *Information, Communication & Society, 15*(5), 739–768. doi:10.1080/1369118X.2012.670661.

Bird, S., Lichtman, R., & Gessner, P. (Directors). (1970). *Finally got the news* [Motion picture]. United States: Icarus Films.

BlackLivesMatter. (n.d.). About the Black Lives Matter network. Retrieved from http://blacklivesmatter.com/about

Black Lives Matter 5280. (2015a, October 25). Amy E Brown, Bianca Williams and members of @BLM5280 ask the question that is really on all of our minds . . . WHERE ARE THE #REPARATIONS? [Facebook status update]. Retrieved from https://www.facebook.com/BlackLivesMatter5280/videos/1508971816086713/

Black Lives Matter 5280. (2015b, October 26). Two hundred fifty years of slavery. Ninety years of Jim Crow [Facebook status update]. Retrieved from https://www.facebook.com/BlackLivesMatter5280/posts/1510379532612608

Black Lives Matter 5280. (2016a). During our #135AndCounting action, we made so many inspiring and soul filing connections with folx from our beautiful communities of color [Facebook status update]. Retrieved from https://www.facebook.com/events/1810462182520893

Black Lives Matter 5280. (2016b, July 8). This is what happens when we ask to be with our people and grieve and love. #135andCounting [Facebook status update]. Retrieved from https://www.facebook.com/BlackLivesMatter5280/videos/1632571923726701/

153

Black Lives Matter 5280. (2016c August 16). We have reached a point in the movement where certain actions and specific behaviors will no longer be tolerated . . . [Facebook status update]. Retrieved from https://www.facebook.com/BlackLivesMatter5280/posts/16522105384 29506

Black Lives Matter 5280. (2016d, August 24). August community meeting—On the ground training (people of color only) [Facebook status update]. Retrieved from https://www .facebook.com/events/1065280796888606/permalink/1069499563133396/?action _history=null

Black Lives Matter 5280. (2017a). Mission. Retrieved from http://www.blacklivesmatter5280 .com

Black Lives Matter 5280. (2017b, January 7). #ReclaimMLK 2017 in 9 . . . [Facebook status update]. Retrieved from https://www.facebook.com/BlackLivesMatter5280/photos/a .1437459096571319.1073741828.1437139253269970/1734297793554113/?type=3&theater

Bock, M. A. (2016). Film the police! Cop-watching and its embodied narratives. *Journal of Communication, 66*, 13–34. doi:10.1111/jcom.12204

Bonilla-Silva, E. (2002). The linguistics of color blind racism: How to talk nasty about Blacks without sounding "racist." *Critical Sociology, 28*, 41–64. doi:10.1177/08969205020280010501

Brenan, M. (2020, September 3). At 65%, approval of labor unions in U.S. remains high. *Gallup*. Retrieved from https://news.gallup.com/poll/318980/approval-labor-unions-remains -high.aspx.

Butler, J. (1997). "Merely cultural." *Social Text, 52*(3), 33–44.

Byrd, A. D., & Tharps, L. L. (2001). *Hair story: Untangling the roots of Black hair in America.* New York, NY: St. Martin's Press.

Canella, G. (2015a, November 24). *BLM5280 stands with Minneapolis* [Video file]. Retrieved from https://www.youtube.com/watch?v=DddYLPiX_k8

Canella, G. (2015b, December 9). *Home healthcare #Fightfor15* [Video file]. Retrieved from https://www.youtube.com/watch?v=KpVzlFxPOmg

Canella, G. (2016a, January 18). *Black Lives Matter 5280 on MLKDay* [Video file]. Retrieved from https://www.youtube.com/watch?v=1zhTvKNMWCE

Canella, G. (2016b, April 15). The SEIU Local 105 marched on Denver yesterday in the #Fightfor15 #J4JDenver [Facebook status update]. Retrieved from https://www.facebook.com /gino.canella/videos/10154161055684365

Canella, G. (2016c, June 24). More than 700 janitors and community members rallied last week in Denver to demand a fair contract for SEIU Local 105 janitors . . . [Facebook status update]. Retrieved from https://www.facebook.com/gino.canella/videos/10154332660324365

Canella, G. (2017a, January 15). In 2016, Amy E. Emery-Brown and Black Lives Matter 5280 demanded "resources not retribution" . . . [Facebook status update]. Retrieved from https:// www.facebook.com/gino.canella/videos/10154974304309365

Canella, G. (2017b, May 1). #MayDay2017 #Denver SEIU Local 105 [Facebook status update]. Retrieved from https://www.facebook.com/gino.canella/videos/vb.589109364/101553 19439504365

Canella, G. (2017c, August 3). Councilman @PaulLopez5280 Talking about #labor and #union solidarity . . . [Twitter post]. Retrieved from https://twitter.com/Gino_Canella/status /893224940421304321

Canella, G. (2017d, December 7). @RonRuggiero105 of @SEIU105 talks about "whole person unionism." #unions #labor #Denver #SEIU [Twitter post]. Retrieved from https://twitter .com/Gino_Canella/status/938908908457832448

Canella, G. (2018, March 9). Radical labor: Aligning unions with the streets. *Roar Magazine*. Retrieved from https://roarmag.org/films/radical-labor-aligning-unions-streets

Canella, G. (2018b). Racialized surveillance: Activist media and the policing of Black bodies. *Communication, Culture and Critique, 11*(3), 378–398.

Carragee, K. M., & Frey, L. R. (2012). Introduction: Communication activism for social justice scholarship. In L. R. Frey & K. M. Carragee (Eds.), *Communication activism: Vol. 3. Struggling for social justice amidst difference* (pp. 1–68). New York, NY: Hampton Press.

Carragee, K. M., & Roefs, W. (2004). The neglect of power in recent framing research. *Journal of Communication, 54*, 214–233. doi:10.1111/j.1460-2466.2004.tb02625.x

Carter, E. (2016, November 8). Denver's independent safety monitor insulated from political whims. *Colorado Independent*. Retrieved from http://www.coloradoindependent.com /162297/amendment-2b-denver

Cartwright, L. (2012). "Art, Feminism and Visual Culture." In I. Heywood and B. Sandywell (Eds.), *Handbook of visual culture* (pp. 310–325). New York: Bloomsbury.

Castells, M. (2007). Communication, power and counter-power in network society. *International Journal of Communication, 1*, 238–266. Retrieved from http://ijoc.org/index.php/ijoc

Castells, M. (2010). *The information age: Economy, society, and culture: Vol. 2. The power of identity* (2nd ed.). Malden, MA: Wiley-Blackwell.

Castells, M. (2011). A network theory of power. *International Journal of Communication, 5*, 773–787. Retrieved from http://ijoc.org/index.php/ijoc

CBS News. (2017, January 21). *Watch legendary activist Angela Davis rally Women's March on Washington* [Video file]. Retrieved from https://www.youtube.com/watch?v=TTB-m2 NxWzA

Chau, C. (2010). YouTube as a participatory culture. *New Directions for Student Leadership, 128*, 65–74. doi:10.1002/yd.376

Cissna, K. N. (2000). Applied communication research in the 21st century. *Journal of Applied Communication Research, 28*, 169–173. doi:10.1089/00909880009365563

Coates, T. (2014, June). The case for reparations. *The Atlantic*. Retrieved from https://www .theatlantic.com/magazine/archive/2014/06/the-case-for-reparations/361631

Coe, K., Kenski, K., & Rains, S. A. (2014). Online and uncivil? Patterns and determinants of incivility in newspaper website comments. *Journal of Communication, 64*, 658–679. doi:10.1111/ jcom.12104

Cole, T. (@tejucole). (2012a, March 8). 5- The White Savior Industrial Complex is not about justice. It is about having a big emotional experience that validates privilege. [Twitter post]. Retrieved from https://twitter.com/tejucole/status/177810262223626241?ref_src=twsrc %5Etfw

Cole, T. (2012b, March 21). The White-savior industrial complex. *The Atlantic*. Retrieved from http://www.theatlantic.com/international/archive/2012/03/the-white-savior-industrial -complex/254843

Colectivo Situaciones. (2020, August 17). Colectivo Situaciones: Complete Works. *Autonomies .org*. Available at: https://autonomies.org/2020/08/colectivo-situaciones-complete-works/

Colorado People's Alliance. (n.d.). Mission and history. Retrieved from https://colorado peoplesalliance.org/about-us/missionandhistory

Corporation for National and Community Service. (2006). Volunteer growth in America: A review of trends since 1974. Retrieved from https://www.nationalservice.gov/pdf/06 _1203_volunteer_growth.pdf

Corral, M. (2016, July 8). Denver janitors win historic victory: A path to $15 in new agreement. *SEIU105.org*. Retrieved from http://www.seiu105.org/2016/07/08/denver-janitors-win -historic-victory-a-path-to-15-in-new-agreement

Couldry, N. (2006). *Listening beyond the echoes: Media, ethics, and agency in an uncertain world*. Boulder, CO: Paradigm.

Couldry, N. (2008). Digital storytelling, media research and democracy: Conceptual choices and alternative futures. In K. Lundby (Ed.), *Digital storytelling, mediatized stories: Self-representations in new media* (pp. 41–60). New York, NY: Peter Lang.

Couldry, N. (2011). Media and democracy: Some missing links. In S. C. Jansen, J. Pooley, & L. Taub-Pervizpour (Eds.), *Media and social justice* (pp. 45–55). New York, NY: Palgrave Macmillan.

Couldry, N. (2015a). The myth of "us": Digital networks, political change and the production of collectivity. *Information, Communication & Society, 18,* 608–626. doi:10.1080/13691 18x.2014.979216

Couldry, N. (2015b). The social foundations of future digital politics. In S. Coleman & D. Freelon (Eds.), *Handbook of digital politics* (pp. 35–50). Northampton, MA: Edward Elgar.

Covert, B. (2016, November 7). Donald Trump's imaginary inner cities. *The Nation.* Retrieved from https://www.thenation.com/article/archive/donald-trumps-imaginary-inner-cities/

Crenshaw, K. (1991). Mapping the margins: Intersectionality, identity politics, and violence against women of color. *Stanford Law Review, 43,* 1241–1299. doi:10.2307/1229039

Dash, P. (2006). Black hair culture, politics and change. *International Journal of Inclusive Education, 10,* 27–37. doi:10.1080/13603110500173183

Daum, M. (2017, March 5). "A day without a woman" is a strike for privileged protesters. *Los Angeles Times.* Retrieved from http://www.latimes.com /opinion/op-ed/la-oe-daum-a-day -without-a-woman-20170305-story.html

Davis, A. Y. (1984). *Women, culture and politics.* New York, NY: Vintage Books.

Dean, J. (2009a). *Democracy and other neoliberal fantasies: Communicative capitalism and left politics.* Durham, NC: Duke University Press.

Dean, J. (2009b). Politics without politics. *Parallax, 15*(3), 20–36. doi:10.1080/13534640902982579

Delgado, D. (2017, April 3). Whites only: SURJ and the Caucasian invasion of racial justice spaces. *Huffington Post.* Retrieved from https://www.huffingtonpost.com/entry/whites-only-surj -and-the-caucasian-invasion-of-racial_us_58dd5cf7e4b04ba4a5e25209

della Porta, D. (2007). *The global justice movement: Cross-national and transnational perspectives.* New York, NY: Routledge.

della Porta, D. (2011). Communication in movement: Social movements as agents of participatory democracy. *Information, Communication & Society, 14,* 800–819. doi:10.1080/13691 18X.2011.560954

Dempsey, S., Dutta, M., Frey, L. R., Goodall, H. L., Madison, D. S., Mercieca, J., Nakayama, T., & Miller, K. (2011). What is the role of the communication discipline in social justice, community engagement, and public scholarship? A visit to the *CM Café. Communication Monographs, 78,* 256–271. doi:10.1080/03637751.2011.565062

Dovey, J. (2000). *Freakshow: First person media and factual television.* Sterling, VA: Pluto Press.

Downing, J. (1984). *Radical media: The political experience of alternative communication.* Cambridge, MA: South End Press.

Downing, J. (2001). *Radical media: Rebellious communication and social movements.* Thousand Oaks, CA: Sage.

Downing, J. (2008). Social movement theories and alternative media: An evaluation and critique. *Communication, Culture & Critique, 1,* 40–50. doi:10.1111/j.1753-9137.2007.00005.x

Downey, J., & Fenton, N. (2003). New media, counter publicity and the public sphere. *New Media & Society, 5,* 185–202. doi:10.1177/1461444803005002003

Edsall, T. B. (2005, July 26). Two top unions split from AFL-CIO. *Washington Post.* Retrieved from http://www.washingtonpost.com/ wp-dyn/content/article/2005/07/25/AR2005 072500251.html

Eisenstein, Z. R. (Ed.). (1979). *Capitalist patriarchy and the case for socialist feminism.* New York, NY: Monthly Review Press.

Elmer, G., & Opel, A. (2008). *Preempting dissent: The politics of an inevitable future.* Winnipeg, Canada: Arbeiter Ring.

Facebook Business. (2016, February 10). Capture attention with updated features for video ads. *Facebook.* Retrieved from https://www.facebook.com/business/news/updated-features-for-video-ads

Ferree, M. M., & Merill, D. (2000). Hot movements, cold cognition: Thinking about social movements in gendered frames. *Contemporary Sociology, 29*(3), 454–462.

Fight for $15. (n.d.). About us. Retrieved from http://fightfor15.org/about-us

Flaherty, R. J. (Director). (1922). *Nanook of the North: A story of life and love in the actual Arctic* [Motion picture]. United States: Pathé Exchange.

Frank, T. (2016). *Listen liberal: Or, what ever happened to the party of the people.* New York, NY: Metropolitan Books.

Fraser, N. (1990). Rethinking the public sphere: A contribution to the critique of actually existing democracy. *Social Text, 25/26,* 56–80.

Fraser, N. (2000). Rethinking recognition. *New Left Review, 3,* 107–120.

Frazier, E. F. (1962). *The Black bourgeoisie: The rise of a new middle class in the United States.* New York, NY: Collier Books.

Freedman, D. (2017). Put a ring on it! Why we need more commitment in media scholarship. *Javnost—The Public, 24,* 1–12. doi:10.1080/13183222.2017.1287963

Freimuth, V. S. (1995). Response to Seibold: Applied health communication research. In K. N. Cissna (Ed.), *Applied communication in the 21st century* (pp. 39–45). Mahwah, NJ: Lawrence Erlbaum.

Frey, L. R., & Carragee, K. M. (2007). Introduction: Communication activism as engaged scholarship. In L. R. Frey & K. M. Carragee (Eds.), *Communication activism* (2 vols., pp. 1–64). Cresskill, NJ: Hampton Press.

Frey, L. R., & Carragee, K. M. (Eds.). (2012). *Communication activism: Vol. 3. Struggling for social justice amidst difference.* New York, NY: Hampton Press.

Frey, L. R., & Castro, N. T. (2016). The inner researcher: Researchers' emotions and identities. In A. Kurylo (Ed.), *Negotiating group identity in the research process: Are you in or are you out?* (pp. 143–167). Lanham, MD: Lexington Books.

Frey, L. R., Pearce, W. B., Pollock, M. A., Artz, L., & Murphy, B. A. O. (1996). Looking for justice in all the wrong places: On a communication approach to social justice. *Communication Studies, 47,* 110–127. doi:10.1080/10510979609368467

Frey, L. R., & SunWolf. (2009). Across applied divides: Great debates of applied communication scholarship. In L. R. Frey & K. N. Cissna (Eds.), *Routledge handbook of applied communication research* (pp. 26–54). New York, NY: Routledge.

Fuchs, C. (2014). *Social media: A critical introduction.* Thousand Oaks, CA: Sage.

Fung, A. (2011, September 9). The constructive responsibility of intellectuals: Using privilege to advance democracy and justice. *Boston Review.* Retrieved from http://bostonreview.net/archon-fung-noam-chomsky-responsibility-of-intellectuals

Funke, P. N., Robé, C., & Wolfson, T. (2012). Suturing working class subjectivities: Media Mobilizing Project and the role of media building a class-based social movement. *tripleC, 10,* 16–29. Retrieved from http://www.triple-c.at/index.php/tripleC/index

Funke, P. N., & Wolfson, T. (2017). From global justice to Occupy and Podemos: Mapping three stages of contemporary activism. *tripleC: Communication, Capitalism & Critique, 15,* 393–405. Retrieved from http://www.triple-c.at/index.php/tripleC/index

Garza, A. (n.d.). A herstory of the #BlackLivesMatter movement. *Black Lives Matter*. Retrieved from http://blacklivesmatter.com/herstory

Gerbaudo, P. (2012). *Tweets and the streets: Social media and contemporary activism*. London, United Kingdom: Pluto Press.

Giroux, H. A. (2013, October 29). Public intellectuals against the neoliberal university. *Truthout*. Retrieved from http://www.truth-out.org/opinion/item/19654-public-intellec tuals-against-the-neoliberal-university

Gitlin, T. (1980). *The whole world is watching: Mass media in the making and unmaking of the New Left*. Berkeley: University of California Press.

Glaser, B. G., & Strauss, A. L. (1967). *The discovery of grounded theory: Strategies for qualitative research*. Chicago, IL: Aldine.

González-Bailón, S. & Wang, N. (2016). Networked discontent: The anatomy of protest campaigns in social media. *Social Networks, 44*, 95–104. doi: https://doi.org/10.1016/j.socnet .2015.07.003

Gramsci, A. (1971). *Selections from the prison notebooks* (Q. Hoare & G. N. Smith, Eds. & Trans.). London, United Kingdom: Lawrence & Wishart.

Grierson, J. (1939, August). The story of the documentary film. *Fortnightly Review, 152*(146), 121–130.

Habermas, J. (1989). *The structural transformation of the public sphere: An inquiry into a category of bourgeois society* (T. Bruger, with F. Lawrence, Trans.). Cambridge, MA: MIT Press.

Habermas, J. (1992). Further reflections on the public sphere. In C. Calhoun (Ed.), *Habermas and the public sphere* (pp. 421–461). Cambridge, MA: MIT Press.

Habermas, J. (1996). *Between facts and norms: Contributions to a discourse theory of law and democracy* (W. Rehg, Trans.). Cambridge, MA: MIT Press.

Habermas, J. (1998). *Inclusion of the other: Studies in political theory*. Cambridge, MA: Polity.

Hall, S. (1977). Culture, the media and the "ideological effect." In J. Curran, M. Gurevitch, & J. Woollacott (Eds.), *Mass communication and society* (pp. 315–348). London, United Kingdom: Edward Arnold Press.

Hall, S. (1980). Encoding/decoding. In S. Hall, D. Hobson, A. Lowe, & P. Willis (Eds.), *Culture, media, language: Working papers in cultural studies, 1972–1979* (pp. 128–138). New York, NY: Unwin Hyman.

Hall, S. (1997). The spectacle of the "other." In S. Hall (Ed.), *Representation: Cultural representations and signifying practices* (pp. 223–290). Thousand Oaks, CA: Sage.

Harvey, D. (2005). *A brief history of neoliberalism*. New York: Oxford University Press.

Hatewatch Staff. (2016, December 16). Update: 1,094 bias-related incidents in the month following the election. *Southern Poverty Law Center*. Retrieved from https://www.splcenter .org/hatewatch/2016/12/16/update-1094-bias-related-incidents-month-following -election

Hendee, C. (2016, June 7). Here's where metro Denver ranks on population growth. *Denver Business Journal*. Retrieved from http://www.bizjournals.com

Henley, P. (1998). Filmmaking and ethnographic research. In J. Prosser (Ed.), *Image-based research: A sourcebook for qualitative researchers* (pp. 42–59). Philadelphia, PA: Falmer Press.

Hennepin Attorney. (2016, March 29). *Ambulance Hayes rear view—Reversed 4* [Video file]. Retrieved from https://www.youtube.com/watch?time_continue=10&v=tdtE9dYOKos

hooks, b. (1992). *Black looks: Race and representation*. Boston, MA: South End Press.

hooks, b. (2007, April 1). Straightening our hair. *Z Magazine*. Retrieved from https://zcomm .org/zmagazine/straightening-our-hair-by-bell-hooks

Incite! Women of Color against Violence (Eds.). (2007). *The revolution will not be funded: Beyond the non-profit industrial complex.* Cambridge, MA: South End Press.

It's Time for Accountability. (2020, November 30). #BLM10Plus Statement. Retrieved from https://www.blmchapterstatement.com/no1/

Jacobs-Huey, L. (2006). *From the kitchen to the parlor: Language and becoming in African American women's hair care.* New York, NY: Oxford University Press.

Jacoby, R. (1987). *The last intellectuals: American culture in the age of academe.* New York, NY: Basic Books.

Jaffe, S. (2019, November 16). The Chicago teachers strike was a lesson in 21st-century organizing. *The Nation.* Retrieved from https://www.thenation.com/article/chicago-ctu-strike-win/

Jenkins, H. (2006). *Convergence culture: Where old and new media collide.* New York: New York University Press.

Jenkins, H., Ford, S., & Green, J. (2013). *Spreadable media: Creating value and meaning in a networked culture.* New York: New York University Press.

Jenkins, J. C. (1983). Resource mobilization theory and the study of social movements. *Annual Review of Sociology, 9,* 527–553. doi:10.1146/annurev.so,.09.080183.002523

Jones, J. (2017, February 13). The racial wealth gap: How African-Americans have been shortchanged out of the materials to build wealth. *Economic Policy Institute.* Retrieved from http://www.epi.org/blog/the-racial-wealth-gap-how-african-americans-have-been-shortchanged-out-of-the-materials-to-build-wealth

Juris, J. (2007). Practicing militant ethnography with the movement for global resistance in Barcelona. In S. Shukaitis, D. Graeber, and E. Biddle (Eds.), *Constituent Imagination* (pp. 164–176). Oakland, CA: AK Press.

Juris, J. (2012). Reflections on #Occupy everywhere: Social media, public space, and emerging logics of aggregation. *American Ethnologist, 39,* 259–279. doi:10.1111/j.1548-1425.2012.01362.x

Kilgo, D. K., & Harlow, S. (2019). Protests, media coverage, and a hierarchy of social struggle. *International Journal of Press/Politics, 24*(4), 508–530.

Klein, N. (2007). *The shock doctrine: The rise of disaster capitalism.* New York, NY: Metropolitan Books.

Kraidy, M. M. (2016). *The naked blogger of Cairo: Creative insurgency in the Arab world.* Cambridge, MA: Harvard University Press.

Laclau, E., & Mouffe, C. (2001). *Hegemony and socialist strategy: Towards a radical democratic politics* (2nd ed.). New York, NY: Verso.

Lambert, J. (2006). *Digital storytelling: Capturing lives, creating community* (2nd ed.). Berkeley, CA: Digital Diner Press.

Lassiter, L. E. (2005). *The Chicago guide to collaborative ethnography.* Chicago, IL: University of Chicago Press.

Lecklider, A. S. (2017, September 10). The real victims of anti-intellectualism. Hint: They aren't professors. *Chronicle of Higher Education.* Retrieved from http://www.chronicle.com/article/the-real-victims-of-anti-intellectualism/

Lee, F. (2017, October 13). Why I've started to fear my fellow social justice activists. *Yes! Magazine.* Retrieved from http://www.yesmagazine.org/people-power/why-ive-started-to-fear-my-fellow-social-justice-activists-20171013

Lopez, G. (2019, August 19). I was skeptical of unions. Then I joined one. *Vox.com.* Retrieved from https://www.vox.com/policy-and-politics/2019/8/19/20727283/unions-good-income-inequality-wealth

Lopez, I. H. (2014). *Dog whistle politics: How coded racial appeals have reinvented racism and wrecked the middle class.* New York, NY: Oxford University Press.

Lorde, A. (1981). The uses of anger: Women responding to racism. *Black Past.* Retrieved from https://www.blackpast.org/african-american-history/speeches-african-american-history/1981-audre-lorde-uses-anger-women-responding-racism/.

Lorde, A. (1984). *Sister outsider: Essays and speeches.* Trumansburg, NY: Crossing Press.

Martin, Christopher R. (2019). *No longer newsworthy: How the mainstream media abandoned the working class.* Ithaca, NY: ILR Press.

McAlevey, J. F. (2016). *No shortcuts: Organizing for power in the new Gilded Age.* New York, NY: Oxford University Press.

McLaughlin, E. C., & Sanchez, R. (2016, October 21). Minneapolis police clear officers in fatal shooting of Jamal Clark. *CNN.* Retrieved from http://www.cnn.com/2016/10/21/us/jamar-clark-shooting/index.html

McHale, J. P. (2007). Unreasonable doubt: Using video documentary to promote justice. In L. R. Frey & K. M. Carragee (Eds.), *Communication activism: Vol. 2. Media and performance activism* (pp. 195–222). Cresskill, NJ: Hampton Press.

Mikati, I., Benson, A. F., Luben, T. J., Sacks, J. D., & Richmond-Bryant, J. (2018). Disparities in distribution of particulate matter emission sources by race and poverty status. *American Journal of Public Health, 108,* 480–485/ doi:10.2105/AJPH.2017.304297.

Milne, E.-J., Mitchell, C., & De Lange, N. (Eds.). (2013). *Handbook of participatory video.* Lanham, MD: AltaMira Press.

Mirzoeff, N. & Halberstam, J. (2018). Decolonize media: Tactics, manifestoes, histories. *Cinema Journal, 57*(4), 120–123. Retrieved from https://cdn.ymaws.com/www.cmstudies.org/resource/resmgr/in_focus_archive/InFocus_57-4.pdf

Moody, K. (2000). The rank and file strategy: Building a socialist movement in the U.S. *Solidarity.* Retrieved from https://solidarity-us.org/rankandfilestrategy/

Mouffe, C. (1989). Radical democracy: Modern or postmodern? (P. Holdengraber, Trans.). *Social Text, 21,* 31–45. doi:10.2307/827806

Mouffe, C. (1999). Deliberative democracy or agonistic pluralism? *Social Research, 66,* 745–758.

Mouffe, C., & Holdengraber, P. (1989). Radical democracy: Modern or postmodern? *Social Text, 21,* 31–45. doi:10.2307/827807

Murdock, G. (1999). Rights and representations: Public discourse and cultural citizenship. In J. Gripsrud (Ed.), *Television and common knowledge* (pp. 7–17). New York, NY: Routledge.

Murray, J. (2015, September 14). Denver's new $1.8 billion budget would boost jail, child welfare staffing. *The Denver Post.* Retrieved from http://www.denverpost.com/2015/09/14/denvers-new-1-8-billion-budget-would-boost-jail-child-welfare-staffing/

Murray, J. (2017, April 20). Denver spent $14.5 million to settle lawsuits against police and sheriff in just 3 years. *The Denver Post.* Retrieved from http://www.denverpost.com/2017/04/20/denvers-settle-police-sheriff-cases-14-5-million/

Murray, S. (2008). Digital images, photo-sharing, and our shifting notions of everyday aesthetics. *Journal of Visual Culture, 7,* 147–163. doi:10.1177/1470412908091935

National Employment Law Project. (2015, December 21). 14 cities & states approved $15 minimum wage in 2015. Retrieved from http://www.nelp.org/news-releases/14-cities-states-approved-15-minimum-wage-in-2015

Negt, O., & Kluge, A. (1972). *Public sphere and experience: Towards an analysis of the bourgeois and proletarian public sphere.* Minneapolis: University of Minnesota Press.

Nielsen, R. K. (2016). Democracy. In B. Peters (Ed.) *Digital keywords: A vocabulary of information, society and culture* (pp. 81–92). Princeton, NJ: Princeton University Press.

Nigg, H. (Ed.). (2018). *Rebel video: The video movement of the 1970s and 1980s—London, Bern, Lausanne, Basel, Zurich*. Zurich, Switzerland: Scheidegger & Spiess.

Ngai, M. M. (2004). *Impossible subjects: Illegal aliens and the making of modern America*. Princeton, NJ: Princeton University Press.

Pateman, C. (1970). *Participation and democratic theory*. Cambridge, United Kingdom: Cambridge University Press.

Pateman, C. (2012). APSA presidential address: Participatory democracy revisited. *Perspectives on Politics, 10,* 7–19. doi:10.1017/S1537592711004877

Papacharissi, Z. (2016). Affective publics and structures of storytelling: Sentiment, events and mediality. *Information, Communication & Society, 19,* 307–324. doi:10.1080/1369118X.2015 .1109697

Petronio, S. (1999). Translating scholarship into practice: An alternative metaphor. *Journal of Applied Communication Research, 27,* 87–91. doi:10.1080/00909889909365527

Phillips, K. (2017, May 22). "Radical Islamic terrorism," Trump said over and over. But not in Saudi Arabia. *Washington Post*. Retrieved from https://www.washingtonpost.com/news /the-fix/wp/2017/05/22/radical-islamic-terrorism-trump-said-over-and-over-but-not-in -saudi-arabia/

Piven, F. (2008). "Can power from below change the world?" *American Sociological Review, 7,* 1–14.

Polletta, F. (2002). *Freedom is an endless meeting: Democracy in American social movements*. Chicago, IL: University of Chicago Press.

Rancière, J. (2000). *The politics of aesthetics: The distribution of the sensible* (G. Rockhill, Trans.). New York, NY: Continuum International.

Reilly, K. (2016, August 31). Here are all the times Donald Trump insulted Mexico. *Time*. Retrieved from http://time.com/4473972/donald-trump-mexico-meeting-insult

Robé, C. (2017). *Breaking the spell: A history of anarchist filmmakers, videotape guerillas, and digital ninjas*. Oakland, CA: PM Press.

Robé, C. & Wolfson, T. (2020). Reflections on the inheritances of Indymedia in the age of surveillance and social media. *Media, Culture, & Society*. doi:10.1177/0163443720926056

Roberts, M. (2016, August 16). Proposal to put Independent Monitor's Office in Denver charter makes ballot. *Westword*. Retrieved from http://www.westword.com/news/proposal -to-put-independent-monitors-office-in-denver-charter-makes-ballot-8200241

Rodriguez, C., Ferron, B., & Shamas, K. (2014). Four challenges in the field of alternative, radical and citizens' media research. *Media, Culture & Society, 36*(2), 150–66.

Roediger, D. R. (1991). *The wages of whiteness: Race and the making of the American working class*. New York, NY: Verso.

Rosanvallon, P. (2008). *Counter-democracy. Politics in an age of distrust* (A. Goldhammer, Trans.). New York, NY: Cambridge University Press.

Rose, J. (1986). *Sexuality in the field of vision*. London, United Kingdom: Verso.

Rose, M. (2014). Making publics: Documentary as do-it-with-others citizenship. In M. Boler & M. Ratto (Eds.), *DIY citizenship: Critical making and social media* (pp. 201–212). Boston, MA: MIT Press.

Ross, M. (2014). Vertical framing: Authenticity and new aesthetic practice in online videos. *Refractory, 24,* Article 3. Retrieved from https://refractory-journal.com

Rothman, L. (2017, May 1). The bloody story of how May Day became a holiday for workers. *Time*. Retrieved from http://time.com/3836834/may-day-labor-history

Ryan, C., Carragee, K. M., & Schwerner, C. (1998). Media, movements, and the quest for social justice. *Journal of Applied Communication Research, 26,* 165–181. doi:10.1080/009098898093 65500

Said, E. (1993). Speaking truth to power [Episode 5 of six-part lecture]. *BBC.* Retrieved from http://www.bbc.co.uk/programmes/p00gxqyb

Sandercock, L., & Attili, G. (2010). Digital ethnography as planning praxis: An experiment with film as social research, community engagement and policy dialogue. *Planning Theory & Practice, 11,* 23–45. doi:10.1080/14649350903538012

Santana, A. D. (2014). Virtuous or vitriolic: The effect of anonymity on civility in online newspaper reader comment boards. *Journalism Practice, 8,* 18–33. doi:10.1080/17512786.2013.813194

Scheufele, D. (2009). Agenda-setting, priming, and framing revisited: Another look at cognitive effects of political communication. *Mass Communication and Society, 3,* 297–316. doi:10.1207/S15327825MCS0323_07

Schradie, J. (2019). *The revolution that wasn't: How digital activism favors conservatives.* Cambridge, MA: Harvard University Press.

Schroeder, J. E. (2008). Visual analysis of images in brand culture. In E. F. McQuarrie & B. J. Phillips (Eds.), *Go figure! New directions in advertising rhetoric* (pp. 277–296). Armonk, NY: ME Sharpe.

Schrum, W., Duque, R., & Brown, T. (2005). Digital video as research practice: Methodology for the millennium. *Journal of Research Practice, 1*(1), Article M4. Retrieved from http://jrp.icaap.org/index.php/jrp

Scott, D. (2019, August 28). The catch-22 for labor unions enjoying newfound public support. *Vox.com.* Retrieved https://www.vox.com/policy-and-politics/2019/8/28/20837207/labor-unions-gallup-poll-great-recession

Sears, D. O., & Freedman, J. L. (1967). Selective exposure to information: A critical review. *Public Opinion Quarterly, 21,* 194–213. doi:10.1086/267513

SEIU Local 105. (2017a, June 13). Today, we marched to Senator Cory Gardner's office to let him know so many in our community benefit from the ACA. #Fixit [Facebook status update]. Retrieved from https://www.facebook.com/SEIULocal105/videos/1526350287422377

SEIU Local 105. (2017b, November 3). Melissa Benjamin has been a home care worker for 16 years . . . [Facebook status update]. Retrieved from https://www.facebook.com/SEIULocal105/videos/1668122193245185/

SEIU Local 105. (2018a, February 9). We're here at Denver International Airport today standing up and speaking out on behalf of airport security workers! [Facebook status update]. Retrieved from https://www.facebook.com/SEIULocal105/posts/1769979359726134:0

SEIU Local 105. (2018b, February 9). Today at Denver International Airport security workers stood together for better wages, benefits, and working conditions. [Facebook status update]. Retrieved from https://www.facebook.com/SEIULocal105/videos/1769985796392157/

Service Employees International Union. (n.d.). About. Retrieved from http://www.seiu.org/about

Shawki, A. (2017, February 21). The legacy of Malcolm X. *Jacobin Magazine.* Retrieved from https://www.jacobinmag.com/2017/02/malcolm-x-assassination-legacy

Shearer, E., & Gottfried, J. (2017, September 7). News use across social media platforms 2017. *Pew Research Center.* Retrieved from http://www.journalism.org/2017/09/07/news-use-across-social-media-platforms-2017

Shirky, C. (2008). *Here comes everybody: The power of organizing without organizations.* New York, NY: Penguin Books.

Showing Up for Racial Justice. (n.d.). About. Retrieved from http://www.showingupforracialjustice.org/about

Silverstein, J. (2013, June 27). I don't feel your pain: A failure of empathy perpetuates racial disparities. *Slate.* Retrieved from http://www.slate.com/articles/health_and_science/science/2013/06/racial_empathy_gap_people_don_t_perceive_pain_in_other_races.html

Singh, N. P. (2004). *Black is a country: Race and the unfinished struggle for democracy.* Cambridge, MA: Harvard University Press.

Spargo, J. (1911). *Sidelights on contemporary socialism.* New York, NY: B. W. Huebsch.

Sylte, A. (2017, November 1). Denver agrees to pay $4.65 million to family of inmate who died in jail. *9News.* Retrieved from http://www.9news.com/news/local/denver-agrees-to-pay-465-million-to-family-of-inmate-who-died-in-jail/488000988

Thompson, C. (2008). Black women and identity: What's hair got to do with it? *Michigan Feminist Studies,* 22(1). http://hdl.handle.net/2027/spo.ark5583.0022.105

Thompson, C. (2008–2009). Black women and identity: What's hair got to do with it? *Michigan Feminist Studies,* 22(1). Retrieved from https://quod.lib.umich.edu/m/mfsg

Tometi, O., & Lenoir, G. (2015, December 10). Black Lives Matter is not a civil rights movement. *Time.* Retrieved from http://time.com/4144655/international-human-rights-day-black-lives-matter

Touraine, A. (1988). *Return of the actor: Social theory in postindustrial society* (M. Godzich, Trans.). Minneapolis: University of Minnesota Press.

Trawalter, S., Hoffman, K. M., & Waytz, A. (2012). Racial bias in perceptions of others' pain. *PLoS ONE,* 7(11), 1–8. Retrieved from http://journals.plos.org/plosone

Tremayne, M. (2014) Anatomy of protest in the digital era: A network analysis of Twitter and Occupy Wall Street. *Social Movement Studies,* 13(1), 110–126. doi: 10.1080/14742837.2013.830969

Tufecki, Z. (2017). *Twitter and tear gas: The power and fragility of networked protest.* New Haven, CT: Yale University Press.

Uribe, L. G. V., & Rappaport, J. (2011). Rethinking fieldwork and ethnographic writing. *Collaborative anthropologies,* 4, 18–66. doi:10.1353/cla.2011.0015

U.S. Census Bureau. (2019). Quick facts: Denver, Colorado. Retrieved from https://www.census.gov/quickfacts/denvercountycolorado

U.S. Department of Labor, Bureau of Labor Statistics. (2005, January 27). Union membership trends in the United States. Retrieved from https://www.bls.gov/news.release/archives/union2_01272005.pdf

U.S. Department of Labor, Bureau of Labor Statistics. (2015). Volunteering in the United States, 2015. Retrieved from https://www.bls.gov/news.release/volun.nr0.htm

U.S. Department of Labor, Bureau of Labor Statistics. (2016). Household data. Employed persons by detailed occupation, sex, race, and Hispanic or Latino ethnicity. Retrieved from https://www.bls.gov/cps/cpsaat11.pdf

U.S. Department of Labor, Bureau of Labor Statistics. (2017a, January 26). Union members—2016. Retrieved from https://www.bls.gov/news.release/pdf/union2.pdf

U.S. Department of Labor, Bureau of Labor Statistics. (2017b, February 8). Labor force statistics from the current population survey. Retrieved from https://www.bls.gov/cps/cpsaat18.htm

U.S. Department of Labor, Bureau of Labor Statistics. (2018, February 28). Union members in Colorado—2017. Retrieved from https://www.bls.gov/regions/mountain-plains/news-release/unionmembership_colorado.htm

Wahl-Jorgensen, K. (2019). Questioning the ideal of the public sphere: The emotional turn. *Social Media + Society,* 5(3), 1–3.

Walker, C. (2016, November 23). Black Lives Matter 5280 recaps trip to Standing Rock to oppose oil pipeline. *Westword.* Retrieved from http://www.westword.com/news/black-lives-matter-5280-recaps-trip-to-standing-rock-to-oppose-oil-pipeline-8526506

West, C. (1993). *Race matters*. Boston, Massachusetts: Beacon Press.

White, S. A. (Ed.) (2003). *Participatory video: Images that transform and empower*. Thousand Oaks, CA: Sage.

Who We Are. (n.d.). Mission Statement. Retrieved from https://www.blacklivesmatter5280 .com/about

Williams, B. (2015, November 11). Making Black Lives Matter: Reflections on the declaration of the movement (introduction and part I). *Savage Minds*. Retrieved from https:// savageminds.org/2015/11/11/making-black-lives-matter-reflections-on-the-declaration -and-the-movement-introduction-part-i

Williams, B. (2017, March 20). Precarious publics: Bianca C. Williams, Black feminist politic of teaching & organizing with emotion. *Humanities Futures*. Retrieved from https:// humanitiesfutures.org/media/radical-honesty-subjective-truths-black-feminist-politic -teaching-organizing-emotion/

Williams, R. (1976). *Keywords: A vocabulary of culture and society*. New York: Oxford University Press.

Williams, R. (1977). *Marxism and literature*. New York, NY: Oxford University Press.

Windham, L. (2017, September 7). The media still gets the working class wrong—but not in the way you think. *Washington Post*. Retrieved from http://washingtonpost.com/news /made-by-history/wp/2017/09/03/the-media-still-gets-the-working-class-wrong-but -not-in-the-way-you-think/

Wolf, S. (2015, August 26). Why Black Lives Matter 5280 says Stapleton neighborhood should change name. *Colorado Public Radio*. Retrieved from https://www.cpr.org/news/story /why-black-lives-matter-5280-says-stapleton-neighborhood-should-change-name

Wolfson, T. (2014). *Digital rebellion: The birth of the cyber left*. Champaign: University of Illinois Press.

Zitzman, A. (2016, August 15). Proposed independent monitor charter change goes to Denver voters. *Fox 31 Denver*. Retrieved from http://kdvr.com/2016/08/15/independent-monitor -charter-change-goes-to-denver-voters

Žižek, S. (1998). The interpassive subject. *Lacan.com*. Retrieved from http://www.lacan.com /zizek-pompidou.htm

Žižek, S. (2002). *Welcome to the desert of the real! Five essays on September 11 and related dates*. London, United Kingdom: Verso.

INDEX

accomplice, 63–64

active membership, 53

activist media, as term, 2

Adler, Patricia A., 53

Adler, Peter, 53

affective publics, 22–26

Affordable Care Act, 85, 113

Afro (hairstyle), 120–121

agonistic pluralism, 13

Aguayo, Angela J., 3, 41

ally, 63–64

alternative media, radical, 8–11

Althusser, Louis, 11

Amendment 70 (Colorado), 112–113

American Federation of Labor and
  Congress of Industrial Organizations
  (AFL-CIO), 32

analog era, of ethnographic filmmaking,
  41–43

apparatus, 11

applied communication research, 27

Argentina, 134

Atton, Chris, 10

Aurora TV, 114–115

Bayat, Asef, 25

Benjamin, Melissa, 134; documentary on, 39,
  72–79, 124; documentary on, at media
  workshop, 126–128; editorial oversight given
  to, 73; Fight for $15 campaign and, 72–73,
  76–79; on home health care work, 75–76;
  interviewing, 74–75, 78–79; at Justice 4
  Janitors rallies, 82; in *Radical Labor*, 97, 100
  See also home health care work

Bennett, W. Lance, 24–25

bias-related incidents, 130

Black feminism: Black Lives Matter and, 17–19;
  intersectional, 18; radical honesty in, 47

Black hair, 119–122

Black Is a Country (Singh), 15

#BlackIsBeautiful, 119–122

Black Lives Matter (BLM), 1; Black feminism
  and, 17–19; #BLMDebate, 86–87; chapters

of, 35–37; color blindness, post-racial
discourses, and, 54–55; global protest
movement for, 2020, 5, 36; intersectionality, human rights in, 54; Minneapolis,
87–90; Service Employees International
Union compared with, 99; social media
and, 34–35, 148n19

Black Lives Matter 5280 (BLM5280), 15, 26,
30–32, 64–65, 136; applied communication
research with, 27; #BlackIsBeautiful,
119–122; #ChangeTheNameStapleton, 48,
117–119; collaborative ethnography with,
44; on Colorado Public Radio, 117–119;
Columbus Day protests of, 110–111;
democracy in, 35–36; editorial control
shared with, 72; founders of, 36–37;
homophobia, patriarchy rejected by, 17;
Indigenous rights and, 110–112; in Justice 4
Janitors docuseries, 82; local news and,
114–115, 117–118, 117–119; on Marshall,
93–95; mission statement of, 36–37, 48;
MLK Day march, 52–53, 90–96, 98–99, 124,
150n16, 150n20; #135HoursAndCounting,
58, 60; researcher membership in, 53; social
media and, 87–90, 103–104, 119–122

Black Lives Matter 5280 (BLM5280),
community meetings of, 39–40, 47–49, 52,
134; closed, 37–38, 58–61; with Service
Employees International Union Local 105,
38, 53–57; Showing Up for Racial Justice
compared with, 62–63

Black Lives Matter 5280 (BLM5280),
documentaries on, 40, 44–45, 71, 102, 134;
#BLMDebate, 86–87; interview questions
for, sample list of, 141; Minneapolis vigil,
87–90, 95–96; MLK Day march, 52–53,
90–96, 124, 150n20; pre-production and,
46–53

Black Lives Matter Global Network
  (BLMGN), 36

Black Power, 120–121

Black workers, in labor movement, 32–34

Bliss, Roshan, 49, 87–88

ABOUT THE AUTHOR

GINO CANELLA is a documentary filmmaker and assistant professor of journalism and media studies at Emerson College. His research and creative work explore activist media, documentary filmmaking, and labor. Gino studies how organizers use media to foster solidarity among grassroots groups and to frame conversations about race, labor, and social justice.